The Economy of Northern Ireland

The Economy of Northern Ireland

PERSPECTIVES
FOR STRUCTURAL CHANGE

Edited by Paul Teague

LAWRENCE & WISHART
LONDON

Lawrence & Wishart Limited
144a Old South Lambeth Road
London SW8 1XX

First published 1993 by Lawrence and Wishart

© Editor and contributors 1993

This book is sold subject to the condition that it shall not, by way of trade or otherwise, be lent, re-sold, hired out or otherwise circulated without the publisher's prior consent in any form of binding other than that in which it is published and without a similar condition including this condition, being imposed on the subsequent purchaser.

Typeset in Garamond by Ewan Smith
48 Shacklewell Lane, London E8
Printed and bound in Great
Britain by Redwood Books
Trowbridge

Contents

Preface	vi
Contributors	viii
Acknowledgements	ix

1. Northern Ireland – Typology of a Regional Economy   1
   VANI K. BOROOAH
2. Economic Performance in Northern Ireland: A Comparative Perspective   24
   D.M.W.N. HITCHENS, J.E. BIRNIE AND K. WAGNER
3. Governance Structure and Economic Performance   60
   ROBERT CLULOW AND PAUL TEAGUE
4. The Public Sector and the Economy   121
   MICHAEL SMYTH
5. Discrimination and Fair Employment in Northern Ireland   141
   PAUL TEAGUE
6. Women in the Northern Ireland Labour Market   170
   NORMA HEATON, GILLIAN ROBINSON AND CELIA DAVIES
7. Foreign Investment and Industrial Development in Northern Ireland   190
   DOUGLAS HAMILTON
8. The Labour Market Impact of New and Small Firms in Northern Ireland   217
   MARK HART
9. The Potential and Limits to North–South Economic Co-operation   240
   RORY O'DONNELL AND PAUL TEAGUE

Index   271

PREFACE

The essays in this volume are not intended to be a complete account of the N. Ireland economy. Rather, the more modest objective is pursued of promoting more informed discussion of some controversies and developments relating to economic life in the province. Regrettably, little of this type of discussion takes place. Part of the problem is that some of the issues involved are politically sensitive which has caused economists to beat a hasty retreat. Thus for instance because the question of alleged discrimination in the labour market is closely associated with the nationalist–unionist divide in the province, there has been no satisfactory economic assessment of the controversy. A consensus has emerged that the topic belongs almost exclusively to the political science and demography worlds. Contrast this situation with the U.S.A. experience when racial discrimination exploded into the open in the 1960's. At the time, economists led the academic stampede to examine the scale and causes of black–white differentials. A rich new body of economic theory emerged from these investigations. Yet twenty years after the outbreak of the present troubles not one aspect of this theory has been applied to the question of Catholic labour market disadvantage. As a result, discussions on the issue remain imprecise and unconvincing.

Perhaps another problem is that the collection of data has taken priority over wider theoretical discussions about the economy. Over the past seven years or so because of the worthwhile efforts of the Northern Ireland Economic Research Centre, and notable individuals like Richard Harris, detailed and comprehensive economic information now exists about the province. In the mid eighties, this was probably the right strategy to pursue, but now there needs to be a shift to developing theoretical insights that give meaning to the figures. Thus whilst a large amount of statistics exist about the N. Ireland labour market, understanding of the dynamics of unemployment or the search strategies of the jobless for example remains rudimentary. Although the huge growth in the public sector is well documented, the impact of this development on the economy as a whole remains speculative. Other examples could be cited but the basic point is that understanding of important aspects of the N. Ireland economy is unsatisfactory. No claim is being made that this book will completely reverse this shortcoming, but hopefully it will make a contribution to changing the scope and direction of economic analysis about N. Ireland.

PAUL TEAGUE

Contributors

ESMOND BIRNIE is Lecturer in Economics at The Queen's University of Belfast.
VANI BOROOAH is Professor of Applied Economics at the University of Ulster at Jordanstown.
ROBERT CLULOW is Principal Economist in the Department of Economic Development, N. Ireland.
CELIA DAVIES is Professor of Women's Studies, University of Ulster at Coleraine.
DOUGLAS HAMILTON is Senior Research Officer at the Northern Ireland Economic Council.
MARK HART is Senior Lecturer in Applied Economics at the University of Ulster at Jordanstown.
NORMA HEATON is Lecturer in Human Resource Management at the University of Ulster at Jordanstown.
DAVID HITCHENS is Senior Lecturer in Economics at The Queen's University of Belfast.
RORY O'DONNELL is Senior Research Fellow at The Economic and Social Research Institute in Dublin.
GILLIAN ROBINSON is Lecturer in Social Policy at the University of Ulster at Coleraine.
MICHAEL SMYTH is Senior Lecturer in Applied Economics at the University of Ulster at Jordanstown.
PAUL TEAGUE is Senior Lecturer in Applied Economics at the University of Ulster at Jordanstown.

Acknowledgements

I owe a great many debts to people who helped in the production of this book. First and foremost are my debts to Beverly Coulter, Pamela King and Jacqueline Ferguson who typed some almost ineligible scripts with speed and efficiency. Secondly, I would like to thank Sally Davison at Lawrence and Wishart for supporting the project and for her consistent commitment to publishing material that encourages debate on N. Ireland. Thirdly, I am grateful to the contributors who met almost impossible deadlines. Finally, I would like to thank Ann for her tolerance and support.

PAUL TEAGUE, BELFAST   FEBRUARY 1993

1
NORTHERN IRELAND – TYPOLOGY OF A REGIONAL ECONOMY

Vani K. Borooah

INTRODUCTION

The last forty years have, arguably, seen no economic event more remarkable than the rise – out of the ashes of the Second World War – of Japan, Germany and France and the parallel decline of the economies of the UK and the USA. One can quantify these changes by noting that, in 1950, gross domestic product (GDP) per person in Japan was slightly over a fourth that of the UK, Germany's was less than two-thirds that of the UK and France's was less than three-fourths. By 1987 Japan Germany and France all had GDP per person higher (respectively 6, 9 and 3 per cent higher) than that in the UK. Although the USA maintains its position as the richest country in the world the gap between it and its competitors has narrowed considerably – in 1950 Japan's GDP per head was only 17 per cent of the USA's; by 1987 Japan had come to within 72 per cent of the USA's per-capita GDP.

The engine for these reversals of fortune has, of course, been manufacturing – the decline of the UK and USA economies has, in large measure, been due to a failure of their manufacturing sectors to hold their own against those of Japan and Germany. Again the disparity of performance in manufacturing between the two sets of countries may be quantified: in 1950, the UK's share of world manufacturing exports was 25 per cent, Germany's was 7 per cent and Japan's was 3 per cent; by 1988 the UK share had fallen to 8 per cent and the German and Japanese shares had risen to, respectively, 20 and 18 per cent. To portray the UK's manufacturing decline differently: in 1950, half of UK employment was in industry; by 1990, this had fallen to 25 per cent.

How does one explain these events? Why should a group of countries, pre-eminent both politically and economically in the aftermath of the Second World War, lose, within the space of four decades, their economic superiority? Conversely, how did it come about that another group of countries, whose economies were destroyed by the war, were able, over the same period, to become so economically successful? In providing an explanation for these events a word that is becoming increasingly fashionable is 'competitiveness'. Thus a 'loss of competitiveness' by the British and US economies is increasingly cited as the reason for their post-war economic decline; while 'regaining the competitive edge' is upheld as the means by which this decline can be arrested and, perhaps, even reversed.

This picture of relative economic decline in the UK becomes particularly dramatic when one narrows the focus to Northern Ireland (NI): arguably, on every economic indicator NI has performed more poorly than the UK as a whole and, indeed, relative to most regions of the UK. Judged in terms of standard of living NI continues to be the poorest UK region – the Family Expenditure Survey (FES) for 1990 showed that the average weekly income of households in NI was 31 per cent lower than the rest of the UK. The same conclusion emerges when the unemployment rate is used as a welfare indicator: the unemployment rate in NI, in February 1992, was 14.2 per cent as compared with the UK average of 9.4 per cent. If manufacturing is used as a yardstick for judging an economy's health, then again it emerges that the slump in manufacturing has been more precipitous in NI than in the UK: manufacturing employment in NI has fallen almost continuously from a post-war peak of 195,000 in 1950 (comprising 36 per cent of total NI employment) to 104,000 in 1990 (comprising 18 per cent of total NI employment).

Against this background of poor economic performance in NI, this chapter attempts to examine, in some depth, those aspects of economic failure which are either especially significant, or different, relative to the economic experience of the UK and its other regions. In our judgement, on such a comparison, four features of the NI economy deserve special mention: (i) the labour market; (ii) the nature of its manufacturing base; (iii) dependence on the public sector; and (iv) special problems with the distribution of economic welfare. The structure of this chapter is built around these four themes and they are discussed in the following sections. In taking this view of the NI economy and its special problems we do not intend to imply that other issues are unimportant. Issues pertaining to agriculture, energy, the environment, and the service sector, to name but a few, are all of justifiable concern to policy makers in NI. Given the limitations of space, however, it is not possible to deal with these issues in this chapter.

THE NORTHERN IRELAND LABOUR MARKET

The outstanding characteristic of the NI labour market is the rate at which its labour force increases every year. Table 1.1 shows that between 1971 and 1986 the NI labour force grew by 28.9 per cent, of which 18.6 per cent was due to natural increases in the working-age population and 10.3 per cent to increased participation. These translate, respectively, into average annual rates of 1.7, 1.1 and 0.6 per cent and compare with UK average annual growth rates for the labour force, and for its natural and participation change components, of, respectively, 0.9, 0.5 and 0.4 per cent. Thus, relative to the UK, NI has had a higher rate of growth in its labour force both because its labour force has grown faster due to natural causes and also because its rate of growth in labour-force participation has been greater. No other region of the UK had, over this fifteen-year period, a higher rate of natural increase[1] and only East Anglia (0.9 per cent), the South-West (0.9) and East Midlands (0.8) had a higher rate of participation increase.

The most significant feature of participation in NI is the increase in female labour force participation that has taken place since 1971: then only 35.2 per cent of the female working-age population was in the labour force (as opposed to 43.9 per cent for GB); by 1986 the NI female participation rate had risen to 45.7 per cent as compared with the UK rate of 49.2 per cent. On the other hand, over 1971–86, the male participation rate fell both in NI and in the UK from 75.6 (NI) and 80.5 (UK) in 1971 to 73.6 (NI) and 73.4 (UK) in 1986: overall, labour market activity rates in NI, in 1986, aggregated across the sexes, were slightly lower than those prevailing in the UK.[2]

Paralleling this increase in the labour force was the fact that between 1971 and 1986 employment opportunities in NI remained static: the number of full-time jobs fell by 5.5 per cent and this exactly balanced the increase in part-time jobs so that, in aggregate, no new jobs were created. As a consequence the employment shortfall in NI (ie. growth in the labour force less growth in employment) grew at the same rate as its labour force, that is 1.7 per cent per year. It should be emphasized that employment growth in NI was by no means poor in relation to other regions: Scotland, the North and Wales all reported net job

Table 1.1 Labour market accounts for regions of the United Kingdom, 1971–86 (percentage of 1971 labour force)

	Northern Ireland	Scotland	North	Wales	South East	East Anglia	South West	East Midlands	United Kingdom
Change in labour force due to:									
natural increase	18.6	15.1	8.7	5.8	6.0	9.0	4.8	10.3	8.1
change in participation	10.3	6.4	4.1	4.0	7.8	14.6	14.9	13.4	7.0
Less **Change in employment due to:**									
full-time	-5.5	-8.2	-14.3	-11.3	-0.6	19.4	10.5	5.2	-4.6
part-time	5.5	5.6	5.1	5.8	3.9	8.6	8.0	7.5	5.1
Equals employment shortfall	28.9	24.0	22.2	15.7	10.5	-4.2	1.2	11.0	14.7
Of which rise in number on									
Government schemes	2.1	4.1	4.4	5.0	2.0	2.4	3.8	-4.1	3.4
net outward migration	12.2	9.6	5.5	-1.4	0.8	-15.6	-12.5	-3.5	1.3
rise in registered unemployed	14.6	10.4	11.9	12.4	7.7	8.9	9.9	10.7	10.0

Source: Jefferson (1990)

losses, with particularly severe job losses in respect of full-time employment. However, the higher rate of growth in NI's labour force meant that its rate of growth of employment shortfall was the highest among the UK regions and, at 1.7 per cent, compared unfavourably with the UK average annual rate of 0.9 per cent.

There are essentially two solutions to a growth in employment shortfall: either people migrate and seek employment elsewhere or they become unemployed. As Table 1.1 shows the increase in employment shortfall in NI of 28.9 per cent over 1971–86 was almost evenly divided between unemployment (14.6 per cent increase) and migration (12.2 per cent increase). The balance of 2.1 per cent is explained by a growth in government training schemes which had the effect of taking people off the unemployment register while keeping them in NI. This high rate of migration out of NI, over 1971–86, was unique among the regions of the UK: even in Scotland, which reported the next highest migration rate, the number of migrants over the period grew by only 9.6 per cent.

Recent research on migration patterns from NI to the rest of the UK[3], i.e. Great Britain (GB), comes to two conclusions. First, during periods of relative prosperity in GB, migration out of NI is bi-modal, involving the movement both of persons possessing high levels of skills and training and also of persons possessing little by way of formal qualifications. In this respect NI–GB migration differs from inter-regional movements within GB, which are restricted mainly to the former category of person. Second, there appears to be considerable 'reverse' migration from GB to NI, both of persons unemployed in GB who remain unemployed in NI and also, more worryingly, of persons exchanging employment in GB for unemployment in NI. These findings cast doubt on the credibility of schemes which seek to address NI's unemployment problem through an encouragement of migration. As we have shown not only does NI, through migration, lose its unskilled unemployed: it also loses its most skilled and employable citizens. Thus, in the face of increased migration, the job-creating capacity of NI's economy must shrink as its best and brightest people leave. Moreover much of its export of unemployment is re-imported, through 'reverse' migration, at a later date.

Analysis of unemployment in NI also reveals several disquieting features. First is the fact that the overall unemployment rate (in February 1992 this was 14.2 per cent) compares unfavourably with the UK rate of 9.4 per cent; moreover, on a historical basis, NI has always had a higher unemployment rate (by approximately five percentage points) than the UK. Second is the geographical distribution of unemployment within NI: this varied, in February 1992, from 11 per cent in the Ballymena Travel-to-Work-Area (TTWA) to 30 per cent in the Strabane TTWA.[4] Third is the problem of the long-term unemployed (ie. those unemployed for over a year) which affects NI particularly badly: in January 1992, 49.7 per cent of the unemployed in NI were long-term unemployed; the corresponding percentage for the UK was only 27 per cent. Since the probability of finding a job falls sharply with the duration of unemployment – both because skills and motivation depreciate the longer a person is unemployed and also because employers are suspicious of the 'employability' of persons who have been unemployed for long periods -the solution to an unemployment problem, of given size, becomes more intractable the larger its make-up in terms of the long-term unemployed.[5]

NI'S MANUFACTURING BASE

Nothing illustrates the precipitous decline of manufacturing in NI better than the fact (noted earlier) that employment in this sector fell from 195,000 in 1950 (36 per cent of NI employment) to 104,000 in 1990 (18 per cent of NI employment). There are three -partly competing, partly complementary – hypotheses which attempt to explain this occurrence. The first is that NI manufacturing – even across identical industries – is less efficient than that in GB. The second hypothesis is that it is not so much that NI industry is inefficient but that NI has the 'wrong' industrial structure – a disproportionate concentration in declining industries and, with the onset of the troubles, the 'wrong' climate for industrial growth. The third hypothesis is that it is not so much inefficiency or wrong structure as ownership of NI industry that is to blame for the decline in NI manufacturing: the emphasis on inward investment, as an instrument for industrial development, has meant that NI industry is, disproportionately, of a branch-plant nature (with head quarters located elsewhere) and hence is particularly vulnerable to closures.

Productivity and Unit Labour Costs in NI Manufacturing

The first hypothesis is most closely associated with the work of Hitchens and Birnie (1989). They argued that NI's productivity level[6] in manufacturing as a whole was, in 1984, only 82 per cent of that achieved in GB: only in food, drink and tobacco and in man-made fibres did NI record a higher productivity level; in office machinery and data processing equipment it achieved only 58 per cent of the GB level. Nor was this differential of recent origin: NI has always had a productivity gap vis-a-vis GB in manufacturing though the size of the gap has fluctuated from 10 per cent in 1975 (i.e. NI productivity was 90 per cent of the GB level) to as much as 26 per cent in 1978.

Since these comparisons were on the basis of equivalent industries in NI and GB it was not possible to blame poor performance on poor industrial structure: Hitchens and Birnie (1989) argued that NI had lower productivity than the GB in most industry comparisons. Nor was this productivity gap compensated for by a gap of equivalent size in labour costs: unit labour costs in manufacturing, at least since 1978, were, in fact, higher in NI than in GB. This lack of competitiveness in costs was aggravated by the fact that NI products were generally of poorer quality than those manufactured in GB.[7]

There are several problems inherent in the Hitchens and Birnie (1989) analysis. First, their analysis was entirely in terms of labour productivity. However, labour is but one factor of production – it combines with capital, another factor, to produce output. What is therefore needed is a measure of productivity in terms of output-per-input where the input is a composite of labour and capital. Measuring productivity in terms of labour input alone may give a misleading picture of efficiency: for example, the construction of a complex plant with substantial capital expenditures but only minimal labour requirements may generate an impressive labour productivity index; however, when the total amortized value of the capital is taken into account the project might not appear quite so impressive.

Second, the analysis is in terms of value-added per worker not per hour. This could make a difference to the magnitude of the productivity gap, which is more properly measured in per hour rather than per person terms. For example, if one normalizes the UK at 100, then, in 1986, relative to the UK, Japan's GDP per head of population was 106, its GDP per person employed was 94 and its GDP per hour worked was only 67.[8] In part this reflects the fact that the number of hours worked per year is higher in Japan; in part it reflects the fact that average hours worked per employed person are lower – because of the relative preponderance of part-time working – in the UK. Extending this to inter-regional comparisons we could have workers working longer hours, say in the South-East, because the pressures of demand require them to work overtime. Then output-per-worker in the South-

East, relative to NI, would be high but output-per-hour might be less impressive.

Third, while differences in productivity levels might be of some interest, the real issue is one of rates of growth in productivity – in other words, regardless of how far behind NI is, is it, or is it not, 'catching up'? Two examples to illustrate the importance of growth (rather than levels) will suffice. The 'Thatcher miracle' of the 1980s was so termed because (notwithstanding the fact that the level of manufacturing productivity in the UK continues to be low in relation to its competitors[9]) the rate of growth of manufacturing productivity in the UK was surpassed only by Japan.[10] The second example, which is, in fact, cited by Hitchens and Birnie (1989), is that of the US, which is extremely concerned about its manufacturing base in relation to Japanese competition; this is not because the Japanese have a higher productivity level (the US level of manufacturing productivity is much higher than that in Japan) but because the Japanese have a higher productivity growth rate.

In terms of productivity growth the NI picture is not quite so gloomy as that painted in terms of levels. Table 1.2 shows the performance of the NI manufacturing sector vis-a-vis that of the UK for the period 1960–83. Up to 1973 the experiences of both NI and the UK were broadly similar: both enjoyed annual rates of growth in manufacturing output of slightly under 6 per cent and annual rates of labour productivity growth of just under 7 per cent. One can aggregate labour and capital to form a composite or 'total' factor of production. The productivity of this total factor, termed Total Factor Productivity (TFP), is then a weighted average of the productivity of labour and capital, the weights being determined by the respective shares of labour and capital in the value of output. Over 1960–73, NI had a lower rate of TFP growth mainly because its capital stock was growing faster than the UK's and hence, because of diminishing returns, its capital productivity was growing more slowly.

Between 1973 and 1979, NI suffered a greater loss of output than the UK but an even greater loss of employment: hence, over this period, labour productivity grew faster in NI than the UK . Both NI and the UK had, however, over the same period, negative rates of TFP growth caused mainly by the fact that rates of growth of capital productivity were negative. The recession of 1980–81 saw a shake-out of labour in both NI and the UK: manufacturing employment fell by an average, annual rate of 8.2 per cent in NI and 7.3 per cent in UK. The result was a sharp rise in labour productivity; however, TFP

Table 1.2 Output, input and productivity in the manufacturing sector of Northern Ireland and the UK[1]

	Northern Ireland	United Kingdom
1960–73		
Output	5.8	5.9
Factor input	2.6	1.9
TFP	3.2	5.0
Labour productivity	6.8	6.6
Capital productivity	-1.2	2.0
Unit labour costs	-1.3	-3.3
1973–79		
Output	-2.5	-0.2
Factor input	-0.8	1.1
TFP	-1.7	-1.3
Labour productivity	0.9	0.4
Capital productivity	-6.5	-3.4
Unit labour costs	3.3	-1.9
1979–83(86)		
Output	-2.1	-3.3
Factor input	-5.6	-3.4
TFP	3.6	0.4
Labour productivity	6.2	4.3
Capital productivity	-4.5	5.1
Unit labour costs	-1.6	-1.0

Sources: Borooah and Lee (1991)

Note 1: Output is net manufacturing output (NI) or value added in the manufacturing sector (UK) at constant prices. TFP growth is equal to either: (1) output growth minus factor input growth (a weighted index of capital and labour inputs); or (2) a weighted average of the growth of labour and capital productivity. Differences are due to rounding.

growth rates were considerably lower because capital accumulation continued apace.

When one combines the productivity growth rates with the behaviour of labour costs one sees (Table 1.2) that NI has suffered a loss of competitiveness (when that is defined in terms of unit labour costs) relative to the UK: except for 1979–83 the growth in unit labour costs in NI has always exceeded that in the UK. The reason for this is that factors affecting the demand for labour play little role in the determination of wages in NI. Instead, wages in NI have primarily been determined by aggregate UK rates moderated, to some extent, by local (i.e. NI) labour market conditions. There is an irony in this since the responsiveness of employment to the real wage rate is much greater in NI than in the UK[11] – i.e. real wage reductions could, if they were possible, be an important instrument of employment generation in NI. However, the evidence is that, in NI, it is not possible, with existing wage determination mechanisms, to reduce wage growth below UK levels.

The Structure of NI Industry and the Effect of the Troubles

In 1989 over nine-tenths of NI's GDP was generated from the following sources: agriculture (4 per cent); energy and water (3 per cent); manufacturing (17 per cent); construction (7 per cent); private services (31 per cent); public administration and H M Forces (14 per cent); education and health (15 per cent). The main contributors to manufacturing output were: food (17 per cent); drink and tobacco (12 per cent); leather, footwear and clothing (10 per cent); textiles (8 per cent); transport equipment (9 per cent); minerals, metals and chemicals (3 per cent).

Canning et al. (1987) examined the structural hypothesis in terms of manufacturing employment. The details of their findings are set out in Table 1.3. They identified four factors that, over 1950–83, could have had an effect on NI's manufacturing employment: the national decline in manufacturing; NI's industrial structure; the industrial policies of the NI government; and the 'troubles'. They concluded that while industrial structure was the main culprit in contributing to the decline in manufacturing employment over 1950–71, two other factors combined to produce a sharp fall in manufacturing employment over 1971–83. These were the national decline of manufacturing and the intensification of the 'troubles': Canning et al. (1987) calculated that, over 1971–83, approximately 40,000 manufacturing jobs were lost in NI due to the 'troubles'.[12]

Rowthorn and Wayne (1988) estimated that, over 1970–85, the 'troubles', by creating an atmosphere of uncertainty and doubt, led to the 'loss' of 46,000 manufacturing jobs – the term 'loss' being defined as the difference between the number of jobs that, in the absence of the troubles, would have existed and those that actually existed. Most of this was due to a loss of multinational confidence in NI: over 1966–71 multinationals set up fifty-one new manufacturing units in the province and created 11,600 new manufacturing jobs; by way of

Table 1.3 The contribution of selected factors to the change in manufacturing employment in Northern Ireland, 1950–83

	Actual	Estimated contribution of:			
		National	Industrial	Policy	Troubles
1950–51	-13	17	-34	0	0
1961–71	9	-9	-22	33	-1
1971–83	-74	-51	-2	17	-40

Source: Canning et al. (1987)

contrast, between 1972 and 1976 they established only fifteen new units and created only 900 new jobs. However, from the figure of 46,000 jobs lost in manufacturing must be subtracted the 36,000 jobs in the public sector (police, prisons, health, education, etc.) that, arguably, would not have been created without the conflict[13] and also the 5,000 security-related jobs in the private sector. Thus the effect of the troubles was probably to cause, between 1970 and 1985, a net job loss of 5,000 jobs representing only one per cent of total employment in 1970.[14] Of course underlying the smallness of this job loss was a severe structural shift in NI's economy from employment in manufacturing to employment in the public sector.

In a more recent study, Harris (1990) found that of the regions of the UK, NI had, over 1963–85, the most specialized manufacturing structure, with Scotland having the least specialized structure. Thus the poor economic performance of NI could have been the result of it having a disproportionate share of industries that, in general, had declined the most. If one calculated what NI growth rates *would have been* if it had had, instead, the UK's industrial structure then the finding was that, although NI's growth rate differences with the UK could not be entirely attributed to structural factors, NI's unfavourable structure was an important factor in restricting its growth rate when overall UK growth was high. In a similar vein Black (1992) calculated, on the basis of an analysis conducted at minimum list heading level, that, in 1987, over a third of NI's productivity gap, vis-a-vis the UK, could be explained by its industrial structure. Although this figure was substantially less than the 54 per cent that, on Black's (1992) calculations, industrial structure contributed, in 1935, to NI's productivity gap it was nevertheless substantial.

The Branch–Plant Nature of NI Manufacturing

In common with other peripheral regions, a great deal of industrial development in NI since 1945 – and most especially in the 1960s and early 1970s – was the result of its success in attracting firms from outside NI to set up manufacturing units in the province: between 1947 and 1967, over 90 per cent of all new industrial jobs in NI were created by 'externally controlled' firms setting up branch-plants in NI.[15] Harris (1990) estimated that, in 1986, only 59 per cent of NI manufacturing jobs were with companies whose headquarters were in NI. This last figure appears unusually high when compared to other UK regions: the corresponding figure for the Tyneside, for example, was only 39 per cent.[16] Such an ownership pattern in NI industry – with a disproportionate presence of external ownership and control – has serious implications for its conduct and performance.

First, there was the vulnerability of branch plants to closure whenever adverse economic conditions led the parent company to restructure its operations. The synthetic fibre and the tobacco industry were particularly affected by these closures. The *Financial Times* data base showed that, over 1976–85, of the 44,045 job losses in NI attributable to large UK companies operating in NI only 8,884 were in companies with headquarters in NI.[17] Fothergill and Guy (1990) concluded that NI plants were selected for closure mainly because of the marginal role they played in the operations of their parent companies and not because NI proved to be an unsuitable location.

These findings have serious implications for a policy of job-generation through inward investment. Although such investment provides the quickest way of generating jobs in NI, the fragility of such jobs is a major source of concern. The problem is that many of the branch plants are production-only plants (of the assembly or sub-assembly variety) and do not have R&D functions; nor are they part of divisional headquarters. Given these characteristics they are least likely to survive recessionary conditions. Apart from vulnerability to closure, the nature of NI's branch plants has other adverse implications. First the level of worker skills is, because of the nature of the operations, likely to be low: for every manufacturing industry in 1983, Harris (1990) showed that the proportion of manual to non-manual employees was higher in NI than in the UK. Second, because the branch plants are part of an internal market extending across the parent company's operations, its linkages are likely to be with other plants within the company and not with other firms in NI. This, in turn, has adverse implications for purchases from local suppliers.

The solution to the problem of generating jobs that are more resilient to recessionary conditions would appear to lie in two directions: first, to attract plants which, in addition to their production functions, also have R&D and administrative functions; second, to emphasize the encouragement of local enterprise.

In this connection, it is interesting to observe recent changes in attitude towards inward investment in the Republic of Ireland which, too, has relied greatly on the creation of jobs through externally-owned firms. Last month, the Irish government announced the creation of a new job creation agency with separate divisions for Irish- and overseas-owned industry. The existing Irish Development Agency (IDA) was geared towards attracting foreign investment but it has been recognized that this needs to be complemented by a strong domestic industry with clear linkages between the foreign- and domestically-owned parts of Irish industry.

THE PUBLIC SECTOR IN NI

Despite the decline of manufacturing, employment in NI has remained remarkably stable: in 1951 civilian employment in NI was 556,000; in 1986 it was 549,000. This stability was provided for partly by the rise in public sector employment and partly by the growth of employment in private services. Its most significant feature – apart from the falling share of manufacturing in total employment, a fact already commented upon – is the rise in employment in both public and private services: in 1951 about one in three jobs were service sector jobs; by 1991 services provided 71 per cent of total employment.

Paralleling this rise in service employment was a rise in public sector employment: in 1960 the estimated public sector employment in NI was 97,000 or 22 per cent of total employees in employment; by 1970 this had risen to 124,000 or 25 per cent of total employees in employment; over 1970–74 public sector employment rose by 40 per cent (at an average annual rate of almost 9 per cent) and constituted, in 1974, 35 per cent of employees in employment. Thereafter growth in public sector employment moderated: between 1974 and 1987 it averaged 1.3 per cent per year and between 1987 and 1991 it actually fell by about 1.5 per cent – the latest figures show that, in December 1991, 38 per cent of employees in employment were in the public sector.

There are two features of public sector employment in NI that are a cause for concern. The first is that there is little prospect of further expansion in such employment such as that witnessed in the early 1970s. The major impetus for this expansion between 1970 and 1974 came partly from the expansion in police and prison services (engendered in turn by a deteriorating security situation) and partly from an expansion of health and social services and education programmes with the intention of reaching British levels of provision in these areas. This has now been achieved and the level of provision of these services has, probably, now reached a plateau. Indeed, the most realistic outcome is a slight decline in the numbers that the public sector employs. This in turn raises questions about the employment prospects of new entrants to the labour market: if employment in the public sector is stagnant and if manufacturing is in decline then the only realistic source of employment is either in the construction industry or in private services. But the fact is that employment in both these sectors is heavily dependent on public sector policies: the former on public expenditure on housing and the latter on the demand generated by public sector incomes. Stagnation in the public sector would, consequently, affect employment in these sectors adversely.

The other worrying feature about the public sector in NI is its size in relation to the rest of the economy. It has already been noted that it provides 38 per cent of employment in NI. In the years to come, even though the numbers in public sector employment might not increase, the decline of employment in other sectors would mean that this percentage would rise. Another aspect of public sector dominance is the gap between public expenditure in NI and public revenues raised from NI: this is currently estimated to be about £2 billion and represents the 'subsidy' that NI receives from the remainder of the UK. To put matters differently, if NI were required to balance its budget then each person in NI – man, woman and child – would be worse off by about £1,300 per year.

Although it is difficult to quantify the argument, it is plausible to argue that the size of the public sector in NI creates a 'dependency culture'. At its most benign, job-seekers in NI – particularly the more qualified – would seek public sector jobs rather than private sector employment both because the former jobs would be remunerated at national rates and also because they would be more stable than private sector jobs. At a further remove, because the 'role model' for NI is paid employment (particularly in the public sector) there is no incentive to enter self-employment. Lastly, even for those in the private sector, there is considerable dependency on the public sector in terms of grants to start businesses and subsidies to on-going concerns. The consequence is that the discipline of market forces is considerably weakened in its application to NI.

INEQUALITY IN NI

The fact that the fissures of religion run through NI's society is, of course, well known. What is perhaps less well known is that the religious divide is reflected in economic differences between the Protestant and Catholic communities. These economic differences are revealed most starkly in the labour market experiences of persons in the two communities. The 1991 Labour Force Survey (LFS) for NI showed that participation rates varied considerably between Protestants and Catholics: 76 per cent of Protestants were economically active as compared to 68 per cent of Catholics. This difference persisted when one disaggregated by sex: the male and female participation rates for Protestants were respectively 87 and 65 per cent while for Catholics they were 79 and 56 per cent. Nor did a further disaggregation by age group reverse this finding: for each sex, and for every age group identified by the LFS in the working age population, Protestants had a higher participation rate than Catholics.[18]

Too much should not, however, be read into this: a much larger proportion of economically inactive Catholics were students (40 and 20 per cent of economically inactive Catholic men and women respectively) as compared to Protestants (36 and 15 per cent of economically inactive Protestant men and women respectively). However, notwithstanding the fact that Catholics had a higher proportion of students among their inactive population, the economically active part of the Catholic population was less well qualified than its Protestant counterpart. A higher proportion of the Catholic active population had no qualifications; this statement was also true when economically active Catholic men and women were considered separately.[19] Moreover, for every qualification level, a higher proportion of the Protestant active population possessed that qualification as compared to its Catholic counterpart: again this statement held for men and women considered separately.

Turning from participation to unemployment, the LFS showed that 18 per cent of the economically active Catholic population was unemployed as compared with only 8 per cent of the Protestant population.[20] Indeed, of the total number of unemployed males in the

LFS sample nearly two-thirds were Catholic. Again, for each sex, and for every age-group, Catholics had a higher unemployment rate than Protestants with the largest differences occurring in the twenty-five to thirty-nine age group in which, for both men and women, the Catholic unemployment rate was three times that of the Protestant rate. When unemployment was disaggregated by duration, Protestants had higher unemployment rates in the shorter durations of unemployment[21] but Catholics had higher rates in the longer durations. Thus not only was there an inter-community difference in unemployment rates in NI but it would appear that the disadvantage of the Catholic community, in this respect, became greater for the long-term unemployed.

The problem for policy makers in NI, therefore, is not merely to bring about a general reduction in unemployment but also to devise means by which the burden of unemployment can be more equitably distributed. This, in turn, raises the question of what causes inter-community unemployment rate differences in NI. Like most issues involving NI's religious divide it does not admit a set of answers which command universal support. Smith and Chambers (1991) catalogue a list of possible explanations other than that of direct discrimination and some of these are: (i) Catholics and Protestants operate in different labour markets with different employment opportunities; (ii) the location of jobs in NI does not favour Catholic areas; (iii) Catholics are disproportionately represented in socio-economic groups and age groups that are most prone to unemployment; (iv) Protestants are better qualified; (v) Catholics 'choose' unemployment because the benefit system favours large families (vi) the number of economically active Catholics – perhaps for demographic, perhaps for participation reasons – is growing faster than its Protestant counterpart so that, even if employment opportunities grow at the same rate for the two communities, the unemployment rate for Catholics will rise faster. It is not the purpose of this chapter to present a detailed evaluation of these explanations, or of the alternative hypothesis, that Catholics have a higher unemployment rate because they are discriminated against in the labour market. Some general points might, however, be usefully made.

First, the arguments as presented above are not independent arguments. Thus, explanation (i), Catholics and Protestants operate in different labour markets, is not unrelated to the locational argument of (ii). In other words Catholics and Protestants were concentrated in different areas and each community specialized in the industries that existed in their respective areas. It would be interesting to know if there were reasons, other than location, which constrained the communities to different markets. Rowthorn and Wayne (1988) suggested that no matter where they lived Catholics had a much higher unemployment rate than Protestants. For the segmented labour market argument to hold water it would be necessary to show that, regardless of residence in NI, the industrial/occupational specialization of the two communities remained unchanged. Second, the force of explanation (iii) is somewhat weak when it is argued that because Catholics have a younger population they would – because the young have special difficulty finding jobs – have a higher unemployment rate. The LFS shows that when one controls for youth by considering the age band 16–24 the Catholic unemployment rate for this group at 26 per cent was substantially higher than its Protestant equivalent of 15 per cent.

Third, on the basis of the LFS, explanation (iv) would appear to have some force; the Catholic labour force was, in general, less qualified than its Protestant counterpart. This must, however, be tempered with the observation that Catholics were most disadvantaged, in employment terms, in precisely those occupations for which they were relatively most qualified. For example, a greater proportion – 14 against 13 per cent – of the Catholic labour force had 'higher than A-level' qualifications; however, among the occupational groups where one would imagine such qualifications to be most relevant, only 26 per cent of managers and administrators were Catholic.

Fourth, the argument about differential rates of population growth is one designed to explain why, over time, even with employment opportunities growing equally for the two communities, the difference between the Catholic and Protestant unemployment rates would grow; consequently, after a sufficient accumulation of such a difference, the Catholic unemployment rate would exceed the Protestant rate. It is true that the Catholic population in NI has grown at a rate much greater than that of the Protestant population: between 1951 and 1981 the Catholic population of NI grew by 25 per cent while the Protestant population grew, over the same period, by only 5 per cent. However, this again must be tempered by the fact that Catholics have a lower participation rate so that while they may constitute 40 per cent of NI's population they, in fact, constitute a smaller proportion of the economically active population.

Lastly, it is true that unemployment differences may be an imperfect measure of differences in economic welfare between the two communities: the operation of the benefit system might lead to income differences (arguably a better indicator of relative welfare) being narrower. Research carried out at the University of Ulster, using NI Family Expenditure Survey (FES) data for 1989, shows that on average, the disposable income of a family with a Catholic head was, at £110 per week, 16 per cent less than that of a Protestant family's income. One further feature of this research deserves mention here. Catholic families with an employed head had on average, a weekly, disposable income of £167; 'large' Catholic families (i.e. with three or more children) had a weekly, disposable, income of £108. There is, on this basis, no evidence for the assertion that 'large' Catholic families would be better off on benefits than in employment – on average they clearly would not be.

LESSONS FOR POLICY

This chapter has argued that NI's economic problems have stemmed from essentially three sources. The first is the problem of labour supply as manifest in the fact that the region has the fastest-growing labour force in the UK. The second is the problem of labour demand as evidenced by the fact that the growth of employment opportunities in NI has failed to keep up with the growth of its labour force. The most significant feature of this failure on the jobs front has, of course, been the decline of manufacturing in NI. The conjunction of these two trends has led to high rates of unemployment in NI and also to high rates of migration out of NI. However, for reasons that this chapter has discussed in some detail, policy makers should resist the temptation to believe that migration therefore presents a solution to NI's unemployment problem.

Yet another consequence of the demand/supply imbalance in NI's labour market has been the rise of public sector employment in order to offset the loss of private sector jobs. The growth of the public sector in NI, coupled with a collapse in its manufacturing base, has maintained the level of employment in NI at around 500,000 jobs but at the cost of a greatly distorted economic structure: nearly two-fifths of jobs in NI are in the public sector and less than one-fifth of jobs are in manufacturing. The problem of job creation in NI cannot, therefore, be divorced from the sources of these jobs. It is clear that the public sector, as an engine for job creation in NI, has run out of steam and it is likely that, in its train, the number of jobs in private services and in the construction industry will also stagnate. Therefore there seems no alternative but to rely on a revitalized manufacturing sector to provide jobs in NI. The question is how this is to be brought about?

It is not the purpose of this chapter to attempt to detail a set of policies – assuming that were possible – for the industrial regeneration of NI. However, some general remarks can usefully be made. The role of state intervention in development is one of the oldest issues in economics and debate on this topic has revolved around the question of when, and to what extent, governments should intervene. More recent studies however (cf. Rodrik (1992), Newberry (1992)) emphasize the *quality* rather than the *quantity* of intervention. It is differences in quality, not quantity, that explain why state intervention has proved disastrous for the economies of Latin America, Eastern Europe, Africa and the Indian sub-continent, but has provided the foundation for growth and prosperity in successful economies such as Japan, Korea and Taiwan.

Rodrik (1992) draws a distinction between 'autonomous' and 'subordinate' states. In the former type of state, policies are formulated autonomously and the private sector lacks the ability to avoid compliance or to redefine these policies as they are implemented. In short, government is a leader. In the latter type of state, government decisions are rarely final and outcomes are the result of an interplay between government and private sector interests. In short, government is a follower and compromiser. Rodrik (1992) shows that subordinate states do not have the correct incentives for removing market failures – compared to autonomous states they systematically under-provide desirable interventions and over-provide harmful interventions. An example of the two government types is provided by their respective attitudes to public sector bodies (Sah and Weitzman (1991)). Subordinate governments have problems disciplining such bodies: they automatically absorb the losses of such bodies, routinely obfuscate their objectives and exonerate them when objectives are not met. Autonomous governments control their public sector bodies by getting them to undertake specific commitments and penalizing them – possibly through liquidation – if these commitments are reneged upon.

Given that the first requirement for successful state intervention is that governments provide leadership, Newberry (1992) enquires into the forms that such leadership should take. He argues that the development task facing countries in the last decade of the twentith century is different from that which faced today's developed countries in the nineteenth century. Then the development problem was one of invention and innovation; the problem today is one of imitation and adaptation. The process is one of transferring and applying 'best practice' techniques and this requires one to commit current resources to uncertain future gains. Much of this uncertainty will be institutional – it will arise because institutions to reduce this risk to acceptable levels either do not exist or, if they do, operate imperfectly. The problem of development is one of 'missing markets', namely, that the markets for future outputs and inputs do not exist. It is this 'market failure' that, according to Newberry (1992), provides both the rationale and direction of government intervention. Governments must intervene in the economy to create such 'future oriented' institutions so as to compensate for the missing 'futures' markets for outputs and inputs.

The creation of such institutions is particularly important in the case of manufacturing. This importance stems from the nature of modern industry with its requirements of large scale investment, of specialized and lengthy training for managers and workers, of access to competitively priced inputs both from home and abroad and of access to foreign markets for the sale of some of its output. Investment requires access to financial institutions that will lend long-term at internationally competitive interest rates. The requirements of training need the intervention of government to ensure that the reluctance of firms to train workers, in the face of uncertainty about whether such workers will not be poached by other firms, is not a barrier to the creation of a well-trained labour force. Access to competitively priced inputs has two aspects. First, on the domestic front, the machinery for wage negotiation should not be such that wage growth consistently outstrips productivity improvements. If competitiveness is being lost through the process of 'free' collective bargaining then the task of government is to carry out the necessary reforms and to send the appropriate signals to arrest, and indeed reverse, this process. Second, on the external front, the exchange rate should be both competitive and reasonably stable and the market for imports should not be distorted either through discriminatory quotas or tariffs. The role of government is to set up institutions or to enter into negotiations that will ensure this. Lastly, the desirability of selling for export requires the setting up of arrangements, in which firms have confidence, to provide a structure of incentives for foreign sales.

Against this background it is possible to sketch the outline of a policy scenario for NI. Most importantly, one needs a pro-active government (and government agencies) that will provide leadership first, by defining clearly, after due consultation (with a number of persons), its economic goals, and second by a commitment to predictable rules of behaviour that are consistently, firmly and uniformly applied. The overriding objective of policy must be to generate higher rates of industrial growth, and in adopting this goal, there must be the clear recognition that this may, in the short run, conflict with the creation of jobs. Industrial growth requires greater efficiency, and this, at least in the initial stages of development when output sales do not grow very fast, would mean that the growth in jobs might not keep pace with that of growth of output. It is clear that higher rates of growth can only be generated, and sustained, through a vastly improved export performance and 'export-led growth' must be the key policy objective. If exports are to be NI's industrial salvation then the success, or failure, of the government's industrial policies must be judged by a single, clear, unambiguous and, most importantly, non-manipulable, performance measure, namely, the growth in the volume of NI's exports.

Once goals are established resources should be diverted to encourage and nurture export oriented industries. This may require the primacy of engineers as managers supported by skilled workers; it may require wage subsidies to attract qualified managers and workers; it may require training subsidies and the establishment of a training infrastructure; it may require preferential access to subsidized credit. In putting such policies forward it is important, as Newberry (1992) points out, to read the lessons correctly. Many countries have been attracted to the idea of modern enterprises which reap economies of scale; in many countries, most notably in those of Eastern Europe, state intervention to ensure this outcome has ended in disaster. The reason that such intervention has succeeded among the 'Asian Tigers' is, firstly, that their industries were indigenously owned and, secondly, that such industries were forged on the anvil of foreign competition. It is on this anvil that NI's industry must be reshaped.

ACKNOWLEDGEMENT

I am grateful to Vidya Borooah for comments on an earlier version of this paper. Needless to say, I alone am responsible for its shortcomings.

NOTES

1. The closest was Scotland with a 0.9 per cent annual rate of growth.
2. Jefferson (1990).
3. See Forsythe and Borooah (1992).
4. NI Economic Council (1992).
5. Layard, Nickell and Jackman (1991).
6. Defined as value-added per employee.
7. See Hitchens and O'Farrell (1988).
8. See H. M. Treasury (1989).
9. With UK=100, manufacturing output per person employed was, in 1989: USA (177); France (112); Germany (105.1). See Broadberry (1992).
10. Over 1979–86 the average, annual, rate of growth of real value added in manufacturing per person employed was: Japan (6.3); UK (4.1); USA (3.3); and Germany (2.0). See Nolan (1989) for further discussion on this topic.
11. See Borooah and Lee (1991).
12. It is important to stress that these were not actual job losses but rather jobs that, but for the troubles, would have been created.
13. Canning et al. (1987) and Rowthorn and Wayne (1988) argue that without the conflict fiscal policy would have remained devolved and a balanced budget would have led to the creation of fewer public sector jobs.
14. See Rowthorn and Wayne (1988).
15. Rowthorn and Wayne (1988).
16. Fothergill and Guy (1990).
17. See Harris (1990).
18. For example, the participation rate of prime-age males (25–44) was 96 per cent for Protestants and 91 per cent for Catholics.
19. Both sexes: 44 (C) and 38 (P) per cent; Men: 50 (C) and 43 (P) per cent; Women: 35 (C) and 32 (P) per cent.
20. Note that the fact that a person was unemployed was not, in the LFS, determined by registering as unemployed, but through actively seeking work.
21. Less than 6 months and 6–12 months.

REFERENCES

Black, B. (1992), *Northern Ireland's Manufacturing Productivity Revisited*, Queen's University, Belfast (mimeo).

Borooah, V.K. and Lee, K.C. (1991), 'The Regional Dimension of Competitiveness in Manufacturing: Productivity, Employment and Wages in Northern Ireland', *Regional Studies*, vol. 25. pp. 219–30.

Broadberry, S.N. (1992), 'Manufacturing and the Convergence Hypothesis: What the long run data show', *Discussion Paper No.708*, Centre for Economic Policy Research, No. U2, London.

Canning, D., Moore, B. and Rhodes, J. (1987), 'Economic Growth in Northern Ireland: problems and prospects', in P. Teague (ed.), *Beyond the Rhetoric: Politics, The Economy and Social Policy in Northern Ireland*, Lawrence and Wishart, London.

Forsythe, F.P. and Borooah, V.K. (1992), 'The Nature of Migration Between Northern Ireland and Great Britain: a preliminary analysis based on the Labour Force Surveys 1986–88', *The Economic and Social Review*, Vol.23, pp. 105–27.

Fothergill, S. and Guy, N. (1990), *Branch Factory Closures in Northern Ireland*, Northern Ireland Economic Research Centre, Belfast.

Harris, R.I.D. (1990) 'Manufacturing Industry' in R.I.D. Harris, C.W. Jefferson and J.E. Spencer (eds) *The Northern Ireland Economy*, Longman, 1990.

Hitchens, D.M.W.N. and Birnie, J.E. (1989), *Manufacturing Productivity in Northern Ireland: a comparison with Great Britain*, Northern Ireland Economic Research Centre, Belfast.

Hitchens, D.M.W.N. and O'Farrell, P.N. (1988), 'The Comparative Performance of Small Manufacturing Companies in South Wales and Northern Ireland', *Omega*, vol. 16, pp. 429–38.

H.M. Treasury (1989), 'Productivity in the 1980s', *Economic Progress Report*, no. 201, pp. 1–5.

Jefferson, C.W. (1990), 'The Labour Market', in R.I.D. Harris, C.W. Jefferson and J.E. Spencer (eds) *The Northern Ireland Economy*, Longman, 1990.

Layard, P.R.G., Nickell, S. and Jackman, R. (1991), *Unemployment*, OUP, Oxford.

Newberry, D.M. (1992), 'The Role of Public Enterprises in the National Economy', *Asian Development Review* (forthcoming).

Nolan, P. (1989), 'The Productivity Miracle?', in F. Green (ed.) *The Restructuring of the UK Economy*, Harvester Wheatsheaf, London, 1989.

Northern Ireland Economic Council (1992) *Economic Assessment*, Report 93, NIEC, Belfast.

Rodrick, D. (1992), 'Political Economy and Development Policy', *European Economic Review*, Vol. 36, pp. 329–336.

Rowthorn, B. and Wayne, N. (1988), *Northern Ireland: The Political Economy of Conflict*, Polity Press, Oxford.

Sah, R.K. and Weitzman, M.L. (1991), 'A Proposal for Using Incentive Precommitments in Public Enterprise Funding', *World Development*, Vol. 19, pp. 595–605.

Smith, D.J. and Chambers, G. (1991), *Inequality in Northern Ireland*, Clarendon Press, Oxford.

2
Economic Performance in Northern Ireland: A Comparative Perspective

D.M.W.N. Hitchens, J.E. Birnie and K. Wagner

This chapter traces the long-term comparative performance of the two Irish economies (Northern Ireland and the Republic of Ireland) since the creation of these states in 1921, with special reference being given to the role of institutions as determinants of economic growth. Particular emphasis is placed on living standards (GDP per capita) as a yardstick by which to judge the success or otherwise of the economies, and Britain is used as a benchmark against which to measure performance.

Both Northern Ireland and the Republic of Ireland have been characterized by levels of GDP per capita which are substantially lower than those in Britain and the extent of convergence has been very limited over the last seventy years. This disappointing performance contrasts with that of other small European economies which started from positions comparable to those of Northern Ireland and the Republic of Ireland and were nevertheless able to catch up with and overtake the British economy.

The productivity of the manufacturing sector is considered as a second indicator of the long-term performance of the Irish economies. Comparative performance in terms of living standards is at least in part related to the levels of relative productivity that are achieved. This second indicator of performance also shows that the Irish economies have failed (the manufacturing sector in Northern Ireland and the indigenous manufacturing sector in the Republic of Ireland) to close a chronic shortfall in productivity relative to Britain. Given that British productivity levels were falling back relative to standards of international best practice during most of the period under review, the Irish economies are implied to be characterized by massive productivity gaps relative to North American and western European standards.

Institutions are defined as those factors that set the framework within which the market economy operates and are, at least in principle, amenable to alteration by public policy. The institutions of one country could raise or lower its economic performance relative to another country. It is therefore appropriate to consider the impact of institutions in a comparative framework. Given that the long-term economic performance of the Irish economies could be characterized as a worse case of the 'British disease' in the sense that there has been a longstanding shortfall in performance relative to Britain, the problem is therefore to identify those institutional features which have handicapped performance even by the relatively poor standards set by Britain. The effects of three institutions are considered to be:

1. A *technical and vocational education system* which has given rise to a worse case of the British problem of a lack of appropriate training and skills;
2. A longstanding and relatively high rate of *subsidy support* to manufacturing in both Northern Ireland and the Republic of Ireland (relative to both Britain and most of the rest of the European Community represents a further institutional brake on performance given that in the past these subsidies have cushioned inefficiency rather than act as a spur to greater competitiveness. The subsidies had a range of harmful effects including: leakage into wage levels higher than those warranted by relative productivity, support to the profitability of otherwise marginal firms, wasteful investment, and intensified X-inefficiency (e.g. managerial slack, overstaffing, unco-operative work attitudes).
3. *Industrial policy* in both the Irish economies from the 1950s to the 1980s could be considered as a further harmful institutional effect. It was *biased* towards inward investment and grant assistance to physical capital. Policy makers were therefore giving too little stress to improvements in the indigenous sector and the importance of human capital.

COMPARATIVE ECONOMIC PERFORMANCE

Varying Extents of Convergence in Living Standards

In reviewing the varying impacts of institutions on economic performance in the Irish economies and East Germany, one means of evaluating performance is to consider the differing extents to which these economies were able to achieve rates of economic growth which produced convergence in levels of living standards relative to the top international performers. Table 2.1 compares levels of GDP per capita in NI, the Republic of Ireland (ROI) and the UK and other western economies in 1913 and 1985.

Notwithstanding some limitations on the data[1] some conclusions are clear. Both NI and the ROI have attained some convergence towards the UK level during 1913–85 but it is important to put these gains into perspective. The UK itself was slipping down the international rankings and so, in some ways, represented a poor standard by which to judge the performance of the Irish economies. In 1913 NI, and to a lesser extent the ROI, had levels of GDP per capita which were close to those in West Germany, France and New Zealand, for example, and far ahead of those in Italy and Japan. However, by 1985 the West German level was more than one and a half times that of either of the Irish economies. The other economies had also pulled ahead. Similarly, the advantage of the USA and Canada relative to the two Irish economies also widened.

Apart from falling back relative to two of the major western economies, i.e. the USA and West Germany, it is also striking how undistinguished Irish performance has been when compared to the small economies of central and northern Europe. In 1913 the Benelux economies, Denmark and Switzerland, had a clear advantage relative to NI and the ROI but the Irish economies, and especially NI, were doing at least as well as or better than the remaining Scandinavian economies. However, by 1985 the Irish economies had been left far behind all the Scandinavian, Benelux and Alpine economies.

The Irish economies can also be compared with those members of the EC which along with NI and the ROI have been given the status of Objective One areas and eligibility for special structural and cohesion funds, given their low levels of GDP per capita compared to the EC average. Between 1913 and 1985 Spanish living standards overtook those in the ROI and achieved a level close to those in NI. At the end of the period Portugal and Greece still lay behind the ROI though the gap had closed markedly.

Table 2.1 Comparative GDP per capita, 1913 and 1985 compared in USA $ of 1985 purchasing power (level as a percentage of that in the UK, UK=100)

	1913	1985
NI	62[a]	78
ROI	55[b]	62
UK	100	100
Major market economies		
France	65	105
Italy	56	99
West Germany	67	111
Canada	96	141
Australia	107	108
New Zealand	70	93
USA	126	152
Japan	30	108
Small 'successful' European economies		
Switzerland	91	123
Denmark	72	113
Belgium	78	98
Netherlands	78	104
Sweden	59	116
Austria	64	99
Norway	52	128
Finland	46	105
EC Objective One areas		
Spain	49	70
Greece	28	55
Portugal	26	51

Note: a: 1924. b: 1926.

Source: Comparative figures for 1985 derived from OECD (1987) which were then backcast to 1913 using national volume series of GDP per capita (Maddison, 1982; and for the ROI, Kennedy, Giblin and McHugh, 1988).

In short, by almost every standard of comparison the relative performance of the Irish economies appears disappointing and in the twentieth century there has been divergence rather than convergence when compared to most other western economies (on the basis of large-scale data samples Barro and Sala-i-Martin (1991) identify a 'normal' rate of international and inter-regional convergence within the capitalist world, and by this standard also the Irish economies are found wanting). Admittedly, performance in this respect was not as bad as that implied for East Germany but this is not much of a consolation. It is also worth bearing in mind that these comparisons are couched in those terms (i.e. GDP per capita) which are most favourable from the point of view of the ROI given that in recent years the GNP of the ROI has been about one-tenth lower than GDP (this is a result of interest repayments on foreign debt and the outflows of profits from international companies).

The counterpart of the dismal performance of the Irish economies in terms of slipping down the league table of western market economies is that their rate of growth of GDP per capita during 1913–85 was amongst the lowest recorded by any industrial economy either capitalist or planned. This is illustrated in Table 2.2.

In terms of GDP per capita both the ROI and UK occupy positions at almost the bottom of the table. NI appears to have done rather better, though this result is partly attributable to the fact that the estimated growth rate, unlike those for the other countries, did not include the years 1913–23 which were generally characterized by low rates of growth. The performance of NI and especially the ROI is even less impressive when considered in terms of total output. The comparative growth performance of the Irish economies in per capita terms was boosted by the fact that the number of heads was increasing relatively slowly (i.e. the high rate of emigration from Ireland enabled the Irish economies to attain higher growth of per capita income despite relatively low rates of increase of total product). Given this the comparison of levels of GDP per capita in Table 2.1 may present an unduly favourable impression of the relative performance of the Irish economies in raising living standards for the population inclusive of those who were in effect 'exported' to other countries.

Convergence and Divergence in Manufacturing Productivity

One of the main determinants of the level of GDP per capita is the productivity of the employed labour force (i.e. GDP per person in employment). Admittedly international variations in the level of GDP per capita are also in part explained by differences in the extent of participation in the labour force. Both NI and the ROI have relatively low participation rates, which provides part of the explanation for their relatively low levels of income per head (Hitchens, Wagner and Birnie,

Table 2.2 Comparative real growth rates, 1913-1985

	GDP per capita (Ranked by per capita growth rates)	Total GDP
Japan	3.3	4.5
Norway	2.7	3.5
Finland	2.6	3.3
Bulgaria	2.5	3.5
USSR	2.4	3.3
Greece	2.4	3.1
Portugal	2.4	3.1
Yugoslavia	2.4	3.4
Sweden	2.4	3.0
Italy	2.2	2.9
Austria	2.1	2.2
West Germany	2.1	2.8
Denmark	2.0	2.8
Canada	2.0	3.7
France	2.0	2.5
NI	2.0[a]	2.4[a]
Spain	1.9	2.8
Poland	1.9	n.a
Czechoslovakia	1.9	2.8
Romania	1.9	2.9
Hungary	1.8	2.3
New Zealand	1.8	3.3
Switzerland	1.8	2.6
Belgium	1.8	2.1
Netherlands	1.8	3.0
USA	1.7	3.0
ROI	1.6	1.8
UK	1.4	1.8
Australia	1.4	3.1

Note: a: 1924-1985 only (on a comparable basis the UK GDP per capita growth rate was 1.7 and the ROI 1.8).

Source: Maddison (1982); OECD (1987); Kennedy, Giblin and McHugh (1988).

1990). Nevertheless, levels of productivity can also be used as an indicator of economic performance and the extent of convergence towards international best practice.

A further reason for attention to productivity is that it has implications for competitiveness. Both NI and the ROI have had longstanding problems of an underemployment of labour. In small open economies increased employment is most likely to come about through increased trade share in world markets. Such an increased share is in turn dependent on improvements in competitiveness, which are most likely to be achieved through higher productivity (policies of relative wage reductions or exchange rate devaluations are either impracticable or very tightly constrained). We focus here on the comparative productivity of manufacturing, given the significance of this sector in terms of linkages and large share of the total production of tradeable products.

A number of conclusions can be drawn from Table 2.3 which illustrates the comparative manufacturing productivity performance of NI, the ROI, and East and West Germany. Given that manufacturing in the UK exhibits a substantial productivity gap relative to international best practice (represented here by West Germany and the USA) it can be seen that NI is very far behind the international productivity frontier notwithstanding the so-called 'productivity miracle' experienced by UK manufacturing during the 1980s. An apparently more sanguine conclusion can be drawn for the ROI where levels of net output per head are implied to be similar to those in West Germany (though still lagging behind those found in the USA). However, it should be stressed that a strong contrast can be drawn between the performance of the indigenous and the non-Irish owned sectors in the ROI (see Table 2.4). Thus in 1988 the productivity of the indigenous sector in the ROI was only four-fifths that of the level attained by UK manufacturing. Irish-owned firms, however, had a net out put per head which was only 79 per cent of the UK average.

When the performance of the Irish economies relative to one of the former communist bloc economies, the former East Germany, is considered, this is of particular interest given that development since the onset of German economic and monetary union is equivalent to a controlled experiment for NI and the ROI as to what may happen to a weak low-productivity economy when it is suddenly integrated with a strong high-productivity economy. In 1991 levels of value added per head in East Germany were still lower than those in either NI manufacturing or the indigenous sector in the ROI though the gap was no longer very large (indeed, the physical productivity of a sample of firms, i.e. the volume of output without making allowance for quality or price differences, has been indicated to be comparable to that of NI; Hitchens, Wagner and Birnie, 1993). It is significant given the chronic nature of the productivity deficiencies of NI manufacturing and of Irish-owned firms in the ROI that firms in East Germany have been shown to have made very rapid progress in narrowing the productivity differential relative to best practice in western Europe (levels of output per head rising by 50 per cent in the first year of German monetary and economic union; Hitchens, Wagner and Birnie, 1993).

Table 2.3 Manufacturing productivity of NI, the ROI and East Germany compared to international best practice, 1935–1990 (net output per head as per cent of average for UK, UK=100)

	1935	1968	1985	1987	1989	1990	1991
ROI	88	82	148[a]			154[b]	
NI	62	85	76		73		
East Germany	n.a.	n.a.	n.a.			34[c]	51[d]
West Germany	102	135[e]	127[f]			110[f]	
UK	100	100	100			100	
USA	208[g]	289[e]		187[h]			

Note: see note 2 at the end of the chapter.

Source: As in note 2 and comparisons of NI, ROI and the UK derived from Hitchens and Birnie (1992).

Despite an apparently strong position relative to NI and perhaps even the UK average, the ROI's productivity and competitive achievement remains seriously flawed in two crucial respects. First, high performance is unevenly distributed between the indigenous and external sectors. Secondly, the extent to which the social benefits of inward investment policy exceed the costs may not be large. Thus, in some respects, the ROI shares the manufacturing problems experienced in NI.

The comparatively high level of productivity is primarily the responsibility of foreign owned firms in a limited number of industrial sectors (especially pharmaceuticals, electronics, office machinery and data processing equipment and soft drinks; the role of industrial structure is considered in the next section).

Table 2.4 shows the gulf separating the average productivity performance of ROI-owned and externally-owned firms in the ROI.

Table 2.4 ROI's comparative manufacturing productivity by ownership type (ROI/UK, UK=100)*

	1985	1987	1988
Indigenous ROI	81	85	79
External ROI	198	211	210
All ROI	132	139	137
All NI/UK	76	74	72

Note: * Net output per head using average market exchange rates (ROI data includes firms in the 3–19 employees size band, the UK data does not).

During the late 1980s levels of output per head in the external sector were about twice as high as those achieved by manufacturing in the UK. However, productivity levels in the indigenous sector remained 15–20 per cent below those in the UK. Indeed the productivity performance of the locally-owned firms in the ROI is much closer to that of manufacturing in NI than it is to the foreign subsidiaries operating within the ROI.

In fact the substandard performance of the indigenous sector is demonstrated by a range of indicators. For example, whereas the indigenous manufacturing sector experienced an employment decline of 13 per cent during 1973–80, the decline for the whole of manufacturing was only 5 per cent. During the 1980s employment in the foreign-owned sector actually grew by 3 per cent (to 93,000 in 1990) but the numbers engaged in Irish-owned firms dropped by 21 per cent (to 120,000). The indigenous firms have proved able to increase the share of output exported; 19 per cent in 1960, 26 per cent in 1973, 31 per cent in 1984, 36 per cent in 1988 (the figures for 1960 and 1973 are those of O'Malley (1989) for 'all firms other than new external', [a] i.e. firms which were established in the ROI before 1960 and will include some foreign owned establishments). However, even though exports have been increased imports have expanded even more rapidly. O'Malley (1989) estimates that for a number of sectors such as wood and furniture, metal goods and engineering, chemicals, textiles and clothing and footwear, competing imports expanded their market share in the ROI by more than 2 per cent per annum. The consequence of this market penetration has been that the bulk of ROI indigenous firms are now found in those sectors (e.g. mineral products, food, drink and tobacco) which are somewhat sheltered from international competition.

ARE THE IRISH ECONOMIES A WORSE CASE OF THE BRITISH DISEASE?

Given that NI and the ROI have, over the long run, lagged behind the UK in terms of both living standards and manufacturing productivity, this suggests that they could be characterized by a worse case of the British disease (i.e. prolonged relative economic decline with particularly poor performance in manufacturing). This in turn raises the questions as to how far the British disease was caused by factors which apply to the Irish economies as well.

Investigations of the causes of the British disease suggest that certain factors are not of crucial significance. For example, the structure of manufacturing industry has been shown to be similar to that in the USA and West Germany (Smith, Hitchens and Davies, 1982). (Though a more up- to-date comparison of UK and German productivity suggests that the two industrial structures were less alike in 1987 than in 1968 and that up to one-seventh of the overall productivity gap may have been attributable to this differential structure; O'Mahony (1992).) Moreover, the UK does not appear to be generally disadvantaged in terms of the relative size of British companies (UK firms have a larger representation amongst the 100 or 500 largest public companies in Europe than would be expected given the overall size of the UK economy). Admittedly, certain large chemicals, car and engineering producers in the UK are substantially smaller than competitors in West Germany or Japan (Pratten, 1986), though this could be as much the consequence of a lack of competitiveness as its cause. Prais (1981) found little difference between the overall median plant size in West Germany and UK manufacturing in 1970–73, though there were some marked sectoral variations. By 1987 the overall UK median plant size had fallen back relative to Germany though those sectors with the largest reductions in plant size were also those with the strongest productivity growth, which suggests that they had been subjected to the greatest shock effects in the 1980s and consequently experienced the so-called productivity miracle (O'Mahony 1992).

Careful matching of the productive capital stock in manufacturing suggests that a deficiency in terms of the quantity of capital may be less marked than comparison of the aggregate economy-wide capital and investment data would suggest(Maddison, 1982). (O'Mahoney (1992), following the method of Maddison (1991) and Summers and Heston (1991) which assumes the same service lives in the different countries, estimates German manufacturing to have a capital–labour ratio 28 per cent higher than its UK counterpart, but this gap would be narrower if the service lives of British assets are indeed longer than in other industrial countries. Indeed, one survey suggested that the capital intensity of British metal working companies exceeded that of counterparts in the USA (Prais, 1986). Certain high-technology items of equipment (e.g. computer numerically controlled machine tools, CNCs) may be less well represented in UK companies (Daly, Hitchens and Wagner, 1985; Hitchens, Wagner and Birnie, 1990) but UK firms are not always at a disadvantage in terms of the quality of their machine stock. In fact, a mix of statistical and survey evidence suggests that the machine stock in UK industry is not substantially older than that in either West Germany or the USA (Rostas, 1948; Bacon and Eltis, 1974; Daly, Hitchens and Wagner, 1985; Hitchens, Wagner and Birnie, 1990.)

Given that industrial structure, size of firms, and quantity and quality of the capital stock may not be major explanations of the UK productivity gap, most commentators have focused on a range of other factors, many of which could be considered as institutional; e.g. a short-termist bias in the capital market, inadequate levels of spending on R&D, failure to develop formal technical and vocational training,[3] systems of industrial relations which encouraged confrontation and disharmony (Barnett, 1986; Crafts, 1988, 1991). As a region within the UK it is not unreasonable to claim that NI would share some of these institutional weaknesses. Although the ROI has been an independent country since 1921 the legacy of institutions inherited from Britain is still substantial (O'Farrell, 1986). Nevertheless, NI and especially the ROI have enjoyed some scope for separate development so, in tracing the impact of institutions in performance, we consider not only the factors which are like Britain, but also those which are particular to the Irish economies.

We now proceed to review the impact of institutional factors (training and education; industrial subsidies; and industrial policy as a whole), which may have had negative impacts on economic growth and productivity. In tracing the harmful effects of these institutions we are not denying that there may be certain other hindrances to the economic development of NI and the ROI which are not discussed here but are worthy of attention.[4]

Training and Education

It is in the area of training and education that both NI and the ROI have followed Britain with crucial effects. The parallels between the experience of ROI and the UK arise because the common administration of Ireland and Britain during 1800–1921 implies that ROI may also have developed at least some of those attitudes and institutions which were to the detriment of productivity growth. Whilst the NI education system has not developed along identical lines to that in the rest of the UK, the irony is that it may display the features of the general British problem but with an even greater intensity (e.g. the proportion of unqualified school leavers is higher).

In the UK there has been a longstanding failure to provide technical and vocational training and education to a standard comparable with that achieved in other industrial economies. As Table 2.5 illustrates, the deficiency is one of both quantity and quality (i.e. the stock of skills in UK manufacturing is comparatively small and the quality of those qualifications which are produced by the training and education system is suspect). Both Irish economies share the quantitative problem and it can be assumed that at best they do no better than Britain on the qualitative side.

The case for considering the ROI as a case of the British disease is strengthened by consideration of the experience of NI. Matched plant comparisons between larger firms in NI and West Germany implied that the NI companies were victims of a more intense version of the British disease particularly with regard to low levels of technical and vocational skills (Hitchens, Wagner and Birnie, 1990). We have already seen that levels of value added per head in the indigenous sector in the ROI are similar to those in NI. The implication is that Irish-owned firms in the ROI share the difficulties of their counterparts in the North with respect to low levels of physical productivity and comparatively poor product quality. This problem is, in turn, the outcome of a lack of production skills and restricted management capabilities.

NI's competitiveness problems would seem to be part of a general problem in the UK where there has been a longstanding failure to provide technical and vocational training and education to a standard comparable with that achieved in other industrial economies. In 1921 the Irish Free State, as the ROI then was, inherited an education system which was strongly influenced by the English model and though this has since been modified, it is highly unlikely that the ROI has been able to increase the output of its technical and vocational education much beyond that of the UK both in terms of quantity and quality.

Tables 2.5 and 2.6 are illustrative and require further refinement for a more accurate comparison, but for what they are worth indicate the scale of the skills differences between the ROI and Britain and European best practice, and that in this respect the ROI has more in common with either Britain or NI than West Germany.

Some of these figures relate to flows rather than stocks and these cannot conclusively prove that the ROI shares the UK's problems of a lack of technical skills. Where stock figures can be used they are sometimes dogged by problems of lack of comparability. For example, the ROI might appear to have proportionately as many workers at the technician level as West Germany, however, this rests on the assumption that everyone who qualifies from a Regional Technical College (perhaps with no more than a one-year Diploma) has attained the level of a German Meister (two to three years on top of two to three years of training as an apprentice) or Techniker (four years of study). Nevertheless, the figures are strongly indicative of the conclusion that the ROI has a skills gap. Even when the favourable assumption is made that the definitional basis of the statistics is comparable, the ROI has proportionally twice as many 'unqualified' as the West German labour force (Table 2.5). Moreover, the annual inflow of formally qualified craft apprentices and supervisors into West German manufacturing is several times greater than that into industry in either the ROI, or Great Britain or NI regardless of the way in which the figures are standardized for varying sizes of industry and population (Table 2.6).

Emigration and the Demand for Skills in the Republic

It should also be stressed that the ROI's experience is not an exact replica of that of Britain. It is, for example, unusual in the sense that a very high proportion of annual output of those qualifying at the higher levels have been lost to the domestic economy through migration (in 1987–88 about 40 per cent of the ROI engineering graduates left the ROI to find work elsewhere). Such out-migration indicates that the level of skills in the ROI is not simply a supply-side issue but a demand-side one as well. Indeed, when the output of graduate and technician engineers is considered relative to the size of manufacturing employment in the ROI, it might appear that the ROI is producing too many of these qualifications and therefore that it is natural for

Table 2.5 Comparative stock of skills in manufacturing, end 1980s. Per cent of labour force qualified to each level ROI, NI and UK shown as a percentage of West Germany* (per cent in WG=100)

Level of Qualification	Quantity	Quality
Graduates (all subjects)	UK 110 NI 45 ROI 88	German degrees longer, more technical.
Technician level	UK 53 NI 49 ROI 100[a]	German Meister Techniker, compared with HND, HNC in UK and output of Regional Technical Colleges in ROI (some only one-year courses).[a]
Lower intermediate level 'craftsmen'	UK 47 NI 60[b] ROI 51[b]	In UK and WG apprenticeships similar in content, though WG may have more rigorous theoretical application. NI figures include all A levels and ROI all Leaving Cert.[b]
Without any of the above	UK 212 NI 180[c] ROI 196[c]	

Note: * The per cent of the manufacturing labour force with each qualification level as its highest qualification is shown as a percentage of the per cent level for West Germany (UK and WG relate to 1987, NI and ROI per cent results for 1989 were compared to these WG results). a: The ROI figures include all diplomas and certificates from the Regional Technical Colleges and many of these are unlikely to be comparable with the UK and WG qualifications in terms of length of study or depth of content. b: The inclusion of non-vocational qualifications in the NI and ROI figures inflates performance relative to the UK average and WG. c: ROI and NI performance relative to the UK average and WG is again inflated for the reason given under note b.

Sources: UK/WG; the NIESR studies, i.e. Prais and Wagner (1988), Steedman (1988), Prais (1989), O'Mahoney (1992). NI; figures supplied by DENI. ROI; figures by the education authorities in the Republic.

migration to be so marked. This conclusion would, however, be a misperception. The fact that industry in the ROI is unable to employ all of the graduates and technicians coming out of the universities and colleges is less an indication of over-production of technological skills

Table 2.6 Comparison of the flows of technical qualifications standardized by manufacturing labour force and population size, end 1980s*

		Labour force	Population	
Graduate engineers:				
	UK	100	71	German degrees
	NI	100	61	longer + more
	ROI	167	82	practical
Technician engineers:				
	UK	100	71	
	NI	na	na	
	ROI	150	75	
Supervisors (formally qualified)		Many times higher in WG		Usually time served in UK rarely equivalent to WG *Meister*.
Craftsmen:				
(formally qualified)	UK	41	31	Fewer written
	NI	41	17	theoretical tests
	ROI	41	20	in UK apprenticeship

Note: standardized on output per 100,000 manufacturing employees (5 million in the UK, 7 million in WG, 100,000 in NI, and 200,000 in the ROI), and on output per million of the population (57 million in the UK, 61 million in WG, 1.5 million in NI and 3.5 million in t he ROI).

Sources: UK/WG; the NIESR studies, i.e. Prais and Wagner (1988), Prais (1989), O'Mahoney (1992). NI/WG; Labour Force Survey and City and Guilds. ROI/WG; Higher Education Authority and FAS.

and more a measure of the relatively small size of manufacturing in the ROI and a consequent lack of use of these graduates and technicians when compared with population size (in the late 1980s less than 6 per cent of the population of the ROI were employed in manufacturing compared to 11.5 per cent in West Germany 8.8 per cent in the UK). When population is used as the standardization factor then the ROI's output of these skills is indicated to be substantially lower than that of West Germany (with the implication that the supply side of the ROI's economy will be correspondingly weaker).

There is also the possibility that, even given the relatively small size of manufacturing in the ROI, the demand for these higher skills is lower than might be expected. If this were the case, there would also be some similarities with the British disease. For example, the relatively low numbers of graduate engineers in UK manufacturing (Finneston, 1980) has sometimes been attributed to a cultural aversion to industrial activity as opposed to professional and financial careers (Wiener, 1980; but see Rubinstein, 1988), Silberston (1987) argues there is also a demand-side problem which is reflected by the relatively low salaries which British companies offer to engineering and production management specialists as compared to those with financial, accountancy and marketing specialisms. The high rates of out-migration of Irish graduates may be partly because industry in the ROI does not perceive the need to offer them employment. It is also likely to be driven by the significant difference between the marginal tax rate facing a single person at the average industrial wage in the ROI compared to his/her counterpart in Britain (Arthur Andersen, 1991). (The imbalance in the ROI tax system whereby labour is very heavily taxed while capital is taxed at a relatively low rate could be considered in its own right as a negative institutional impact on economic performance.)

Low levels of demand for technical skills in the ROI could indicate a certain amount of complacency about the ROI's training needs. Tony O'Reilly, Chief Executive of Heinz, argued in 1981 that 'Irish workers properly led are as good as any', and Milton Glass, Treasurer, Gilette, claimed (1983), 'The Irish worker is just as good as the legendary German worker' (O'Malley, 1989). In a survey study (Roche and Tansey, 1991), the chief executives of the 1,000 largest private companies ranked the technical (14 per cent) and production management (6 per cent) training needs of top managers relatively low (far behind the perceived need for more training in general management, finance, marketing and industrial relations). Such results are indicative of one aspect of the British disease, i.e. a complacency about technological matters with the accountancy side of business being given priority. Moreover, a lack of experience of world-class manufacturing standards (Roche and Tansey, 1991) may make ROI managers poor judges of their own training requirements. (A number of exchange visits between managers in the NI and West German clothing industries revealed a similar myopia on the part of the managers in the low-productivity NI sector, who were similarly reluctant to admit how much they had to learn from the higher training standards they had observed in the West German factories; Hitchens, Wagner and Birnie, 1991.) At the same time, some critical skill deficiencies have been identified, e.g. 36 per cent of clothing companies surveyed reported problems relating to machinists and 29 per cent to production managers, design and technicians (FAS/Colin McIver as reported in Roche and Tansey, 1991). For example, lack of technical skills meant that operatives could not repair their own machines when these broke down. This represented a classic symptom of the British disease.

The Need for Research on Links between Training and Performance

The British skills shortfall and its probable impact on comparative productivity has been intensively researched – for example, by the National Institute of Economic and Social Research and usually through the technique of matched plant comparisons (Prais, 1981; Prais and Wagner, 1983; Daly, Hitchens and Wagner, 1985; Steedman and Wagner, 1987; Prais and Wagner, 1988; Steedman and Wagner, 1989; Prais, 1989). It could be argued that there is a need for similar kinds of research programmes in the Republic.

These would focus on measures of the stock of skills in Irish-owned firms together with qualitative measures (e.g. how Irish training courses compare with those in Europe in terms of breadth and depth of content). For example, the matched plant comparisons of small firms in the ROI with those in regions of Britain (O'Farrell and Hitchens, 1989) collected data on the proportion of persons designated as skilled, but this revealed nothing about the quality of those skills. Skill quality was a problem for small firms in all the regions considered, but it was indicated as critical in the case of the ROI (as it was for Northern Ireland; Hitchens and O'Farrell, 1988). Many of the criticisms of Irish products which were reported by the managers of British firms may be interpreted largely as a consequence of poor-quality skills, lack of attention to detail and inadequate supervision and quality control procedures. Furthermore, in skill-intensive product segments such as precision engineering, injection mould and tool making, many Irish companies, when showed samples from matched English firms, conceded under questioning that they could not produce to the tolerances and finish displayed by the English samples, especially those in the Bristol area. Matched plant comparisons with European counterpart firms would allow the impact of training levels on physical productivity and product quality to be traced (the intention would be to identify the specific links which the general statistical studies of education and economic performance have usually only been able to assert without strong proof (OECD, 1987)). At the same time research should be directed to the multinational sector in the ROI to ascertain how far they locate complex processes and products in their Irish operation. The extent to which they do this would prompt the question as to how they were able to achieve high productivity levels with a predominantly unskilled or semi-skilled labour force. Given the small size of the industrial base in the ROI and the historical lateness of industrialization it is likely that the ROI shares with NI a problem of a lack of diversity of skills (i.e. certain precision engineering, mechanical and electrical skills are likely to be under-represented in Ireland). Research should be focused to identify gaps and the possibility that selectively encouraged in-migration by talented outsiders could be used to fill holes in the skills base.

What seems to be clear is that NI and the ROI are deficient in terms of the output from the education system of technically skilled persons (OECD, 1991) but these weaknesses are reinforced by the relatively low priority given to the training/retraining of those in employment. A variety of recent sample surveys in the ROI suggest that only 21 per cent of employees receive off-the-job training, – 35 per cent of managers and 11 per cent of craftsmen (as compared to 25–40 per cent, 50 per cent and 15–48 per cent respectively amongst other industrial economies (Roche and Tansey, 1991)). It has been estimated that private companies devote the equivalent of 0.9 per cent of payroll costs to training (compared to 1.4 per cent in the US, 2.1 per cent in France and 2.9 per cent in West Germany). All this is notwithstanding a recognition in some quarters that some aspects of the ROI's skill base are weak, for example, management training (e.g. CIP, 1973).

The National Institute studies linked poor training standards to relatively low rates of physical productivity and inferior product quality. In the case of the ROI it has been noted that greater training would enable the absorption of changes in product and process technology and facilitate the adoption of more advanced capital equipment (Roche and Tansey, 1991). The same is certainly true in NI where a dearth of technical skills has contributed to the underutilization and ineffective application of the technically sophisticated machinery already in operation (Hitchens, Wagner and Birnie, 1990, 1991). The relatively low rates of R&D spending in the ROI and NI are in part a function of the lack of technically qualified personnel. During the 1970s the rate of R&D spending in ROI industry actually declined and in 1975 stood at only one-quarter of the EC average and one-sixth of the US average (Maguire, 1979). In 1990 ROI manufacturing was estimated to spend the equivalent of 0.5 per cent of value added on R&D and NI manufacturing 0.9 per cent compared to around 2 per cent in most major industrial economies (CBI, 1992). Moreover, even more than in the case of the UK, it might be anticipated to yield further benefits through providing an incentive to foreign investors to locate plants (including those which engaged in higher value added activities) in the ROI (Reich, 1990)). As things stand, the unskilled or semi-skilled status of most plants in the ROI is notable. In Telesis' (1982) survey of thirty-four mechanical engineering factories only half employed even a couple of qualified engineers and skilled blue-collar workers.

In addition to the link between a lack of training and inadequate performance regarding innovation, a second mechanism through which poor skills standards are translated into poor competitiveness is that of product quality. In a matched plant comparison of productivity between NI and West Germany the authors used a simple method to partition responsibility for the West German value added advantage between physical productivity (i.e. number of units per worker) and quality (i.e. the value added arising from each of these units).[5]

The excess of value added per head at the West German firm over that of the NI company after allowing for the physical productivity difference is a measure of the relative importance of quality (and other factors) to productivity. Although the method is unsophisticated it was derived from a detailed and time-consuming set of managerial interviews and is (as far as the authors are aware) the first attempt which has been made to separate out the responsibility for the international productivity gap between physical productivity and other factors inclusive of quality. Table 2.7 shows that, on average, three-fifths of the value added gap is attributable to physical productivity differences and two-fifths to other factors inclusive of quality. Alongside the figures is shown the proportion of products matched which were agreed by managing directors at the matched plants to be superior in the West German case.

Like their counterparts in NI, sample surveys of small firms in the ROI have found a general gap in product quality performance relative to firms in regions of Great Britain (Hitchens and O'Farrell, 1989). The generally low levels of value added per head throughout the indigenous sector in the ROI suggest that this could be a widespread problem. The owner of an outstanding Irish small firm included in the matched comparisons commented, 'I have to manage for quality and constantly fight for high standard ... There is no tradition of standards in Ireland ... In Italy even the poor people are used to high standards in their own clothes'.

Table 2.7 Importance of differences in product quality in West German/NI comparisons 1987/88

	Percentage of cases where W German quality greater	Percent of W German productivity advantage attributable to:*	
		Physical productivity	Other factors
Engineering	50	40	60
Food, drink etc	0	100	0
Textiles	50	48	52
Clothing	57	53	47
Miscellaneous	60	62	38
Total cases	48	61	39

Notes: * The partition of the value-added gap between quality and physical productivity is based upon a total of twenty-two matched pairs where it was possible to compare both value-added and physical productivity.

Total number of matched comparisons: engineering 10, food 5, textiles 6, clothing 16, miscellaneous 5, and total manufacturing 42.

Source: Hitchens, Wagner and Birnie (1990).

The Subsidization of Inefficiency

The extent of subsidization

In terms of education and training NI and the ROI could be considered to have an institutional problem similar in type to that of Britain, though of greater intensity. Turning to industrial policy and particularly the extent to which heavy subsidization may have prolonged inefficiency, the difference between NI and the ROI on the one hand and Britain is one of degree.

NI and the ROI were not unusual in making grant payments to manufacturing but what does stand out in either a British or EC context is the relatively high rate of subsidization in the Irish economies.

Even when comparison is restricted to Scotland and Wales which, like NI and the ROI, have active development agencies and a peripheral location, manufacturing in the two Irish economies emerges as the most heavily subsidized.

Table 2.8 Subsidy rates in Britain and Ireland, 1985–1986 (total assistance as a per cent of manufacturing GDP factor cost)

England	0.5
Wales	4.5
Scotland	3.7
NI	18.3[a]
ROI	13.0[b]

Notes: a, see note 6; b, see note 7 at end of chapter.

Sources: UK regions: Regional Trends 1988; Northern Ireland Appropriation Accounts 1985–86, 1986–7. ROI: National Income and Expenditure 1990; IDA Survey 1986.

The rate of subsidy to manufacturing in NI and the ROI is also one of the highest in western Europe. The European Community Survey of State Aid (1989) suggests that none of the ten EC members (i.e. excluding Spain and Portugal) for which data were available had a national average rate of subsidy to manufacturing (excluding aid to steel and shipbuilding but inclusive of tax and loan-based incentives) as high as that in NI (*Financial Times*, 1989, November 20). The EC members with rates of support closest to NI were: Italy (amounting to a 1981–1986 average of 15.8 per cent of value-added, though this estimate has since been revised downwards (*Financial Times*, 1990, February 28)), Greece (13.9 per cent) and the Republic of Ireland (12.3 per cent). Danish manufacturing received the lowest subsidy rate (1.7 per cent) followed by manufacturing in the UK and Germany (both receiving state aids equivalent to 2.9 per cent).

Notwithstanding reductions in the level of industrial and regional spending in NI and the ROI during 1986–1992, the rate of support would still be relatively high given that similar or even greater reductions in industrial assistance were experienced in Great Britain.

The Impact of Subsidies

An evaluation of the impact of subsidization on economic performance and productivity is complex given the range of possible outcomes. For example: a boost to wages, higher profits, wasteful capital investment, and X-inefficency. We will now consider each of these possibilities in turn (it should be noted that these are the negative impacts of subsidization which have to be weighed against the positive effects on output and employment through effects on the cost of labour or capital and relative product competitiveness).

(i) *Higher Wages* It is in principle possible, given a strong enough bargaining position, that those in employment would be able to extract all or most of the potential gain from subsidies by raising their wage level. It is also true, notwithstanding high rates of unemployment and relatively low productivity, that wage levels in NI and the ROI converged towards those in Britain during the 1960s–1980s (the extent of this convergence was greater in the case of the ROI and since the late 1980s there have been indications of a trend reversal to divergence in the case of NI relative wages; Black, 1987; Hitchens, Wagner and Birnie, 1990; Ray, 1990). What is unclear is how far subsidy payments were in effect leaking into higher wage payments.

(ii) *Supporting Profitability* To the extent that firms had a greater bargaining power than workers, then it is possible that the benefits of subsidization leaked into profits instead.[8]

A detailed sample study conducted by the authors throws more light on the role of subsidies as a cushion against market discipline in NI (Hitchens, Wagner and Birnie, 1990). Four-fifths of the NI firms had a reasonable level of profitability in spite of an undistinguished record in terms of comparative productivity. The fact that NI labour costs were under 50 per cent those of Germany provides part of the explanation for the paradoxical relationship between productivity and profitability. The other major explanation is the very large implicit subsidy to profits provided by grant aid to industry in NI. Table 2.9 considers Selective Financial Assistance (i.e. discretionary grants).

SFA payments averaged about 3 per cent of turnover in a given year. Whilst this may not seem too much it should be stressed that value-added is itself only about 30 per cent of turnover. Hence selective assistance averages one-tenth of value-added. Moreover, whilst it was not possible to obtain complete information on the amount of capital grant received by the firms, standard capital grants averaged about three-fifths of total SFA for NI manufacturing during 1981–87 (Appropriation Accounts (NI)). Thus by implication SFA and capital grants combined might amount to about one-sixth of the value-added of our sample firms. For ten companies within our sample it was possible to match data on profits with those for SFA (both as a per cent of sales). Profits averaged 7.3 per cent whereas SFA averaged 5.2 per

Table 2.9 Selective financial assistance (SFA) to sample companies in NI

	Total 1981–87 £ million (1987 prices)	Total 1981–87 £ per employee	SFA in one year as % of sales
Engineering	16.1 (21.4)	2,651 (3,561)	3.6
Textiles	22.1	11,961	3.1
Food etc.	6.5 (21.0)	3,024 (9,738)	1.3
Clothing	20.0	3,935	3.5
Miscellaneous	8.8 (9.5)	8,018 (8,666)	1.3
All manufacturing	73.5 (94.0)	4,526 (5,790)	2.6

Note: Values in parentheses include additional estimates for standard capital grants where these could be made. Unfortunately the published data for these grants are less useful than those for SFA. This is because many companies lease their capital from separate financial firms. In such cases the purchases are recorded to the financial firm rather than the NI firm which uses the machine. As a result the values in parentheses do not represent the full amount received in terms of both standard capital grants and SFA together. They should therefore be treated as minimum estimates.

Sources: SFA data from British Business 10 October 1986, 3 February 1987, 8 May 1987, 7 August 1987, and 27 November 1987 and earlier editions.

cent. So that even without considering capital grants, let alone subsidized buildings, training, marketing, and research and development, grant aid is 'explaining' most of the profitability of the NI companies. Whilst it might be objected that a sample of ten companies is too small to be meaningful, it should be noted that total state assistance to industry in NI is about one-fifth of manufacturing GDP (this remains so even when Harland and Wolff and Shorts are excluded).

This very high rate of state support to industrial profits makes any failure of the market to produce the signals to move to greater efficiency worse. Without the grants, some firms with very low productivity levels would be driven out of business, thus raising the average performance of manufacturing in NI. Other firms would adapt to the harsher environment by achieving gains in their performance. It could be argued that the comparatively lavish rates of state assistance in NI is at the very least a permissive cause of NI's comparatively low productivity within the UK.

Consideration of the impact of subsidies on profitability in the ROI is, if anything, more complex than in the case of NI. This is because strong implicit subsidization of profits (given the relatively low rate of corporate profit taxation) may have induced transfer pricing, i.e. subsidization would have led to the measured value added per head being higher than it would otherwise have been given manipulation of prices to redistribute profits within international companies towards their ROI subsidiaries. This could be considered a somewhat artificial boost to productivity in the ROI since it would be compatible with continued production of standardized products with little R&D or advanced skills input (Telesis, 1982). Attempts to estimate the scale of transfer pricing using various methods suggest that it may explain only a relatively small part of the total productivity advantage of international firms in the ROI relative to their counterparts in the UK.

(iii) *Waste of Capital* Prolonged and heavy subsidy of investment may have cheapened the relative cost of capital in NI and the ROI to such an extent that purchase of machinery has gone past the level which could be justified. What is certainly true is that since the late 1960s average investment rates in manufacturing in the Irish economies have been substantially higher than those in Britain (Hitchens, Wagner and Birnie, 1990; CBI, 1992). Moreover, matched plant comparisons between NI and West German firms indicated that the NI firms were not in general outclassed by their German counterparts in terms of the technological 'up-to-dateness' of equipment (in this a very strong contrast could be drawn with counterparts in East Germany where machinery was usually antiquated; Hitchens, Wagner and Birnie, 1990, 1993). Indeed in one sector, clothing, the NI firms were characterized by the most advanced machinery found anywhere in the world (Hitchens, Wagner and Birnie, 1990, 1991). Similarly, matched comparisons of small firms in regions of Britain and Ireland indicated the relatively advanced state of machinery in NI and the ROI.

However, is it legitimate to argue that some of this investment was excessive? Once again the evidence of the matched firms studies are indicative. NI firms had lower rates of machine utilization than West German counterparts. Indeed, there were particularly severe problems arising in the use of the aged computerized equipment. Breakdowns and machine unreliability were marked (as they were in the comparisons of small firms with regions in Britain). This was notwithstanding a much larger representation of maintenance workers than in West Germany.

(iv) *X-inefficiency* Following Leibenstein (1966), this is considered as generalized slack of management and labour which lead to higher average costs. Forms of X-inefficiency emerged in matched comparisons between West German and NI firms. None of the West German firms surveyed reported any overstaffing, whereas almost three-fifths of NI sample firms judged themselves overstaffed in at least one department (admittedly this problem could not be entirely attributed to grant payments, given that absenteeism and functional inflexibility of labour required firms to carry some excess labour). In 68 per cent of matched comparisons the NI firms had a higher proportion of indirect employees than the West German counterpart (Hitchens, Wagner and Birnie, 1990). Poor motivation towards work could represent another form of X-inefficiency induced by heavy subsidization. In the matched comparisons 31 per cent of NI managers reported poor attitudes to work compared to 24 per cent of West German managers. However, the complaints in West Germany were mainly concentrated in plants employing *Gastarbeiter* and none of the German complaints approached the intensity of the complaints in NI: 'greedy', 'sludge', 'a mind bending attitude', 'reluctant to work, lazy and late'.

Moreover, 43 per cent of the NI sample plants had experienced strikes and disruptions during a three-year period compared to none of their West German counterparts. During the 1960s–1980s the strike rate in NI was also higher than in Britain when individual matched manufacturing sectors are considered. In 1980–1985 however the average strike rate in NI was only 64 per cent that of the UK level (or 72 per cent if allowance is made for differences of industrial structures). Comparisons of small firms including the ROI did not suggest that the ROI shared NI's problems of poor work attitudes (Hitchens and O'Farrell, 1989). Moreover, taking the economy as a whole the ROI strike rate has tended to be similar to that of the UK. However, it should be recognized that the ROI has a higher representation of the predominantly non-unionized agricultural sectors whilst having a negligible level of mining activity (which generally has a high strike rate). During 1983–1987 strike rates in manufacturing, utilities and transport services in the ROI averaged about twice the levels of counterpart sectors in the UK (216 per cent, 235 per cent and 182 per cent of the UK level respectively).

Impact of Subsidies: Summary

In short, the manufacturing sectors in NI and ROI have been characterized by rates of subsidy which are relatively high by EC standards when considered as a percentage of total output. One inference which could be drawn is that firms have become dependent on subsidies as a substitute for the gains to profitability that might be expected to arise through productivity and efficiency improvements.

Kornai (1980) and Winiecki (1988) have described the allocative, productive and X-inefficiencies which were widespread throughout the former communist bloc economies and arose from the so-called soft budget constraint which firms had under the planning system. To the extent that the generous grant payments to firms in the Irish economies can be thought of as milder forms of soft budget constraint, then there would be similarities between NI, the ROI and East Germany in terms of some of the explanations of relatively low productivity levels. However, in the next section the causes of low productivity particular to the Irish economies are considered.

Failure of Policy to Promote a Strong Indigenous Sector

Even if the hypothesis that subsidies led to lower productivity and growth is rejected, it still seems the case that industrial policy in both the ROI and NI has failed to achieve positive benefits commensurate with its cost. Kennedy, Giblin and McHugh (1988) note that industrial policy in the ROI has historically been very costly in social terms. During the 1930s–50s phase of protectionism the cost was mainly carried by the consumer (e.g. through higher prices and restricted choice). The switch to inward investment from the 1950s onwards did not remove the social cost but shifted its incidence to the taxpayer. Had the indigenous sector developed at a more rapid pace, these heavy costs to either consumers or taxpayers would not have been necessary. As measured by rates of grant payments industrial policy in NI has if anything proved even more expensive than that in the ROI (Hitchens, Wagner and Birnie, 1990). However, in contrast to the ROI, as a region within the UK the taxpayers of NI have not had to shoulder this burden.

However, is it possible to go a stage further and argue that not only was policy unsuccessful but it actually represented a negative institutional effect on economic performance? The policy of protectionism pursued by the ROI during the 1930s–1950s probably reinforced the undue dependence by most ROI firms on the home market with the consequence that when this policy was reversed many of the Irish-owned firms were unable to stand against foreign competition (indigenous firms are now predominantly concentrated in those sectors where exposure to international trade is low; O'Malley (1989)). The inward investment policies pursued by both the ROI and NI during the 1950s–1980s may have involved some displacement of locally-owned firms (though it is not clear how far this happened as a consequence of a discriminating effect of the package of industrial incentives or to what extent it was an inevitable result of the inefficiencies of the indigenous sector).

In the case of ROI industrial policy, the relatively low rate of tax on corporate profits (10 per cent) has probably also had a harmful indirect effect. Unfortunately, the counterpart of the relatively low rate of taxation on capital has necessarily been a relatively high rate of taxation on labour (*Report of the Industrial Policy Review Group*, 1992). The *Report of the Industrial Policy Review Group* (1992) expressed the hope that the ROI would move towards a broader tax base with fewer distortionary effects, i.e. capital would eventually be taxed more heavily with lower rates on personal incomes. Unfortunately, earlier commitments by the government mean that the 10 per cent rate of corporate profit tax is unlikely to be raised before 2010.

It is certainly true that the authorities in either Irish economy are yet to develop a set of policies which would successfully promote a strong indigenous sector (Telesis, 1982; DED, 1990; *Report of the Industrial Policy Review Group*, 1992). It is also true that inward investment by international firms has traditionally received the lion's share of attention and resources from the policy makers. Less clear is how far the lack of priority given to the indigenous sector contributed to the lack of competitiveness evidenced in home firms (Hitchens and O'Farrell, 1987, Hitchens, Wagner and Birnie, 1990). Given certain supply-side weaknesses in locally-owned firms (e.g. with respect to human capital as described above), it is possible that a different institutional set-up which gives more priority to the indigenous sector would of itself have achieved little. Nevertheless, it is probably the case that policy makers over-emphasized the externally-owned sector given that the competitive problems of indigenous firms were poorly understood. The use of grants to attract outside companies was therefore an easier option than attempting to reverse the specific competitive failures of local firms.

The New Competitiveness Strategies in NI and the ROI

We have already noted the relatively high rate of subsidies in the two Irish economies and those grants concentrated especially on physical capital (as opposed to human capital; Harris, 1990). During the last five years there has been a switch of emphasis such that the development agencies in both economies lay more stress on 'software' (i.e. work-force training, management courses, marketing, consultancy, business services and R&D). It is therefore appropriate to review the effect of recent policy reviews in both the economies (DED, 1990; *Report of the Industrial Policy Review Group*, 1992) to test whether this latest institutional change will have any positive effects on productivity and performance.

The Review Group in the ROI deserves credit for producing a thorough and critical evaluation of industrial policy as it had operated in the ROI during the 1980s. The depth of analysis employed exceeded that of the corresponding series of policy documents which have been appearing in NI as part of the rethink of economic policy in the province (DED, 1990; IDB, 1991a, 1991b; LEDU, 1991; TEA, 1991a, 1991b). The range of economic sophistication employed in the supporting reports is impressive. Although the re-think in NI government strategy is welcome it displayed a much less impressive grasp of the theoretical issues than did its counterpart in the ROI.

In fact one of the most damning criticisms of the review in NI is that in some respects it represents only a catching up with the ROI policy ideas of six to eight years earlier. The *Telesis Report* (1982) had already attacked the intellectual basis of a policy which relied heavily on inward investment and at the same time questioned the validity of the performance indicators (e.g. job creation) which had hitherto been used by the IDA. However, it is possible to identify some limitations in both sets of policy documents.

For example the *Report of the Industrial Policy Review Group* (1992) rightly took a very broad view of the range of factors which could impact on industrial performance (in this it contrasted with its predecessor Telesis (1982) which largely restricted itself to industrial policy as traditionally defined). Unfortunately, the resultant list of areas where the Republic's economy was judged to be weak (e.g. a narrow tax base, misallocated savings, high costs of infrastructural services, inadequate focus of the education and training system on closing a relative skills gap, lack of management training, low levels of R&D, the continued failure of the food sector to fulfil its apparent potential, the weakness of indigenous firms in general etc.) did not include any attempt to identify priorities for public action. In other words, the Review Group was able to identify those factors which were hindering the ROI performance, but they could not weight their importance as contributions to the overall competitiveness problem of the ROI. Similarly, when DED (1990) considered how state intervention would now be targeted to remove market failure and obstacles to growth it did not provide any priorities for action.

The *Report of the Industrial Policy Review Group* (1992) displayed novelty as compared to the earlier Telesis report (1982) when it argued that in general industrial policy should be directed towards creating clusters of indigenous firms operating within appropriate market niches. There was the vague advice that such clusters should be based upon local strengths. Underlying this argument seems to be some idea of comparative advantage, i.e. there are certain economic activities at which the ROI is good and developmental efforts should be concentrated on these. However, the notion of comparative advantage should be treated with caution because it need not imply absolute advantage, i.e. the ROI may not be highly efficient in food processing, it may simply lag behind international competitiveness standards to a lesser degree than in other sectors. To focus too strongly on food, for instance, might be to make the mistake that because the ROI has always had a lot of food industries in the past it should have a lot in the future.

In the case of NI any recommendations of selectivity were vague. IDB (1991a, 1991b) implied that assistance would in future be conditional on the companies receiving such grants attaining certain improvements in competitive performance, however defined. Unfortunately, the definition of the 'competitive' company remained unclear and subsequent indications from the NI authorities suggest that the policy is now one of 'backing winners'. To the extent that it is reminiscent of earlier policies of 'picking winners', this sounds similar to the ROI's policy of 'picking niches' albeit the ROI is aiming to foster clusters rather than individual companies.

In fact there are some general weaknesses to this approach of identification of niches or backing winners. It ignores the extent to which NI manufacturing and the indigenous sector in the ROI lags very far behind average British standards and, to an even greater extent, average continental European standards. To expect any more than a small number of local firms to propel themselves into international niches may be too optimistic. The fundamental problem may be an inadequate elasticity of response on the part of the private sector in the ROI and NI to government initiatives designed to boost competitive performance.

CONCLUSIONS

In stressing the institutional impact on long-term economic growth in NI and the ROI we have been implicitly downgrading certain non-institutional factors which have traditionally received much attention as possible causes of under-performance in NI and the ROI: small size of economy and firms, peripherality and the direct impact of political violence.

In addition, we have not considered the effects of more general aspects of national (or regional) culture because institutions are part product of, and part input to, that culture. For example, to some extent the behaviour of firms, banks, development agencies and government departments was determined by the cultural background of the decision makers. Even where NI and the ROI shared similar institutions to those found in Britain there may have been differentially poor performance given the role of culture. The impact of 'Irish culture' (Northern or Southern) on economic performance is a vexed question, usually majoring on such issues as whether economic growth and efficiency was given a high enough priority relative to other alternative social goals or whether the work ethic in NI and the ROI is inadequately developed (Hitchens, Wagner and Birnie, 1990; Lee, 1990). What is clearly evidenced is that both NI and the ROI are more insular societies than that of Britain or most other western countries (as indicated by the proportion of the population who are outsiders or members of ethnic minorities; Hitchens, Wagner and Birnie, 1990). Such insularity is most marked in the case of NI, where the 'troubles' have reduced migratory in-flows. Thus institutions in NI especially, and the ROI to a lesser extent (given possible return immigration from the Irish diaspora in the USA and elsewhere), are restricted to a local/domestic talent pool when recruiting for top positions (it is notable that the industrial development of Ireland in the nineteenth century was heavily dependent on immigrant entrepreneurs). Such narrowness of experience is bound to have a crippling effect on long-term economic development given that there is inadequate knowledge of standards of international best practice.

NOTES

1. For example, the comparisons of GDP per capita presented in Table 2.1 rely largely on the use of national volume series of changes in real national output (together with series for population size) to project back to 1913 a comparison of relative per capita national income in 1985. If it had been possible to measure directly the comparative level of GDP per head in 1913 this would have been likely to have given a different answer in some cases. A number of commentators have noted that contemporaneous comparisons of output per head are generally likely to more be more reliable than those based on projections which rely on indices of real output, which are likely to get progressively more unreliable as they are applied to longer and longer stretches of years (Smith, 1985; Hitchens, Wagner and Birnie, 1990; O'Mahoney, 1992).

    A data limitation particular to the cases of NI and the ROI is that the volume series are not available for the years prior to the mid-1920s (following Kennedy, Giblin and McHugh (1988); the assumption was made that the standing of the two Irish economies relative to the UK did not alter between 1913 and the mid-1920s.

2. a ROI adjusted by removal of firms employing less than twenty workers (this was to increase compatibility with the size ranged in the UK Census of Production).
   b 1985 result updated using national volume series for output and employment.
   c An estimate of East German/West German value added per head (assuming like levels of utilization) was derived from the sample study of Hitchens, Wagner and Birnie (1993) and linked to the UK using O'Mahony (1992) estimate of West Germany/UK in 1990.
   d Method as in c with the assumption that Germany/UK comparative productivity in 1991 was the same as in 1990.
   e Currency conversion using weighted average relative price of principal products (Smith, Hitchens and Davies, 1968).
   f Unit value ratios used to compare gross value added per head in 1987 which was then adjusted using national volume series of output and employment (O'Mahony, 1992).
   g Weighted comparative physical output per head (Rostas, 1948).
   h Unit value ratios used to compare net output per head (Van Ark, 1992).

3. O'Mahoney (1992) estimated that when relative labour inputs were adjusted for quality differences this could account for 55 per cent of the UK–West German productivity gap (physical capital was estimated to account for a further 35 per cent).

4. Over and above the institutional handicaps on economic performance which are considered in this chapter, there are certain other institutional factors which may have effected that performance: for example, the extent to which the Border has limited the attainment of those gains which would be realized by greater north–south co-operation, the cost effects on firms of compliance with fair employment legislation, the impact of the 'troubles' and the possibly limited accountability of policy determination and administration in NI.

5. In previous work by the authors (Hitchens, Wagner and Birnie, 1990) an attempt was made to separate the contributions of product quality and physical productivity from the comparative productivity shortfall when making a comparison of thirty-nine matched plants between NI and West Germany in 1987/88. Estimates of physical productivity differences were made during visits to matched companies (e.g. dozens of garments, thousands of screws, etc.). In addition data were collected on gross output and value added achieved in production with a view to providing measurement and explanation of productivity differences. The results of this research have already been published (Hitchens, Wagner and Birnie, 1990) but the purpose of this note is to discuss more fully the method used and its relevance.

The relative price level of the West German product is equal to the ratio of West German gross output to NI gross output divided by the ratio of West German physical output to NI physical output. This conclusion is trivial, but if the assumption is made that the market exchange rate maintains purchasing power parity for goods of homogenous quality, then any difference between the West German relative price level as calculated from the firm data from that implied by the market exchange rate is suggestive of the fact that the products are not of the same quality.

6. The NI subsidy rate excludes aerospace and shipbuilding to ensure comparability with the GB results where no attempt was made to apportion Department of Trade and Industry spending (e.g. on shipbuilding, steel, motor vehicles and aerospace) on a regional basis within GB.

7. Total grants include all capital grants and selective assistance and the cost of publicly financed land and premises. The estimate for the ROI includes the implicit subsidy of profits given by a corporate profit tax of only 10 per cent as compared to 35 per cent in the UK; for grant payments alone the ROI's subsidy rate was 3 per cent. (Total profits were estimated from the IDA Survey. ROI grant expenditure in 1986 recorded in the national accounts was compared to manufacturing GDP as estimated from the same source.)

8. Or at least, with grant payments firms are able to tolerate lower levels of profitability than would otherwise have been the case.

It is also likely that the grant regime favoured NI firms through reducing their reliance on borrowing. Roper (1992) found that NI companies held only 26 per cent of their liabilities as bank loans and short-term liabilities (compared to a UK average of 43 per cent). With interest rates at 15–20 per cent during 1989 and 1990 the gain to Northern Ireland companies in lower interest payments was equivalent to one-third of pre-tax profits.

ACKNOWLEDGEMENT

The figures presented here on the comparative productivity of the ROI derive from a forthcoming Ph.D. thesis by J.E. Birnie.

REFERENCES

Akerlof, G.A., Rose, A.K., Yellen, J.L. and Hessenius, H. (1991), 'East Germany in from the cold: the economic aftermath of currency union', *Brookings Papers on Economic Activity*, no. 1, pp. 1-87

Arthur Andersen (1991), *Report to the Industrial Policy Review Group on Reform of the Irish taxation system from an industrial point of view*, Stationery Office, Dublin.

Bacon, R.W. and Eltis, W.A. (1974), 'The age of US and UK machinery', *Monograph*, no. 3, National Economic Development Office, London.

Barnett, C. (1986), The Audit of War: *The Illusion and Reality of Britain as a Great Power*, Macmillan, London.

Barro, R.J. and Sala-i-Martin, X. (1991), 'Convergence across states and regions', *Quarterly Journal of Economics*, no. 106, pp. 407–43.

Black, J.B.H. (1987), 'Conciliation or conflict', *Industrial Relations Journal*, vol. 18, no. 1, pp. 14–25.

Chubb, B. (1992), *The Government of Ireland*, Longman, London.

CIP, (1973), *General Report*, (Prl 2927), Stationery Office, Dublin.

Coopers and Lybrand Deloitte (1992), *Northern Ireland economy: Review and prospects*, Belfast.

Crafts, N.F.R. (1988), 'British economic growth over the long-run', *Oxford Review of Economic Policy*, vol. 4, no. 1, pp. i–xxi.

Crafts, N.F.R. (1991), 'Reversing relative economic decline? the 1980s in historical perspective', *Oxford Review of Economic Policy*, vol. 7, no. 3, pp. 81–98.

Culliton Report (1992), otherwise known as the *Report of the Industrial Policy Review Group*, Stationery Office, Dublin.

Daly, A., Hitchens, D.M.W.N., and Wagner, K. (1985), 'Productivity, Machinery and Skills in a Sample of British and German Manufacturing Plants', *National Institute Economic Review*, no. 111, pp. 48–62.

DED (1990), *Northern Ireland Competing in the 1 990s: The Key to Growth*, Department of Economic Development, Belfast.

DENI, (1992), *The Funding of Higher Education Research in Northern Ireland*, Discussion Paper, Department of Education Northern Ireland, Bangor.

Economist, (1990, April 21), 'The training trap'.

Finegold, D. and Soskice, D. (1988), 'The failure of training in Britain: Analysis and Prescription', *Oxford Review of Economic Policy*, vol. 4, no. 3, pp. 21–53.

Finneston, Sir M. (1980), *Engineering our future*, Command 7794.

Gorzig, B. and Gornig, M. (1991), *Produktivitat und Wefibewerbsfahigkeit der Wirtschaft der DDR*, DIW, Heft 121, Berlin.

Gudgin, G., Hart, M., Fagg, J., Keegan, R., and D'Arcy, E. (1989), 'Job generation in manufacturing industry 1973-1986: a comparison of Northern Ireland with the Republic of Ireland and the English Midlands', *Northern Ireland Economic Research Centr Report*, Belfast.

Hitchens, D.M.W.N. and Birnie, J.E. (1991), 'Productivity in the Irish Economies', *Irish Banking Review*, (Spring).

Hitchens, D.M.W.N. and Birnie, J.E. (1992), 'The scope for economic co-operation between Northern Ireland and the Republic of Ireland: Reversing the competitive failure of the Irish economies', *Department of Economics Working Paper*, no. 34, Queen's University of Belfast.

Hitchens, D.M.W.N. and O'Farrell, P.N. (1987), 'The Comparative Performance of Small Manufacturing Firms in Northern Ireland and South East England', *Regional Studies*, vol. 21, no. 6, pp. 543–554.

Hitchens, D.M.W.N., Wagner, K. and Birnie, J.E. (1990), *Closing the Productivity Gap: A Comparison of Northern Ireland, the Republic of Ireland, Britain and West Germany*, Gower-Avebury, Aldershot.

Hitchens, D.M.W.N., Wagner, K. and Birnie, J.E. (1991), 'Improving Productivity through International Exchange Visits', *Omega*, vol. 19, no. 5, pp. 361–368.

Hitchens, D.M.W.N., Wagner, K. and Birnie, J.E. (1993), *East German Productivity and the Transition to the Market Economy*, Avebury, Aldershot (forthcoming).

IDB (Industrial Development Board for Northern Ireland) (1990a), *Forward Strategy 1991–93*, IDB, Belfast.

IDB (1990b), *Forward Strategy 1991–93 Competitiveness and its Measurement*, IDB, Belfast.

Katz, E., and Ziderman, A. (1990), 'Investment in general training', *Economic Journal*, vol. 100, pp. 1147–58.

Kennedy, K.A., Giblin, T. and McHugh, D. (1988), *The Economic Development of Ireland in the Twentieth Century*, Croom Helm, London.

Kornai, J. (1980), *Economics of Shortage*, North-Holland, Amsterdam.

LEDU (Local Enterprise Development Unit), (1991), *Forward Thinking: LEDU's Corporate Plan 1989–1994*, LEDU, Belfast.

Lee, J.J. (1990), *Ireland 1912–1985, Politics and Society*, Cambridge University Press, Cambridge, England.

Leibenstein, H. (1966), 'Allocative efficiency versus "X efficiency"', *American Economic Review*, vol. 56, June, pp. 392–415.

Maddison, A. (1982, 1991), *Phases of Capitalist Development*, Oxford University Press, Oxford (First/Second edition).

Maguire, C. (1979), *Research and Development in Ireland 1977*, National Board for Science and Technology, Dublin.

OECD, (1987), *Structural Adjustment and Economic Performance*, Organization for Economic Co-operation and Development, Paris.

OECD, (1991), *Review of National Policies for Education – Ireland*, Organisation for Economic Co-operation and Development, Paris.

O'Farrell, P.N. (1986), *Entrepreneurs and Industrial Change*, Irish Management Institute, Dublin.

O'Farrell, P.N., and Hitchens, D.M.W.N. (1989), *Small Firm Competitiveness and Performance*, Gill and Macmillan, Dublin.

Olson, M (1982), *The Rise and Decline of Nations*, Yale University Press, New Haven, Connecticut.

O'Mahoney, M. (1992), 'Productivity levels in British and German manufacturing industry', *National Institute Economic Review*, no. 138, pp. 46–63.

O'Malley, E. (1989), *Industry and Economic Development: the challenge for the latecomer*, Gill and Macmillan, Dublin.

O'Malley, E.; Kennedy, K.A. and O'Donnell, R. (1991), *The Impact of the Industrial Development Agencies*, Stationery Office, Dublin.

Osborne, R.D. (1985), 'Religion and educational qualifications in Northern Ireland', *Research Paper no. 8*, Fair Employment Agency, Belfast.

Porter, M. (1990), *The Competitive Advantage of Nations*, The Free Press, New York.

Prais, SJ (1981), 'Vocational qualifications of the labour force in Britain and Germany', *National Institute Economic Review*, no. 98, pp. 47–59.

Prais, S.J. (1986), 'Some international comparisons of the age of the machine stock', *Journal of Industrial Economics*, vol. XXXIV, pp. 261–87.

Prais, S.J. (1989), 'Qualified manpower in engineering in Britain and other industrially advanced countries', *National Institute Economic Review*, no. 127, pp. 76–83.

Prais, S.J. (1991), 'Vocational qualifications in Britain and Europe: theory and practice', *National Institute Economic Review*, no. 136.

Prais, S.J., and Wagner, K. (1988), 'Productivity and management: the training of foremen in Britain and Germany', *National Institute Economic Review*, no. 123, pp. 34–47.

Pratten, C.F. (1986), 'The importance of giant companies' *Lloyds Bank Review*, no. 159, pp. 33–48.

Ray, G.F. (1990), 'International labour costs in manufacturing', *National Institute Economic Review*, no. 132, pp. 67–71.

Reich, R.B. (1990, August 31–September 6), 'But now we're global', *Times Literary Supplement*, pp. 925–926.

Roche, F.W., and Tansey, P. (1991), *Industrial Training in Ireland: a study prepared for the Industrial Policy Review Group*, Stationery Office, Dublin.

Roper, S. (1992), 'The profitability of Northern Ireland manufacturing firms', *NIERC Report*, Belfast.

Rostow, W.W. (1962), *The Stages of Economic Growth*, Cambridge University Press, Cambridge, England.

Rowthorn, R. and Wayne, N. (1988), *Northern Ireland: The Political Economy of Conflict*, Polity Press, Cambridge.

Ruane, F. (1991), 'The Traded Sector: manufacturing', in J.W. O'Hagan (ed.), *The Economy of Ireland: Policy and Performance*, Irish Management Institute, Dublin.

Report of the Industrial Policy Review Group, (1992), 'A time for change: industrial policy for the 1990s', Stationery Office, Dublin.

Rubinstein, W.D. (1988), 'Social class, social attitudes and British business life', *Oxford Review of Economic Policy*, vol. 14, no. 1, pp. 51–58.

Schumpeter, J. (1939), *Business Cycles*, McGraw-Hill, New York.

Scott, R. and O'Reilly, M. (1992), Northern Ireland Manufacturing Exports, *Northern Ireland Economic Research Centre Report*, Belfast.

Silberston, A.(1987), 'The supply and demand for scientists and engineers in Britain', *Paper given to the Economics Section of the British Association for the Advancement of Science*, Annual Meeting (August 25), Queen's University of Belfast.

Smith, A.D., Hitchens, D.M.W.N., and Davies, S.W. (1982), *International Industrial Productivity*, Cambridge University Press, Cambridge, England.

Steedman, H. (1988), 'Vocational training in France and Britain', *National Institute of Economic and Social Research Discussion Paper*.

Steedman, H. and Wagner, K. (1987), 'A Second look at productivity, machinery and skills in Britain and Germany', *National Institute Economic Review*, no. 122, pp. 84–95.

Steedman, H. and Wagner, K. (1989), 'Productivity, machinery and skills: clothing manufacturing in Britain and Germany', *National Institute Economic Review*, no. 128, pp. 40–57.

Summers, R. and Heston, A. (1991), 'The Penn world table (mark 5): an expanded set of international comparisons, 1950–1988', *The Quarterly Journal of Economics*, May, pp. 327–68.

TEA (Training and Employment Agency) (1991a), *Strategy*, TEA, Belfast.

TEA (1991b), *Management Development: A Discussion Document*, TEA, Belfast.

Telesis (Report), (1982), 'Review of Industrial Policy', *National Economic and Social Council Report*, no. 64, Dublin

Van Ark, B. (1990), 'Comparative Levels of Manufacturing Productivity in post-war Europe: measurement and Comparisons', *Oxford Bulletin of Economics and Statistics*, vol. 52, no. 4, p p. 343–374.

Wiener, M.J. (1980), *English Culture and the Decline of the Industrial Spirit 1815–1980*, Penguin Books, Harmondsworth.

Wilson, T. (1989), *Ulster Conflict and Consent*, Blackwell, Oxford.

Winiecki, J. (1988), *The Distorted World of Soviet-type Economy*, Routledge, Kegan Paul, London.

3

GOVERNANCE STRUCTURES AND ECONOMIC PERFORMANCE

Robert Clulow and Paul Teague

PROBLEMS OF THE NORTHERN IRELAND ECONOMY

Since 1973 the manufacturing sector in Northern Ireland has been in relative and absolute decline. In absolute terms, manufacturing output has fallen by 25 per cent and the sector's share in total regional output has fallen from about 31 per cent in 1973 to 17 per cent in 1990. Now less than 20 per cent of the Northern Ireland workforce are employed in manufacturing. A number of factors are responsible for this sharp deindustrialization. One is the structural composition of Northern Ireland industry. In the mid-1960s, the province was dominated by a select group of industries, particularly tobacco, textiles, shipbuilding and aircraft manufacture. However, with the collapse of the golden age of economic growth in the early 1970s, these sectors fell into steep decline. As a result, the region's industrial base contracted dramatically. A second and related factor has been the withdrawal of multinationals from the province and the reluctance of others to invest there. In the 1960s the influx on inward investment was responsible for Northern Ireland experiencing the largest annual increases in manufacturing output amongst UK regions. By 1973 over half of all manufacturing jobs in the province were in the externally-owned sector. Since then the importance of inward investment to the local economy has been withering away. In 1990 there were 210 externally-owned plants in Northern Ireland, representing a decline of 40 per cent since 1973. In terms of employment, the externally-owned sector now contains 50 per cent fewer jobs than in 1973. The indigenous manufacturing sector has also fared badly over the past twenty years.

In the early 1970s local small firms in the manufacturing sector employed about 19,000 people but by the late 1980s this figure had fallen to around 12,000.

Considerable effort has been made to arrest this industrial decline. Extensive and generous subsidies have been developed for enterprise development and for improving commercial performance. However, the success of this panoply of schemes has not been great. As a result, a consensus has emerged that current industrial policies need recasting. Yet devising alternative policies that could have more positive effects is clearly going to be difficult. Much of the current reappraisal of policy focuses on how *firm* level performance could be improved. However, in this chapter it will be argued that such an enterprise level focus is misplaced. Instead, it is argued that good competitive performance results from wider systemic arrangements in the economy: the institutions and the norms governing industrial relations, for instance. In other words, the competitiveness of firms emerges from the structure and dynamics of the wider economy and polity and not the other way. As a result, to improve the competitiveness of firms we must first discuss the type of economic model or system that should be in place.

Thus this chapter departs from the mainstream discussion and assesses which is the most appropriate economic model for the promotion of commercial competitiveness in the province. The argument is that Northern Ireland would be best off if it created a governance structure which promoted agglomeration economies. But it is also argued that the construction of such a system will be difficult given the distortions bedeviling the local economy. Thus to obtain better commercial performance may require a series of institutional changes. Before the argument is entered into properly, the institutions and policies that have been used to promote industry are sketched out.

A Sketch of Institutions and Policies for Industry

Initial Institutions and Policies

During the 1950s and 1960s industrial development policy in the province was administered by the Ministry of Commerce. In 1971, the Local Economic Development Unit, LEDU, was established to specialize in the support of small firms (those employing below fifty employees). The following year the Northern Ireland Finance Corporation was set up to assist companies threatened with closure; however, this was replaced by the Northern Ireland Development Agency (NIDA) in 1976. NIDA's remit was to strengthen local companies, set up state enterprises, promote technology transfer and supervise restructuring of declining industries.

In 1982, NIDA was replaced by the Industrial Development Board (IDB). This body, staffed by civil servants and short-term contract employees, with an Advisory Board drawn from outside government, was a move towards as much autonomy as the requirements of ministerial responsibility would permit. IDB's responsibility lies with larger companies (those which employ more than fifty employees), while smaller companies remain the responsibility of LEDU. Currently the three main development agencies in Northern Ireland are thus IDB, LEDU and the Training and Enterprise Agency (T & EA). The overall direction of policy and responsibility for these agencies lies with the Department of Economic Development (DED) in Northern Ireland.

The principal objective of industrial strategy and economic development policy after the Second World War was the promotion of new employment to compensate for the loss of jobs in older industries and to reduce unemployment. This involved two approaches to industrial restructuring: (i) the attraction of new industry to the province using a wide range of financial incentives allied to an effort to promote the province as a suitable location for internationally mobile project; and (ii) encouraging where possible the expansion of existing industry.

It was accepted at an early stage that to diversify the industrial base in the province, a significant proportion of the capital and expenditure required would have to be attracted from outside Northern Ireland. The principal instrument used to encourage companies to locate in Northern Ireland has been a package of financial incentives periodically revised to maintain a competitive position relative to other regions seeking internationally mobile projects. The incentives have involved capital grants and employment-related assistance. The main thrust of assistance, under the original approach to policy, was directed towards restructuring and re-equipping indigenous industry in Northern Ireland to arrest decline and encourage diversification into new markets. The instruments used to achieve these goals were various forms of financial assistance for capital investment, together with a wide range of measures designed to promote other business activities such as marketing and R&D.

In 1971, there was a significant strengthening of the range of financial support available to industry, including assistance for the maintenance and safeguarding of existing jobs as well as the creation of new employment. Called 'Broad Focus' the objective of the policy in the 1970s was to maximize employment opportunities and this was pursued by spreading exchequer funding across the industrial spectrum – from assisting new start-ups at one end to attracting inward investment at the other. The policy mix in the original strategy was comprehensive. Restructuring was encouraged through the use of accelerative policies to boost investment by indigenous companies and attract new inward investment projects to the province. Decelerative policies were used extensively to rescue viable but ailing firms and to safeguard employment, particularly in national recessions. Capital and employment grants were used extensively.

Despite its encompassing scope, the original approach had some weaknesses. First, it only addressed the symptom of economic malaise in Northern Ireland rather than the root causes of the province's failure to provide employment for its population. Second, the specific policies appeared not to work. Although relatively generous public support was on offer, manufacturing performance was not particularly good. Third, past policy was very expensive in terms of taxpayers' money. By spreading resources widely, problems of deadweight and displacement were considerable. Finally, past policies may have given rise to a dependency culture within Northern Ireland. Grant aid can distort or mask market signals essential to the efficient conduct of businesses far beyond the immediate receipt of that assistance. Over time the expectation is created that public support will always be available, thus discouraging self-reliance in industry and undermining market discipline. This is most acute in the case of assistance to maintain employment in ailing companies in Northern Ireland which essentially overrides the judgement which the market has already passed on these companies.

The failure of past policy to improve the performance of industry, coupled with the possibility that a dependency culture could be prevalent within manufacturing (a case of too much medicine killing the patient) led to a radical rethink of Industrial and Economic Strategy in the mid-1980s, which began with the Pathfinder Process.

The Pathfinder Process

In July 1987 the Department of Economic Development published 'Building a Stronger Economy, The Pathfinder Process'. This was a discussion document intended to raise debate on future economic strategy in Northern Ireland and its objective was to find new and better ways of building a stronger local economy. Pathfinder characterized Northern Ireland's economic position as that of a 'dependent economy', dependent on external funding, ideas and initiatives. The question Pathfinder raised was how Northern Ireland could achieve a stronger, more resilient economy. A more resilient economy was defined as one that would:

— build on its own resources and strengths;
— be diversified;
— be capable of accepting, and indeed initiating, positive change rather than resisting it;
— be outwardly directed, not isolationist, protectionist or parochial; and
— still be supportive at the personal level of those who are not employed, be responsible for the rehabilitation, remotivation and retraining of the unemployed, and offer opportunities for personal enterprise.

The Department also identified six root causes of weakness in Northern Ireland's economic performance:

(a) *Lack of an Enterprising Tradition*   The symptoms of the lack of an enterprising tradition include the province's high degree of external ownership of industry and the low rate of business start-ups, which means that Northern Ireland does not generate new and replacement jobs and products as rapidly as other regions.

(b) *Deficiencies in Training, Work and Managerial Competencies*   Just as there has been concern about the level of the UK's training, work and managerial competence by comparison with competitor countries, Pathfinder also highlighted that a similar problem existed with regard to Northern Ireland.

(c) *Distance Penalties and the Small Local Market*   Pathfinder also highlighted Northern Ireland's peripheral geographical position in Europe as imposing costs and limitations which go beyond transport cost differentials. These relate to isolation from major markets where new products are launched and developed and from major production areas where product and process innovations cluster. When combined with a small and relatively low-income local market, this was seen to impose obstacles to new product development and the marketing of new or existing products.

(d) *Small Manufacturing Sector, Large Public Sector* At the time of Pathfinder, the public sector accounted for around 42 per cent currently around 39 per cent (1992) of employees in employment in Northern Ireland. Pathfinder highlighted that the public sector, in general, tends to be concerned with the distribution of wealth rather than its creation and is frequently seen as inward-looking and passive rather than outward-looking, seeking trading opportunities. Pathfinder saw an opportunity in finding a way to use the public sector in Northern Ireland as an additional economic development resource.

(e) *Dependence on Public Funds* Public funds are a major resource available to Northern Ireland industry. However, as stressed by the document, public assistance, like some medicines, must be used with discretion or a potentially counter-productive dependence can arise. In Pathfinder's view, too many Northern Ireland companies seem to seek relief of their problems in additional public funds rather than in new markets, products or production techniques. As a result, it was concluded that this dependence is potentially a major strategic weakness of the Northern Ireland economy.

(f) *The Northern Ireland Political Situation* Pathfinder outlined what are seen as the economic effects of the local political situation, including:

— a direct impact on investment;
— an overshadowing of the extent of Northern Ireland's economic problems with the economic debate on the sidelines of the political debate;
— a general debilitating effect on morale, self-esteem and self-belief in the Northern Ireland community which influences economic as well as other activities.

In the area of enterprise, the paper concluded that there was a need to generate a more positive attitude to enterprise throughout the Northern Ireland community; generate greater self-confidence and skills among those in Northern Ireland wishing to start a business; and restructure assistance to ensure delivery in a co-ordinated way. In the area of competitiveness, Pathfinder stressed the failure to give due recognition to the critical importance of the managerial resource in Northern Ireland. In the area of exports, the paper suggested that what was needed was a change in the attitudes of local managers towards exporting. With the use of public funds, it stressed the need for greater awareness in the public and private sectors of the dangers of substantial and prolonged dependence by industry on public subsidy.

An Assessment of the Pathfinder Process

Although perceptive in some of its insights, the Pathfinder document had a number of important limitations. First of all, it overlooked the issue of inward investment and its role in economic development. This was surprising given that the spectacular success of the province's manufacturing sector during the 1960s was due in large measure to the presence of outside firms in the local economy. As a result, it seemed somewhat cavalier to rule out inward investment as a policy option given the scale of the province's difficulties. What needs to be borne in mind is that as there are only one and a half million people in the province, a handful of large inward investment projects would dramatically improve the employment opportunities of some sub-regions. Another failure of Pathfinder was that it set down unrealistic policy objectives. In particular, it asserted that the objective of policy should be to transfer Northern Ireland into a self-reliant economy without seriously analysing whether this was a realistic goal. In principle few would disagree with this economic objective. Creating a self-reliant economy in the province would be welcome relief from years of economic crisis and hardship. However, whilst the objectives of Pathfinder could be regarded as laudable, whether they were achievable is an entirely different matter.

If a strict definition of a self-reliant economy is taken, and there is no reason to believe that any other definition was used by Pathfinder, then a key task of policy must be to ensure that Northern Ireland economic balance with the outside is at, or near to, equilibrium. As the province's trading deficit stands at about one and a half billion pounds financed more or less by the British subvention and amounting to about 27 per cent of GDP, this is a formidable task. If an external balance is to be realized then there has to be a spectacular increase in industrial output and productivity.

Existing industry in the province would have to undergo a wholesale transformation if it is to be the engine of economic regeneration. Pockets of the manufacturing sector, most notably aircraft and motor vehicles and parts, have been able to weather the prevailing crisis quite well and to increase output. These industries, however, are very much the exception, since most of the manufacturing sector in the province is heavily subsidized. Moreover, in addition to subsidies, many parts of the manufacturing sector are dependent on public contracts from the British government for their survival. Clearly, the industrial sector in Northern Ireland would have to undergo a wholesale transformation before the objective of a self-reliant growth model could be realized.

Currently, the British government places much store on the role of small firms in the process of economic development, and to a large extent this approach is mirrored in the Pathfinder initiative. But it is questionable whether small firms alone can make a telling contribution to economic revival in the province. A survey by Hitchens and O'Farrell, 1987, found that in comparison with similar enterprises in South East England, the performance of small manufacturing firms in Northern Ireland is distinctly lacklustre. In almost every respect, the quality of design and finished products, pricing levels, levels of expertise and skills within the workforce, the scale of investment in plant and machinery, and registered profits, the Northern Ireland firms performed worse than their English counterparts. This is a fairly systematic catalogue of failings which suggests that the notion of establishing a self-reliant economy through the creation of a large small firms sector is fanciful.

What also needs to be stressed is that whilst a massive expansion in industrial output is an essential condition for the creation of a self-reliant economy, the resultant increase in manufacturing employment will make only a modest contribution to solving the unemployment problem in the province. In an economy without the scale of economic difficulties facing Northern Ireland, a major expansion of industrial output would create the conditions for a substantial increase in employment in non-industrial activities. But if the primary objective is a self-reliant economy, then any increase in industrial output in the province would presumably go towards financing existing levels of service-sector employment, presently funded by the external subsidy. To create the conditions for a further increase in service employment in the province not financed by external sources, an economic miracle would be required in the province unparalleled in modern history. Thus, the evidence suggests that the creation of a self-reliant economy in Northern Ireland is an over ambitious and unrealistic policy goal. For a considerable time to come, Northern Ireland will remain dependent on the outside world.

A third problem with the Pathfinder process was that it ignored the institutional framework and other wider environmental conditions. All countries have a 'economic policy model'. This notion does not refer to a formalized economic model, like the Cambridge or the Liverpool model, but describes the economic policy system of a specific country – hence the idea of a 'Swedish model' or a 'German model'. The key feature of an economic policy model is that it defines the relationship between political, economic and social institutions and the market. The exact nature and form of these institutional/market relationships vary across countries but tend to fall into one of four categories.

Box A refers to relatively successful market-dominated economic systems – examples are the United States and Switzerland. While institutions certainly exist in these countries, they tend to be weak and passive. Markets tend to be the main determinants of economic outcomes. Box B describes the situation where institutions and markets co-exist in an incoherent and asymmetrical manner. It may signify either a case where there are too many of the wrong type of institutions or a case where there is too much unbridled market power. An example of the former situation is the Italian economy during the 1970s. In that decade, Italy tried to replicate the institutional arrangements which made countries such as France and Germany successful during the golden age of economic growth. However, because market conditions had changed considerably as a result of the economic crises these institutions, rather than facilitating growth, imposed enormous rigidities on the economy. The result was a widespread successful drive by the business community to escape these regulatory structures. Ironically enough in doing so they unwittingly established a new cohesive connection between institutions and markets which Piore and Sabel (1984) call flexible specialization. The early years of the Thatcher administration, when Britain experienced a massive drop in its industrial capacity and employment, may be taken as an examples of too much unbridled market power.

	A	C	
Economic Success	Little institutional presence in the market	Symmetrical institutional/market relationships	**Economic Success**
Economic Failure	Asymmetrical institutional/ market arrangements	Excessive institutional involvement in markets	**Economic Failure**
	B	D	

Examples of the scenario of symmetrical institutional/market relations contained in Box C are Sweden, Germany or Japan. In this model, institutional pressures and influences on markets have positive outcomes. Thus, in Sweden, a formalized wage determination system keeps wages higher than they would be under market conditions, thereby preventing employers from implementing cost-reducing competitive policies and obliging them to obtain better performance through product diversification, the introduction of new technology and investing in training and retraining. In a similar way, the training regime in Germany which obliges employers to train more workers and afford them broader skills than required by immediate economic circumstances creates major labour market pressures against low-skill and cost-competitive strategies and in favour of innovative/high skilled initiatives. Thus, by exerting influences and pressures on markets, these institutions close off certain commercial avenues. But at the same time, these institutions also respond to market signals. Thus for instance a major 'qualification offensive' is under way in West Germany in response to the demand of employers for more multiskilled apprentices. Turning to Box D, the previous central planning systems of the Eastern bloc are examples of excessive institutional involvement in markets, in some instances to the extent that the latter hardly function.

Obviously this is a highly stylized representation of the dynamic interactions between institutions and markets. But in a broad sense, it is a useful framework to distinguish between successful and unsuccessful economic policy models. Applying this representation to Northern Ireland, it can hardly be doubted that the province falls firmly into Box B. There is a major disfunction between the regulatory or institutional framework and underlying market conditions, thereby creating economic malaise. By default, Pathfinder appeared to be wanting to establish an economic policy model, which falls into Box A in the province, without any sound or coherent reasons to justify such a course. Notions such as greater competitiveness and improved productivity were evoked in the Pathfinder documents but these are economic aspirations — every country in the world wants greater competitiveness and improved productivity — which are insufficient justifications for a particular economic development method. As a result, Pathfinder failed systematically to address major issues such as the economic dynamics of Northern Ireland's relationship with Britain or the Republic of Ireland, or offer any comments on other key matters such as the role of the multinationals in the province, or to raise questions such as whether Northern Ireland can develop regional institutional arrangements to guide the direction of markets in the province. Given its neglect of the structural and institutional context for economic development in the province, from the very outset Pathfinder was going to find it difficult to be successful.

Competing in the 1990s – the Current Approach

Thus whilst Pathfinder contained pertinent insights into the problems of Northern Ireland and launched some worthwhile individual schemes, it was severely limited as an overall economic development strategy. Unsurprisingly therefore the initiative very quickly fell out of favour and a new policy document was launched by the Department of Economic Development called 'Northern Ireland Competing in the 1990s: The Key to Growth'.

In this document, the authorities set out the new economic strategy to improve growth in the local economy. 'Competing in the 1990s' basically sets out the broad framework for DED and its agencies (IDB, LEDU and T&EA) to guide assistance to industry in the 1990s.

A new set of economic development objectives are outlined for DED and its agencies:

> To promote economic growth which will lead to increased employment and the reduction of unemployment in Northern Ireland by:
> —assisting Northern Ireland industry to become internationally competitive;
> —attracting high quality internationally mobile projects;
> —providing those in employment or seeking employment with the skills necessary to enable industry to become more competitive or to obtain employment wherever they wish; and
> —assisting the development of entrepreneurs and an enterprise culture (DED).

Although the document recognised that the DED had an important role to play in increasing growth in Northern Ireland, it also argued that the private sector should carry the lion's share of this burden.

Many of the perceived weaknesses of the Northern Ireland economy outlined by Pathfinder were reiterated in the document: the dependency of the manufacturing sector on a relatively small number of larger firms which have the ability to compete effectively in international markets; the local focus of so many small firms in the province; the high level of public financial assistance unintentionally masking key market signals which would spur management towards greater competitiveness. In addressing these weaknesses the New Approach has the following components:

— ensuring that government assistance, while not displacing private sector finance, is focused on the obstacles to growth and will help improve the competitiveness of Northern Ireland industry;
— intensifying the drive for inward investment;
— building up management and workforce skills;
— stimulating the development of entrepreneurs and the enterprise; and
— targeting growth areas through detailed sectoral studies.

A key feature of the new approach is that it adopts the stance that resources in the economy are best allocated through markets and that the purpose of public assistance to industry is to help firms in Northern Ireland overcome those problems which they cannot be expected to deal with through their own efforts: the role of policy is to compensate for situations where the market mechanism fails to operate properly. Thus the purpose of public intervention should be to remove market failure or imperfections.

For indigenous industry, public assistance in Northern Ireland will be limited to providing help to overcome constraints to improving competitiveness and growth that cannot be addressed through the normal operation of the market. The rationale for the new policy approach is that since an efficient capital market exists in Northern Ireland there is no justification why public funding should be provided for commercially viable projects. The new strategy heralds a fundamental change in the nature of support for indigenous industry; however, this is not so for inward investment projects. These projects will still be offered financial inducements to locate in Northern Ireland. Finally, in summary the new approach makes it clear that responsibility for economic growth in Northern Ireland rests squarely on the shoulders of the private sector in the province.

During 1991 the new strategy was further developed. In particular DED started to signal that a key component of policy would be 'backing winners': either companies, individuals or groups within Northern Ireland's indigenous sector. 'Backing winners' in the indigenous sector means government working with Northern Ireland companies which have the potential and drive to grow and the ambition to increase their sales and/or market share. Indigenous companies who are 'winners' are defined as those who have marked themselves out by certain characteristics – for example, a record of profitable growth, export orientation and innovation. Assistance will be targeted at areas such as business planning, product/process improvement, quality, market research, marketing and help with export information and advice. The essence of the new policy is, thus, market orientated and accelerative by encouraging Northern Ireland indigenous companies eager to grow to achieve their full potential more rapidly than they could achieve it themselves.

Thus for industrial or economic development policy the key touchstone is whether it can improve competitiveness. But in reality, however, this policy change does not progress matters since competitiveness is a fairly imprecise concept, open to a variety of meanings and interpretations. Some regard it as an *ex post* outcome of a successful economy, involving the presence of a highly dynamic manufacturing sector, low unemployment and high incomes (Zysman and Cohen, 1987). Others view it as a measuring instrument to evaluate the performance of the economy. Macro-economists tend to emphasize the exchange or inflation rate, or wage settlements in assessing the competitiveness of an economy. For their part, industrial economists focus on production functions – the relationship between capital and labour at the firm level. In business schools the concept is seen mostly as a matter of strategy. Competitiveness arises as a result of a firm's strategic decision in areas such as corporate management, marketing or human resources. Yet another view is to regard competitiveness as the product of the right type of institutions being in place (Streeck, 1990). Thus for instance 'proper' labour market institutions encourage good industrial relations practice and produce highly skilled workers. All in all the notion can be interpreted in any number of ways.

An indication of the difficulty of operationalizing the concept of competitiveness was that the Industrial Development Board produced a discussion paper requesting submissions from the private sector on the definition and measurement of the notion. Thus while the new objective of economic policy is generally accepted, few concrete ideas exist about how best it can be achieved. In other words, like Pathfinder and other initiatives the growth of the 1990s strategies may well have limited success because it does not have a clear idea of the processes that underpin competitiveness.

Overall an enduring feature of the policy debate on the Northern Ireland economy is the virtual absence of any discussion on more systemic issues associated with the economic development process. For instance, no satisfactory assessment has been made of the underlying dynamics which attracted large numbers of multinational companies to the province. Nor has there been any examination of the various typologies of regional economic development in the economic literature to see if they are appropriate for Northern Ireland. Thus for example no assessment has been made of the neo-classical economic model and its suitability as an economic strategy for the province. As a result of this shortcoming, economic development strategy has tended to revolve around high-sounding but imprecise terms – addressing market failures, promoting competitiveness, encouraging enterpreneurialism and so on. A major argument of this chapter is that a wider understanding is needed of the economic influences operating on regions before a co-ordinated and successful policy model can be developed for the province. To fill this vacuum this chapter now assesses various policy frameworks or models to see if any of them are appropriate for the Northern Ireland context.

In particular the next section outlines three traditional economic models which point the way towards gaining competitiveness in a region such as Northern Ireland. The three approaches are: (1) the Neoclassical model; (2) the Cumulative Causation Model and (3) the Organizational Approach. The limitations of these more traditional models will be highlighted with the view to examining more contemporary experiences of regions which have enjoyed unprecedented growth.

THE NEOCLASSICAL VIEW AND COMPETITIVENESS

The neoclassical model of economic development and growth is a supply-side approach. The approach looks at the determination of output in an economy in terms of the co-operating factors of production: labour and capital. The approach assumes that output depends on the inputs of the factors of production. The relationship is assumed to be stable over time. It is called a production function, which also assumes that capital and labour can be combined in different proportions to produce a given output: that is, capital and labour are homogenous. The properties of the model can be illustrated using a Cobb-Douglas production function.

$$Q = \text{constant} \cdot L^a K^b$$
$$\text{of Log } Q = \log(\text{constant}) + a \log L + b \log K$$

where Q = output
L = labour input
K = capital input

The constants a and b, in the equation above, represent the respective contribution of capital and labour inputs to aggregate output. Converting the above equation into a rate of growth equation:

$$q = al\dot{} + bk\dot{}$$

where q = rate of growth or output
l$\dot{}$ = rate of growth of labour
k$\dot{}$ = rate of growth of capital

Here, the growth of output is dependent on growth in labour, in part, and a part dependent on capital. Finally, a residual term is introduced which allows output to rise over time at a constant rate even if capital and labour are constant.

$$q = r + al\dot{} + bk\dot{}$$

The growth residual (r) is defined as the rate of growth of output minus the weighted average of the input growth rates and it picks up shifts in technology, working practices and anything else left out of the analysis.

Allowing constant returns to scale, the equation above can be rewritten.

$$q = r + (1-b)\, l\dot{} + bk\dot{}$$
$$\text{which equals } q - l\dot{} = r + b(k\dot{} - l\dot{})$$

Hence, output per worker can only increase if capital growth exceeds the growth of the labour force or if the trend rate of growth rises. The above equation can be applied to a region,

$$q_r - l\dot{}^r = r_r + b(k\dot{}^r - l\dot{}^r)$$

where subscript r refers to a specific region in the economy.

Regional differences in the growth of output per worker are explained by regional differences in technical progress and in the growth of the capital/labour ratio (Armstrong/Taylor, 1985). However, the neoclassical approach also assumes mobility of factors of production between regions in an economy. Capital and labour will move towards those regions which offer the highest expected rate of return. Hence regional growth disparities occur because of regional differences in the rate at which indigenous supplies of capital and labour expand, and also because of inter-regional movements of these two factors. The neoclassical approach also assumes that capital and labour markets are perfectly competitive: in other words, factors are paid their marginal products. Neoclassical models also assume perfect flexibility of factor prices. Factors of production will migrate between regions due to differences in inter-regional prices. It is a market-orientated or equilibrating approach. In other words the model assumes continuous market clearing. Hence, a characteristic of the neoclassical model is that wage levels will be high in regions with a high capital/labour ratio but the rate of return on capital will be low. The high wage region will experience an inflow of labour and an outflow of capital, vice versa for a low-wage region. The operation of market clearing via price flexibility ensures that rates of return, growth rates, wage rates and growth in output per head will be evened out between regions.

Policy Implications

Three possible policy avenues to improve competitiveness arise from the above framework; two are a direct consequence of the model and one, a result of its assumption of wage flexibility:

(1) Encourage capital formation, for example, by the provision of capital grants;
(2) Encourage innovation, for example, by the provision of research and development grants;
(3) Lower real wages in the Northern Ireland economy.

The first recommendation is trying to raise output per worker by raising the quantity of capital per worker. The second is trying to raise the underlying multi-factor productivity growth in Northern Ireland. The third proposition attempts to align wage levels with underlying economic performance. Real wages are too high in Northern Ireland to clear the labour market. If they fell, indigenous firms would be more competitive in external markets, new firms would be attracted into the province and domestic firms would raise their demand for labour. However, a real wage cut would be difficult to achieve without real loss. Indigenous firms may be unwilling to pay lower wages through fear of losing skilled workers to Great Britain. Cutting public sector wages could put downward pressure on wages in the private sector, however, again this could result in the loss of skilled workers through migration. Cutting unemployment benefit would reduce wages. This would create some low-paid jobs, but the benefit cut would cause substantial poverty and hardship.

High levels of unemployment and lack of job opportunity causes net outward migration from Northern Ireland. Thus migration is the mechanism which ensures unemployment is kept to manageable levels in the province. Canning, Moore and Rhodes (1987, p. 274) have argued that:

> wage cutting does not provide a viable economic development programme for Northern Ireland ... Without economic growth, cutting wages simply substitutes one form of hardship, low incomes, for another, unemployment. It is not clear which is preferable, particularly as incomes may have to be very low to have the same effect on migration as high unemployment.

Limitations of the Neoclassical Approach

The first limitation of the neoclassical approach is that it is entirely a supply-orientated model. The approach stresses the influence of basic supply factors such as labour-force growth, the growth of the capital stock and technical change. The model ignores the potential contribution of demand-side factors in determining a region's growth of output and productivity. Once attention is turned to the demand side of the market this allows for the possibility that regional growth differences can occur due to differences in the growth of a region's exports. The export-based approach stresses the crucial role of the external demand for a region's output in determining its growth.

The second limitation of the neoclassical approach is that it views the firm as little more than a black box. The theory pays no attention to the actual operations of production, which is represented by the generalized production function that can generate steamboats as easily as tubes (Storper and Walker 1989). The model assumes a conception of Malleable Capital which can be transferred costlessly and instantaneously from operation at one level of the capital–labour ratio to any other. This assumption by-passes some of the central difficulties of a real growing economy, in which mistakes are made, expectations are unrealised and historically given capital stock can be a constraint on short and medium term growth prospects (Jones, 1975). The model does not examine the firm as an organizational structure and ignores the role of management and hence strategy. The external institutional framework in which the firm operates is also ignored.

The neoclassical model is an equilibrium theory of price. Marshall, in his derivation of equilibrium prices, assumed that decreasing returns dominate. However, Marshall himself suggested that the law of increasing returns will dominate in many industries. But once increasing returns are introduced into the model, it is not possible to derive equilibrium prices. To establish the existence of an equilibrium requires that all goods have perfectly competitive markets and a determinate price.

Increasing returns, on the other hand, lead to indeterminant prices and cause markets in one way or another to work imperfectly. With this dilemma, it has not been possible to integrate a more realistic theory of the firm with an equilibrium theory of price. As a result of this lack of realism in the neoclassical theory of the firm potential concepts to explain economic development such as strategy, production, management, organization, culture, and regulation are suppressed. Thus neoclassical equilibrium theories may be useful as a form of abstract reasoning, but they have little explanatory power in terms of the success or otherwise of firms.

The third limitation of the theory is that, with 'fitted' production functions, it appears that most of the growth can be attributed to the residual factor. Some of the contributory factors explaining the residual could be: the form of industrial relations, innovation and new technology, the quality of workers, management and plant, and also improvements in capital utilization (Muellbauer, 1986). However, by definition, the residual is the term the theory says least about. The neoclassical approach does not explain how to achieve competitiveness but rather imputes economic growth, and growth in output per head, to various contributory factors. One of these factors is the residual. Imputing growth to various factors is all very well; however, in practice, we wish to know how to affect growth. To understand how competitiveness is achieved, we must open the black box of the firm. The neoclassical model just does not do this.

The fourth limitation is the assumption of a perfect market adjustment mechanism. Current advances in economic theory suggest that perfect factor price flexibility and market clearing are unrealistic assumptions. A more plausible and widely accepted view is the New Keynesian approach which assumes the absence of continuous market clearing (Gordon, 1990). According to this view, prices and wages fail to adjust quickly enough to clear markets within a relatively short period of time. Market clearing does not occur because firms and workers are seen as having some monopoly power and because of the existence of limited information and high transaction costs (Mankin and Romer, 1990).

As far as trade unions are concerned, for example, bargaining models have been developed where firms and unions bargain over wages and employment with the result that employment can fluctuate significantly but real wages remaining stable. Thus unions can be a source of resistance to real wage fluctuations. Another explanation of real wage stickiness are insider–outsider theories. The insiders are defined as experienced employees whose jobs are protected by a variety of labour turnover costs which make them costly for firms to replace. The outsiders are either unemployed or work in the casual or secondary labour market. Insiders gain market power without necessarily taking into account the interests of outsiders. Also, unions can organize insider' activities, and via market power, insiders can resist outsiders' attempts to gain employment by underbidding the prevailing insider wage. Union behaviour and insider–outsider models are closely linked. Insider–outsider models show how unemployment for outsiders does not create downward pressure on the real wage. Real wages become sticky.

Efficiency wage theory can also help explain real wage rigidity. Efficiency wage theory is based on the proposition that worker productivity depends on the level of the real wage. With such a link between the wage rate and worker efficiency, firms may rationally pay a real wage above the market clearing level. Firms, here, are refusing to reduce the wage, to hire workers from the pool of unemployed, available to work at a lower wage, fearful that a reduction in real wages for existing workers may reduce productivity by more than the gain in lower wages. For efficiency reasons real wages are rigid downwards.

Thus from a new Keynesian perspective the market adjustment mechanism may be very imperfect. By contrast, neoclassical theory stresses market clearing via price flexibility which ensures that growth rates, wage rates, growth in output per head, and rates of return will be equalized across regions via migration of factors of production in response to price signals. Introducing real wage rigidity in the labour market blunts wages as a signal and hence regions may not automatically grow at the same rate.

In summary then, the neo-classical model can be regarded as having the following shortcomings:

— it is a supply side model which ignores demand-led influences, for example, exports;
— it ignores the actual operations of production;
— it ignores the possibility of the existence of increasing returns;
— the residual term in the model tends to explain most of economic growth;
— the model assumes prices and wages are perfectly flexible, and that markets clear. In reality, this may not be so.

As a result, economists have searched for other explanations of economic growth and of how competitiveness emerges. In particular, economists have looked at demand-side influences. The next section will outline the Cumulative Causation model which highlights the role of the demand-side of the economy.

THE CUMULATIVE CAUSATION MODEL

The cumulative causation model is essentially a demand-led theory of achieving competitive advantage and growth. The cornerstone of the model is the Verdoorn Law:

$$q = a + bQ$$

where a = autonomous productivity growth
b = the Verdoorn coefficient
q = productivity growth
Q = output growth

The law states that productivity growth is positively related to the rate of growth in output. It is a law of increasing returns. The faster the growth in output, the faster will labour productivity increase. This law has important implications for an economy. Increasing output leads to a law of increasing returns where labour productivity rises. If an economy can grow faster than other economies, that is, increase its output faster, then it will achieve a competitive advantage, through faster labour productivity growth. The process is cumulative and self-perpetuating. Rising labour productivity leads to lower product prices, and hence, rising real incomes in that economy. Rising real incomes through multiplier effects feed through to resulting further increases in output. These increases lead to further rises in productivity, real incomes and output, and so the process continues.

What are the implications of the Verdoorn relationships and its resulting process of cumulative causation? The law provides the mechanism whereby a particular region in an economy can achieve a competitive advantage over other regions. The region can achieve this internally in its indigenous industry or externally by way of its export sector. To see how the process can work for a region's export sector, consider the effect of a rise in demand for the region's exports on world markets. Export growth will rise in the region which raises the region's rate of growth of output. The effect of the increase in output growth is to raise labour productivity growth which leads to increasing export competitiveness through falls in the region's export product prices.

The improvement in the competitive position induces a further rise in exports and hence the virtuous circle continues through further increases in output plus productivity.

The cumulative causation model combines two basic assumptions: (i) that demand growth Q favours productivity b; and (ii) that productivity gains induce expansion of demand.

In functional form:

$$b = f(Q)$$
$$Q = g(b)$$

The first equation states a positive relationship between growth rates Q and productivity b, with causation running from Q to b. The second shows productivity growth b causing an increase in demand Q. With regard to the first equation, demand can encourage productivity improvements in a number of ways: (i) work might be reorganized, by redesigning the working time schedule, by taking advantage of learning by doing effects or by re-ordering the division of work between crafts or firms; (ii) new investments and/or the scrapping of old production capacities (within or between firms) may be undertaken, thus raising the level of production per person employed; (iii) some technical change can take place which upgrades the efficiency of new equipment or reduces the time lags and obstacles affecting the links between firms, suppliers and markets.

The way productivity gains lead to an expansion of demand can be best explained in terms of demand regimes. The demand regime can either take the form of productivity gains which feed through to real wage and profit increases which stimulate final demand; or alternatively, productivity gains may be used to reduce product prices, boosting exports or reducing imports which again boosts final demand. Thus the validity of the cumulative causation model depends on the internal workings of the two equations stated above.

Regional Implications of the Cumulative Causation Process

The cumulative causation process raises two policy possibilities for a region like Northern Ireland. One is an attempt to apply the process itself and the other is to attempt to capture some of the spillover benefits from the process.

(a) The Internal Model

The cumulative causation process explains how a region, once it has gained an initial competitive advantage, can surge ahead of other regions on the wave of a virtuous circle of growth. However, it can also show how a region, once it has started to decline, (say due to a dependency on sunset industries), can plunge into a vicious circle of stagnation. The decline is perpetuated by the cumulative process. Overall then the cumulative causation process is an explanation of the differences in growth between disadvantaged and advantaged regions. In particular, it attempts to highlight that the gap between richer and poorer regions can widen rather close as suggested by the neoclassical model.

How does the cumulative causation process provide an internal model for economic development for a poor region like Northern Ireland? For the most part it does so by providing the rationale for a policy which tries to narrow the growth differences between well-off and disadvantaged regions. More specifically the process gives a rationale for fiscal transfers to poor regions. A fiscal transfer to a disadvantaged region is an attempt to bolster up demand in that region and hence raise the size of the domestic local market. Increasing the size of the local market may allow local firms to exploit economies of scale and hence trigger off the cumulative growth process. Any exploitation of scale economies may trigger a virtuous circle of growth.

(b) The External Model

The external model is a consequence of the process itself. The cumulative causation process essentially links demand, growth and productivity with economies of scale. With demand growing steadily and opportunities existing for productivity improvements, firms will be attracted to grow larger to capture economies of scale effects. As a result of this process, the firm itself makes the product from start to finish, including the intermediate components. For instance, a clothing firm could produce and process the fabric; then design, knit and sew the garment and finally even retail the finished clothing. The firm in this case invariably grows large.

During the golden age of economic growth the search for economies of scale produced manufacturing units on a gigantic scale. Initially, these large firms aimed their output at domestic markets. But after a time the scale of investments made required them to seek markets elsewhere. As a result a key feature and a central dynamic of the golden age was the growth and spread of multinational companies in the world economy.

The consequence of the cumulative causation process therefore has been the growth of multinationals which, in their search for economies of scale, have located production facilities internationally. This gives an external model for economic development in Northern Ireland. The policy is the attraction of branch plants of multinationals into the province. The benefits that should accrue are the creation of employment directly, and indirectly in indigenous suppliers, raising output locally and possible external benefits such as training and the possible introduction of new production techniques. As we have seen, Northern Ireland has consistently offered a wide range of financial incentives to branch plants which locate in the province, and this remains a policy of the Industrial Development Board for Northern Ireland today. The heyday of the branch plant in Northern Ireland was during the 1960s, when the number of internationally mobile investment projects attracted to the province grew substantially (Teague, 1987a).

Limitations of the Cumulative Causation Model

During the 1950s and 1960s, the cumulative causation model was the main counterweight to the neoclassical thesis. Clearly it has many positive qualities, but it also suffers from a range of shortcomings. The first limitation of the model is that the Verdoorn relationship is as much a black box as the production function in the neoclassical model. In particular, the relationship between an expansion of output and productivity improvement, however useful, is an over-simplification since it hides a complex set of economic processes which deserve more detailed attention. What are the various explanations which have been postulated to account for the relationship? Verdoorn himself postulated that output growth creates opportunities for the greater division and specialisation of labour. Kaldor (1963) highlighted the importance of economies of scale, both static and dynamic, due to extensions of the division of labour and markets, organizational economies and 'learning by doing' effects. Much of the connection between demand and productivity and vice versa is seen in terms of deepening the division of labour or capturing scale effects. But little attention is given to the institutional context for growth; for instance the type of industrial relations systems in place or the relationship between firms and the financial system. Nor is much weight given to matters such as managerial strategies, the organizational ecology of the firm (i.e. whether internal labour markets exists) the human resource strategies of enterprises and so on.

These drawbacks are reflected in the mathematics of the Verdoorn/ Kaldorian law, as some of the equations are not particularly robust. For instance the relationship between demand and productivity omits a large number of organizational characteristics. The nature of investment behaviour remains opaque, especially with regard to technical change. Moreover, since the exact scale of productivity sharing is not specified and the role of external price shocks entirely omitted, the productivity/demand relationship cannot be regarded as any way steady.

A second shortcoming of the model is that it now has reduced explanatory power since the productivity slowdown of the 1970s. In particular after several decades of slow growth and high unemployment the Verdoorn view that a strong positive relationship exists between output, productivity and employment appears to no longer hold. Certainly it seems unable to account for the events of the 1970s and 1980s. Using estimations on pooled data for a set of sixteen OECD manufacturing industries, Boyer and Petit (1989) show that the correlation between demand and productivity has weakened since 1973. The relationship between output productivity and employment is anything but stable. For instance, in many ways the relationship between productivity and employment is now negative with many countries pursuing high productivity growth through job rationalization strategies. Thus all in all the Verdoorn appears relevant to an economic era that has come and gone.

THE ORGANIZATIONAL APPROACH

The third view of achieving competitiveness is the 'Organizational Approach'. This is basically a pragmatic, empirical way of studying competitiveness. It involves the empirical study of good performance along with bad performance. The characteristics of the economic system in regions or countries which are regarded as competitive are compared with similar characteristics in regions or countries seen as competitive laggards. To a large extent, the method is a checklist approach where problem areas are identified by comparing the good with the bad. Correcting such problems is seen to be the key to achieving good performance. Match plant comparisons are usually the main method of collecting the data for studies in this mould. Thus the characteristics of firms in a high-productivity region or country are compared with those in a low-productivity region or country. Problem areas are then identified by running through this checklist of characteristics.

This approach is exemplified by the study undertaken by D. Hitchens, K. Wagner and J. Birnie entitled: Northern Ireland Manufacturing Productivity compared with West Germany – A Matched Plant comparison (1989). In the study, forty-five plants in Northern Ireland were compared with thirty-nine in West Germany involving thirty-two different product groups within the manufacturing sector. A single Northern Ireland plant was matched with a single plant in Germany within the same product category, and in a number of cases multiple matches were made. The plants were matched as closely as possible by both product type and factory size. The study allowed for a comparison of: physical productivity, product quality, age of machinery, level of technology, the extent of adaptation and customization of machinery, machinery maintenance, the layout and cleanliness of premises, manning levels, the qualifications of management and labour force, absenteeism, labour turnover, strikes, disruptions, and finally, attitudes to work, between Northern Ireland and West German plants. The study found that generally the German plants had higher physical productivity and the edge in terms of quality products despite there being no disadvantage in Northern Ireland as a consequence of machine age. Some of the productivity shortfall could be traced to higher technology in some sectors in Germany. Poor labour productivity in Northern Ireland (NI) was also blamed on overmanning both in direct processes and indirect employees. Northern Ireland labour was outclassed in terms of the quality, quantity, width and intensity of skills, training and practical experience. The cause of the lower productivity in Northern Ireland was blamed on generous provision of financial assistance, in the form of capital grants, which dampened financial pressures on NI companies to improve productivity, and also on the poor labour force standards prevalent in the province. To overcome Northern Ireland's productivity gaps the authors of the study recommended a more effective allocation of government grants together with an improvement in the standards of training to enhance productivity.

Limitations of the Organizational Approach

Unquestionably, the Organizational Approach has its merits. By identifying and then examining the characteristics of firms in low-productivity regions compared with high-productivity regions, problems and weakness can be highlighted. But the approach runs the dangers of emphasizing the symptoms of uncompetitiveness rather than the causes. To a large extent, this is caused by the methodology being heavily empiricist in orientation. Maurice *et al.* (1984) have highlighted that there are two dramatically opposed methodologies that can be adopted under the organizational Approach. The first methodology they highlight is the 'universalistic approach'. This appears to be the methodology that Hitchens, Wagner and Birnie adopted. This approach assumes that the differences observed between countries are the result of comparable agents acting in accordance with a universal rationality but in different cultural environments or under different institutional constraints.

The universalistic approach assumes that deviations – in this case, differences in productivity – are caused by rigidities or a specific characteristic in one of the countries concerned. In this way differences are assumed to be national effects which will disappear as soon as the rigidities justifying their existence have themselves disappeared.

Maurice, Sellier and Silvestre, however, advocate a societal methodology when comparing organizations in two different countries. This approach assumes that it is social relations within society which shape the way a firm is organized. Firms in each country are then 'specific to each type of society'. They argue that it would not be possible really to compare two firms in two different countries unless this was looked at from the point of view of the social relations which have shaped it as well as the microscopic details within each firm. The differences between each firm could then be related to differences between both societies and their social relations which consist of the educational relation (which binds individuals to society through the educational and vocational training system), the organizational relation (which binds individuals to society through the division of labour) and the industrial relation (which binds individuals to a society through systems that establish social identity and economic co-operation, i.e. management, workers and their organizations). Hence, a study looking at productivity would not only examine the microscopic details of say, two firms in isolation, but would also relate it to the way society in each country works.

The Hitchens/Wagner/Birnie study fails to pursue this latter approach and as a result their analysis is a combination of narrow empiricism and amateur sociology. In the absence of more encompassing explanations for poor productivity performance, the policy recommendations from the study must be treated cautiously. Take for instance their proposals for the redirection of government assistance and the enhancement of training as the main way to achieving competitiveness. Now these may be important elements in the drive to upgrade competitiveness in NI, but are they sufficient conditions? Without having an underlying theory which outlines the conditions by which competitiveness emerges in the province, it is not possible to say. Policy prescriptions based on the approach may have intuitive appeal; however, without theory, it is not possible to say whether they are skirting round the edges or if they are really getting to the heart of the problem.

As can be seen from the outline of the three traditional models in this section, the need for a coherent theory as to how competitiveness emerges is crucial to understanding economic development. The next section will outline two new explanations, from which it may be possible to build a strategy for achieving economic advantage. The limitations of the three older models has led to the search for other possible explanations of emerging competitiveness. The three traditional models are somewhat in demise. However, it is not that their features will disappear, but they will be incorporated within the two new models outlined in the next section.

TOWARDS A NEW VIEW OF ACHIEVING COMPETITIVENESS: THE NEW INTERNAL MODEL

This section explores the determinants of a new internal model. This model shows how a regional economy can become highly dynamic by building local agglomeration economies. Rekindling Marshall's argument that dynamic economic structures can emerge from clusters of interdependent firms, the idea is that industrial activity is taking a distinct regional form. Thus Sabel (1989) points to highly dynamic industrial regions like Emilia Romagna and Baden Württemberg as instances of this new internal model. Certainly the economic performance of these regions are impressive. For policy the big question is how these regions have been able to be successful. The argument of the section is that the successful exploitation of the advantages of smalscale production depends crucially on conditions outside the firm. For firms to reap fully the benefits of external economies, the wider environment must enable, foster and encourage firm co-operation. In other words, the successful operation of the new internal model depends on a virtuous governance structure.

Governance Structures and Agglomeration Economies

Comprising three inter-related tiers, the concept of governance structure attempts to explain why agglomeration effects or external economies of scale emerge in a particular region, or country for that matter. Table 3.1 lists the main components of each tier.

Table 3.1 Components of a Governance Structure

(a) The nature and extent institutional frameworks
    (i) the role of 'external' economic and commercial institutions both private public and private;
    (ii) the nature of the local infrastructure;
    (iii) the industrial, political and social traditions of the area;
    (iv) the role of the financial system;
    (v) the type of pressures exerted from the establishment of external bargains;
    (vi) the nature and informal norms and conventions governing the economy.
(b) Commercial connections
    (i) the linkages between companies and the external environment;
    (ii) the networks operating between companies.
(c) The dominant form of enterprise calculation
    (i) the skills formation strategies of enterprises;
    (ii) the production system in place amongst firms;
    (iii) the scale of R&D expenditure;
    (iv) organizational structure:
        (a) the form of decision making, and
        (b) the organization of the labour process;
    (v) logistics planning.

(a) The Nature of the Local Infrastructure Physical and Commercial

If firms are to operate successfully within a region, there must be an adequate physical infrastructure, for example, roads, bridges and telecommunications to enable transport of goods inside and outside the region and adequate transmission of information across the economy. The form which the external commercial institutions take, both public and private, is very important to the successful operation of the industrial district. To reap the benefits of agglomeration effects, external economic and commercial institutions should enable, encourage and foster economic co-operation between firms. Hence, the role which external institutions such as universities, development agencies, and the Chamber of Commerce take is very important. The goal for such regional institutions would be the promotion of economic co-operation.

Best (1989) in his examination of the regional agglomerations of small firms in the Third Italy gives examples of where external institutions can foster economic co-operation among small firms; as he suggests:

> The Third Italy is a goldmine for studying institutions by which individuals can achieve the benefits of joint action that are beyond the reach of individual action ... (p. 137).

In other words, institutions in a region can provide common services to small firms within particular sectors, thereby encouraging collective commercial action.

In the third Italy, for instance, institutions, such as the CNA business association, can assist in solving general problems which affect all small firms in a particular sector such as quality control. In addition they also can provide business services to firms, such as export marketing or bulk purchasing of raw materials, for which substantial economies of scale exist. This demonstrates the benefits of collective action and hence promotes co-operation between independent enterprises. Thus small firms can act through the medium of an institution to co-operate on those issues which are of common interest to all.

Institutions may also attempt to facilitate inter-firm linkages by actively promoting physical infrastructure such as industrial parks where small firms with complementary and similar productive activities may locate. Moreover, as financial consortia in the third Italy show banks can act as independent, unbiased assessors of new business ideas put forward by the small firms who are members of the consortia. If the institution, in this case a consortium, has built up a reputation for impartiality then the independent assessment can facilitate the obtaining of loans for entrepreneurial activity. Through such activity potential market failures can be reduced; in this case risk-averse banking behaviour, which due to opportunism and bounded rationality may be unwilling to lend to the small firm sector for entrepreneurial activity even if the ideas are commercially sound. Institutions can also provide information to client small firms, particularly in areas that are undersupplied by the market. To a large extent this can be seen as overcoming the 'public good' aspect of information by providing it to all firms. Examples of information could be marketing opportunities and new technology.

(b) The Role of the Financial System

Enterprises have relationships with the financial system which may have a direct bearing on the performance of the business or its strategic decisions. For instance, banks may only be willing to lend short-term to firms and stress short-term profitability as a pre-requisite for loans. If the bank adopts such short-term strategies, it may undermine longer-term investments by businesses, thereby causing productive activity to fall short of its maximum feasible potential. Such action by banks may not prove conducive to the development of regional agglomeration effects which are predicated on commercial actors not having short-term horizons.

Aoki (1988) when outlining 'an Economic Model of the Japanese Firm' highlights the distinctive role which the Japanese financial sector plays in creating a co-operative and cohesive business environment. Aoki highlights that in Japan, banks and financial institutions are majority shareholders in businesses. The main result of this equity holding is a sheltering of Japanese enterprises from takeover.

In addition, Japanese banks do not interfere with the management of the businesses unless the company suffers a business crisis. In other words, management in Japan is free from outside interference and can take the necessary long-term decisions needed for business survival.

This type of complementary yet non-interventionist financial sector could also help foster the growth of regional agglomeration effects. One of the main advantages of such a system is that firms are actually encouraged to take the long-term decisions without fear of bank interference. A system such as this will complement the decisions made by firms to undertake long-term co-operative relationships with other firms. It may also allow firms to incorporate the interests of employees in the business strategy. Developing long-term contracts with employees, as well as with other firms, can make it easier for a small firm to be innovative. In exchange for long-term contracts, employees would take on more responsibility for problem solving, ideas and knowledge creation and would have to more readily accept the notion of working with management as a team.

(c) The Nature of External and Political Bargains

External and/or political bargains can be either the result of adversial or co-operative industrial relations. Locke (1990) highlights the differential between the adversial and co-operative arrangements when examining industrial restructuring in Italy. In the case of Fiat Auto the local union adopted a militant oppositional strategy even though market conditions were making firm restructuring an imperative. By adopting such action, the union was not only obstructing attempts to make the enterprise commercially viable but was also putting its own existence on the line.

In contrast, the Biellese Textile District restructured along the lines of the regional agglomeration model. In this case unions positively contributed to the process. In particular the unions and managers agreed a development pact which allowed for the transition from specialized to integrated production. Thus, negotiated industrial relations between employers and unions, based on mutual understanding and compromise, can positively contribute to economic development. Informal social norms and conventions within the region can also contribute to the development of the co-operative relationships between firms. Social traditions such as common educational and professional experience for instance can nurture co-operative and trust relations.

The second part of the regional agglomeration model's governing structure consists of the networks which are created between the firms in the region. An evergreen notion in the literature on industrial policy literature is the effects of experience and learning. At its most simplest the idea is that an enterprise can achieve an increase in productivity or competitive performance in the absence of new investment or added research and development expenditure. Under Fordism, such gains were mostly associated with 'learning by doing' effects. Now the full realization of such effects entails a much wider and sophisticated range of commercial activities. For the most part, the second tier of the governance structure is mainly about whether and how enterprises use linkages with each other to achieve these 'non-tangible effects' (Best, 1989).

The sub-contractual relationship between large firms and their suppliers and the linkages between quasi vertically integrated firms in regional economies are much discussed in the literature (Scott and Storper, 1989). Conventionally, the sub-contractual relationship has been regarded as one of control, whereby large firms use market power to establish dependency, and even exploitative, connections with small firms. When times are good for the large enterprise, the small firm enjoys relative prosperity but when recession hits their services are dispensed with and they are the first to go to the wall. As a result, employment in small firms has generally been regarded as precarious and working conditions as low-grade (Piore, 1980). A number of recent studies have suggested that this traditional scenario is changing and new constructive types of sub-contractual relationships are emerging (Harrison, 1989). At the heart of this transformation is the realization on the part of large firms that it is in their interests to invest in their relationship with suppliers. Thus for instance some large enterprises have entered into long-term contracts with suppliers in which a semi-permanent commercial connection is traded for high-quality supplies. In other cases, the large firm transfers resources to the small firm to help it exploit new or improve products or processes. As a result, the large enterprise may gain from quality improvements made to products by the supplier, whilst simultaneously the value added activities of the small firm are enhanced. All in all, the picture is of a positive symbiosis between large and small firms from which considerable experience and learning effects arise.

Intense interactions between groups of quasi-integrated enterprises either on a sector or regional basis is another source of intangible gains (Hirst and Zeitlin, 1991). In relation to Japan, the Keiretsu industrial group system is the foremost example. These groups connect literally hundreds of 'solar' firms producing all kinds of things with major banking and trading organizations which give them assistance on such matters as financial planning, marketing and so on. From these cross corporate relationships a web of co-operative commitments arise on a whole range of business issues. On a regional basis, some case studies are showing that small firms are establishing networks between themselves to share information on such things as technological development, the organization of the production process and marketing strategies without threatening any of the participants competitive position (Harrison, 1992). Such information sharing is sometimes extended so that collaborative or joint activity is undertaken by a group of enterprises. In addition, enterprises may club together to form marketing consortia and so on. Thus the new name of the game is that forms of business exchange and collaboration actually enhance the competitive performance of the involved firms.

A number of benefits arise from these inter-firm linkages. First of all, they give the individual enterprise the ability and confidence to specialize – a prerequisite to increased productive efficiency in small firms. Furthermore, they generate a high level of trust between enterprises, thereby reducing the likelihood of short-term opportunistic behaviour. In addition, in certain circumstances they allow firms to become innovative along Schumpterian lines, either in terms of product or process development. In other words, the innovative firm does not simply seek the cost route to competitiveness: by being a learning firm, it may be able to capture economies of scope – the ability to move from one product to another – a premium in today's turbulent and fragmented markets, or to realize lower transaction costs by improving information flows with other firms.

On occasions, the connections that exist between enterprises and the external environment can be so intense that they can turn around the economic fortunes of a region. Piore and Sabel (1984) articulate this effect in their theorizing about flexible specialisation. In essence flexible specialisation is about enterprises abandoning the principles of economies of scale and realising economies of scope through a rediscovery of the virtues of small-scale production and by creating external economies of scale. A number of substantial criticisms has been made against this scenario (Amin, 1989). It is not the intention here to debate the validity or otherwise of these criticisms. But it may be that the profound and benign effects which Piore and Sabel envisage being triggered by flexible specialization will only emerge in a handful of cases.

Nevertheless, institutional arrangements and collaborative networks are clearly important in allowing an enterprise to reach its maximum feasible level of competitiveness. But they do not constitute the full story of how a region can obtain a highly dynamic manufacturing sector, otherwise it would simply be a matter of putting in place the right type of external agencies and networks. Saxenian (1989) splendidly shows in her study of the Cambridge phenomena how creating an advanced commercial environment is not a sufficient condition for establishing competitive companies. This is essentially because enterprises, irrespective of the wider environment, have considerable autonomy in choosing the type of production, employment and commercial strategies they pursue. Hence the internal decision-making processes of enterprises are an important aspect of any governance structure. In examining this dimension of a governance structure the notion of enterprise calculation developed by Williams *et al.* (1983) is suggestive. Enterprise calculation essentially refers to the financial, marketing and production strategies firms pursue and the balance between them. A useful distinction is between a defensive and offensive enterprise calculation. Defensive enterprise calculations involve firms implementing decisions largely based on cost considerations. One such calculation is to abandon product lines and through an injection of capital in new technologies focus on being competitive in a narrower range of activities. Although output falls as a result of such rationalisation investments, profitability is either restored or increased. Labour costs are also reduced since the company now uses fewer workers. Another cost-cutting route is the well debated notion of the flexible firm where labour costs are deduced by dividing the workforce into core and periphery groups. Atkinson (1986) suggests that these types of strategies – the emphasis on investments to reduce costs rather than to develop new products or improve processes – have been widespread in British industry during the pase decade or so. All in all, the tactic is to defend or protect the enterprise by reducing exposure to financial or market shocks.

In contrast, an offensive enterprise calculation is about making long term investment decisions, increasing R&D expenditure, pursuing comprehensive skill formation strategies, and implementing new technologies to establish advanced production systems. To highlight the differences between a negative and a positive enterprise calculation Table 3.2 outlines two contrasting models of workplace industrial relations systems. Whereas the cost reduction approach encapsulates the negative enterprise approach, the commitment harmonizing system reflects a constructive approach to business affairs. Such a system is indispensable if a firm wants to create the proper organizational ecology for the full exploitation of advanced technology by multi-skilled workers.

Conceivably firms could follow a hybrid enterprise calculation, incorporating defensive and offensive components. But the proposition here is that if an offensive calculation is not present amongst firms in a sector or region (or both) then the overall governance structure will tend to under-perform. Conversely, if an offensive enterprise calculation is widely present then it is more likely that a virtuous interaction will emerge between all three elements of the governance structure producing powerful dynamic results in terms of the commercial competitiveness of the participating firms (Lipietz, 1990). But the benefits of a virtuous governance structure do not only relate to indigenous industries. They also put the region in a stronger position to capture the positive spillovers from the corporate strategies outside large firms.

Table 3.2 Two systems of workplace employee relations

Employee relations functions	Cost reduction	Commitment harmonizing
Job enlargement	Job tasks narrowly defined; many job classifications; work designed for individuals.	Broadly defined jobs; few job classifications work designed for teams.
Job enrichment	Non-supervisory employees have little influence over 'management' issues.	Blurring of hierarchial lines; link conception with execution of task.
Employee relations participation	No formal mechanism for employee participation.	Quality Circles; labour management committees.
Grievance procedure	No formal policy for employee complaints/ grievances.	Formal dispute resolution procedures.
Communication/ socialization	Informal service.	Regularly share business/economic information with employees.
Staffing	Lack of internal labour markets (use of temporary employees, low skill requirements).	Internal labour markets (career paths; higher skill requirements).
Training	Limited to specific job skills learned 'on the job'.	Problem solving; communication skills; cross training.
Compensation package	Limited benefits.	More extensive benefits.
Pay increase criteria	Individual performance.	Work group or company performance; skill level.
Pay level criteria	External competitiveness local labour markets.	Internal equity.

THE DEMISE OF FORDISM AND THE RE-ORGANIZATION OF LARGE FIRMS

The argument of the last section is that with regard to economic policy we must increasingly think in spatial terms. This is a move away from the traditional models of competitiveness and economic performance which put firms at the centre of analysis. Obviously firms, particularly large firms, are still a powerful force in modern economies, but the massive changes occurring in the corporate world have shifted the boundaries of effective economic policy. This is especially the case with regard to large firms. Under Fordism, firms grew bigger to capture internal economies of scale, producing highly dynamic economy-wide effects. In today's economy it is proving more and more difficult for firms to realize scale economies, and the capturing of systemic spillover effects has proven even more elusive. Thus since the Fordist production system is no longer producing dynamic effects, it is questionable whether economic policy should now be predicated either on encouraging firms to grow bigger or on capturing the indirect benefits from this process. It may be worthwhile to assess this point more fully.

During the golden age of economic growth, economic life was characterized by reasonably high levels of stability and certainty. Today's highly competitive economy is far removed from that environment. The market place is increasingly turbulent and volatile. On the demand side, there is increasing instability as the modern sophisticated consumer continuously seeks new products and product variety. As a result the life cycle of products has shortened and the quality of goods and services must be very high. On the supply side, western firms face increased international competition as a result of the globalization of corporate life. With greater uncertainty in the market place, firms now must be flexible and adaptable. Whether the traditional internal economies of scale model which is predicated on inflexible and rigid production techniques is appropriate for these more volatile demand conditions is open to question.

The 'Fordist' internal economies model has a number of inbuilt disadvantages. First of all, the exploitation of internal scale economies via vertical integration leads to a specialized division of labour within the firm which tends to reduce skill levels and increase repetitive job tasks. This leads to boredom within the workforce and industrial anomie. As a result, problems of shirking, disinterest and worker discontent can arise. Secondly, the production process can become rigid and inflexible. A process which depends on long runs of one product to achieve internal economies is rigid to the extent that it is hard to dismantle or change at short notice. Thirdly, such inflexibility and rigidity, resulting from long production runs, can lead to products which are overly standardized. Fourthly, the need to grow large can create problems of co-ordinating such a large organization. Managerial decision making becomes cumbersome and sluggish. Finally, the firm constantly emphasises production and the exploitation of technical economies within itself. Stress on production reduces the emphasis placed on product quality. As a result, the firm tends not to be sensitive to the needs of the consumer or to changes in tastes or market demand. These advantages, an inconvenience in the 1950s and 1980s, have now become the course of deep rigidities since they create major asymmeteries between the firm and consumption patterns.

Thus the system of mass production appears rigid in the face of market conditions where product variety is at a premium. Modern market conditions are inimical to rigid and inflexible production techniques. Geroski (1989) has pointed out that when the market demands more product diversity incentives will be created for manufacturers to adopt varied rather than mass production strategies. In other words, large firms become to regard market uncertainty and volatility as permanent features of business life. Faced with fragmenting markets, large firms are thus trying to become more adaptable and flexible. Changes in the structure and strategies of large firms can be interpreted as an attempt to establish a new symmetry between corporate structures and market conditions. In particular, it would appear that large firms are trying to simultaneously realise certain of the advantages associated with internal economies of scale and achieve a dynamic flexibility effect which has the aim of eliminating the diseconomies of scale associated with the older model.

INTERNAL DEVELOPMENTS

Internally large firms are vertically disintegrating. Vertical disintegration by the large firm is now seen in most cases as an appropriate strategy. Vertical disintegration typically involves a single or more likely a range of components previously produced internally being subcontracted. Now by vertically disintegrating firms do not necessarily lose the benefits of internal economies of scale. New technological developments have now made it possible for firms to achieve technical economies without vertically integrating. In the 1950s and 1960s the minimum efficient scale of operations was invariably large due to indivisibilities in production machines. As a result of modern technology, it is now possible to have more divisibilities. Capital equipment has become more malleable, and less lumpy, allowing large firms to develop a fairly sophisticated production chain without vertical integration. But by virtually disintegrating, firms are moving away from Fordist productionist techniques and associated corporate strategies, which has profound implications for the shape of economic policy.

The key to new commercial strategies is the development of long-term relationships between large firms and their suppliers which reduces transactions costs. Because of such arrangements it has become cheaper for large firms to buy inputs from subcontractors rather than produce in house. Innovations such as 'just-in-time' stock control have also added to the attraction of subcontracting. As a strategy, large firms can use outsourcing to reduce costs. An example of such outsourcing is given by Donaghu and Barff (1990), in relation to Nike:

> No athletic footwear firm now wholly owns any integrated production facilities: athletic footwear production in general is presently typified by the large scale vertical disintegration of functions and a high level of subcontracting activity ... Despite Nike's history of changing producers, the company maintains very close and persistent ties with a core group of affiliated factories and regular relations with some manufacturers ... The distinguishing aspect of Nike's current production system is that virtually 100% of the company's product is manufactured by production 'subcontractors'.

As well as reducing costs by outsourcing, large firms are also using technology internally to their own advantage. With the organization of large firms becoming more flexible, the phenomenon of 'cost centres' is emerging. In this case, the larger firm splits its internal organization into departments or sections, differentiated by activity. By doing so, it can make each section responsible for their costs and revenues. This involves measuring the output and costs associated with each section. This is a flexible approach to controlling costs. In addition firms are also adopting new managerial techniques for example 'total quality management'. In this particular case, the larger firm dispenses with its separate quality control Department and instead, the workforce at all stages of the production process checks for quality. In other words everyone employed is a quality controller. The advantage here is that flaws in products can be spotted at any stage of the production process, as opposed to right at the very end. This saves on costs as flawed goods can be spotted before significant value added processing is applied to them.

External Changes

Large firms are now pursuing a wider and subtler range of business strategies. One factor forcing them to do so is the role of technology and technical change. Many markets are now obliging firms to become more research intensive. A demanding market requires firms to get better quality and more sophisticated goods onto the market faster. Rapid technical progress has considerably shortened the product life cycle for many goods. In other words, a product which is regarded as innovatory can become obsolete in a few years. As a result, there are now much higher risks in pursuing a pure internal economies of scale strategy in terms of Research and Development. To counter the risks of not recouping any investment made in R&D, large firms are being forced into strategic alliances with other firms with the view to reducing the costs of R&D. As opposed to internal economies of scale in R&D, large firms tend now to pursue external linkages in R&D. Strategic alliances can be regarded as a form of inter-firm agreement for the purposes of R&D, production, marketing or distribution. At one extreme they may be close to a merger, though normally they can take such forms as a joint venture, consortium or co-operative agreement. Thus strategic alliances refer to instances where two different firms undertake a joint agreement to develop new products, or market/distribute each other's product or produce each other's product. In expounding the virtues of strategic alliances Buigues and Jacquemin (1989) suggest that they promote synergies, avoid costly duplication, make it possible to disseminate technological information more widely and reduce the time required to put a new product or process on the market; they also ensure that risks are more widely distributed among the partners.

Strategic alliances can take the form of a contract, subsidiary or joint venture and it is usually for technological reasons that such ventures are set up. They are widely regarded as the best way of spreading risk and pooling resources. Three end benefits are seen as arising from strategic alliances (i) access to new technology; (ii) access to new markets; (iii) acquisition of new skills and expertise. They involve co-operative agreements with other firms to try to remain competitive as the pace of change in technology and product market quicken. Although these sorts of conditions will not affect all types of industries, it can be seen from Figure 3.1 that they are likely to be prevalent in industries where it is important to be a leading firm or where there is high product differentiation. Such conditions can be found in specialised and volume industries. It is in these types of industry where technology is driving large firms to form strategic alliances.

	WEAK	STRONG
HIGH	Fragmented	Specialized
	catering (conventional)	pharmaceutical
	building (conventional)	DP software
	craft industries	luxury cars
	Impasse	Volume
	steel	aerospace
	shipbuilding	tyres
	paper	medium-sized cars
		electronic components
		TV sets and video recorders
		domestic appliances
LOW		

Number of possible differentiations (vertical axis)

Advantages of being a leading firm (horizontal axis)

Figure 3.1 Competitive environment matrix examples of industries
Source: BCG, 1985; Porter, 1985; Buigues 1985

The above sections have outlined the changes which are occurring in larger firms both internally and externally. It will be left to the next section to explain exactly what these changes add up to. However, it is worth stressing that a single large firm may not be adopting all these changes internally or externally. Rather it is likely that certain of these developments will be more apparent in industries where consumer demand is constantly shifting and changing.

To emphasize the implications of these developments for inward investment for a region like Northern Ireland, it is useful to highlight the differences between the older external model and the new external model in this context; see Table 3.3.

Under the 'old style' external model, inward investment to a region took two forms. One is the traditional 'branch plant' concerned mostly with assembly and sub-assembly type functions for the parent external company, in other words, a production platform. The other is the merger with or acquisition of an indigenous company in the region. In this case, the external company 'buys out' the indigenous firm either for diversification reasons, or to enter new markets or because of the

Table 3.3 External model of economic development for a region – international investment

Old Style	New Style
(i) Branch plant	(i) Branch plant
(ii) Acquisition and merger	(ii) Acquisition and merger
	(iii) Large firms buying up innovative small firms in the region
	(iv) Joint venture between small firm in region and large external firm for R&D purposes
	(v) Inward investment to the region as a result of a joint venture (R&D) between two large external firms

local firm's unexploited potential for profitability. Large external firms, in this case, are usually interested in the larger indigenous companies.

Under the 'new style' external model, branch plant and merger/acquisition type inward investment still occur. However there are three new developments in the types of international investment. The 'new style' now includes interest by large external firms in small indigenous companies within the region. The first new type of arrangement occurs when the external firm buys a smaller innovative firm within the host region. This can occur whenever the small firm is at the forefront of knowledge within the particular industry, creating new products and processes. The large firm, in this case, wishes to tap into this know-how – for example, takeovers in the area of biotechnology. The second new type of investment is very similar, here, the larger firm enters a joint R&D venture with an innovative small firm within the host region, again to benefit from its knowhow or 'Schumpeterian' qualities. This spawns a joint R&D and possibly production project in the region. Finally, two larger firms may agree on a joint R&D venture and decide that the most suitable location for the subsidiary project is within the region to gain from the innovative characteristics of small firms within that location. This, again, creates a subsidiary R&D, leading possibly to a production facility within the region.

But the big question is how a region can attract such new forms of inward investment. Large firms are more likely to locate higher value added forms of inward investment in regions which possess agglomeration type economies. In other words, the necessary condition for attracting the new large firm investment is the presence in the region of the regional agglomeration or endogenous model. To forge strategic alliances or develop joint ventures, larger firms will be seeking out regions which possess firms who are innovative and flexible or highly specialised and knowledge intensive. Industrial districts are more likely to have firms with this sort of dynamic effect. In effect a region needs to have the new internal model in place before it will be able to attract quality inward investment. If it is not in place the region may only attract branch plant type inward investment projects. For Northern Ireland the implications are clear: to benefit from the best of both worlds it must develop a regional agglomeration type model internally.

The theoretical analysis which has been outlined in this part of the chapter has clear implications for a region like Northern Ireland. If Northern Ireland is to achieve a competitive advantage and at the same time attract new forms of inward investment, one possible strategy which could be adopted is the promotion of the agglomeration economies within the region. In the next section the possibility of Northern Ireland pursuing an economic strategy along the above lines is explored.

Northern Ireland: A Case of a Faulty Governance Structure

The argument so far is that if a region wants to achieve good industrial performance either through the internal or external routes it must have a highly symmetrical governance structure. Virtuous interaction between the three tiers of the governance structure produces a number of gains. First of all, it can create the external economies similar to those found in Marshallian industrial districts. With the presence of external economies for example, the moral hazard problem of firms being reluctant to pursue certain types of investment because they cannot internalize all the benefits is to some extent eased. Secondly, governance structures create a low transactions cost environment. With dense networks of firms and with institutions making market connections that might not otherwise exist, information is more freely available and better processed which makes enterprises more sensitive to market developments. Moreover, commercial collaboration is likely to generate a high level of trust thereby reducing opportunistic behaviour and competitive dynamics based on price. Now it is unlikely that all the benefits will arise simultaneously, but a benign governance structure may produce enough benefits to make a significant difference to regional economic performance.

However, an equally plausible scenario is that for some reason or another a governance structure may function in a disjointed or distorted manner. The consequences of a malfunctioning governance structure are no less far reaching than in the case of a virtuous governance structure. Conceivably, where the malfunctioning is deep seated and systematic a region could be locked into a scenario of chronic economic failure. The argument of this section is that the Northern Ireland economy must be seen as an example of a malfunctioning structure which involves each tier operating sub-optimally.

Kind Aunties and Soft Budgets

One way the governance structure is distorted is by the public sector playing a key role in the local economy. With the private sector – particularly the tradeable sector – so weak, the public sector has come to dominate the local economy. About 40 per cent of the workforce is employed directly in the public sector and probably many more indirectly owe their jobs to public expenditure. In the short run a large public sector can exist alongside a weak private (tradeable) sector by the public authorities borrowing and raising taxes. But beyond the short term, this situation is not sustainable as international money markets become reluctant to lend and revenue raised through taxes reaches its upper limits. Thus for this situation to exist on any prolonged basis requires the economy to have some type of external benefactor. The UK exchequer is Northern Ireland's benefactor. Public expenditure in the province outstrips locally raised taxes by some £2 billion. To meet the shortfall, the British government gives a subvention to the province in the form of a fiscal transfer. It is important to note that expenditure on security is not included in the subvention. Most of it comes in the form of public sector wages and in social security and pensions. Approximately the subvention amounts to £1,300 per annum for each Northern Ireland resident and the cost to British taxpayers is equivalent to one penny on income tax. If Northern Ireland were obliged to live within its means public expenditure would fall by more than a third and regional GDP by about 25 per cent. Thus even with the multitude of problems outlined earlier, Northern Ireland enjoys a standard of living not warranted by the performance of the underlying economy. Unquestionably the British exchequer operates as the province's economic lifeline.

This situation is interpretated in a number of contrasting ways. One view is that since Northern Ireland is part of an economic union with Great Britain, in which the principle of parity in public expenditure prevails, the fiscal transfer from Whitehall to the province is relatively unproblematical. The subvention merely represents a form of redistributive regional policy characteristic of many fiscal federalist arrangements and which other parts of the UK such as Wales and Scotland also receive. Thus so long as Northern Ireland remains part of the UK, the province can benefit from British financial support until the fortunes of the local economy pick up. Up to a point, this argument has much validity. Northern Ireland is better off with the fiscal transfer than without it. But it is a narrow and static approach to the matter which marginalizes some key issues. In particular, it inadequately addresses the question of whether the scale of the subvention may be having negative spillover effects in the local economy. After all, per capita public spending in Northern Ireland is about 50 per cent above the national average while in Scotland it is about 20 per cent above.

The public sector is twice as big in the province as in any other UK region. With the public sector being so large the question must be asked as to whether the subvention has created asymmetric incentive structures in the local economy to the extent that it is now in the perverse role of simultaneously smothering key dynamics in the tradeable sector, such as entrepreneurship, while being the province's financial saviour. It is precisely this question that the above argument fails to tackle.

A view that deals with the question head on is a variant of Bacon and Eltis's (1978) 'crowding out' thesis. According to this view the public sector in the province has become too large, diverting resources – financial, human and so on – away from the private sector. As a result, the local economy suffers from a deep structural sclerosis which if left unchecked will permanently prevent the emergence of a more balanced and self-reliant productive system. The remedy of course is to cut the subvention thereby administering a 'shock' to the local economy which hopefully will kick-start private enterprise. Again elements of this view have validity but, in its entirety, it has important shortcomings. Theoretically there is no way of determining the optimal size of a public sector and as a result it is misleading to argue *a priori* that a large public sector is harmful to an economy (Beckerman, 1986). As the Nordic countries showed in the 1980s, it was possible to expand public provision without damaging the competitive dynamics of tradeable sectors (Glyn, 1990). With regard to Northern Ireland the large public sector probably has negative spillover effects but the 'crowding out' thesis more or less assumes this to be the case and thus fails to precisely identify what form these effects take. More importantly, the idea that administering a shock through cutting public expenditure will have a positive and benign impact appears highly questionable. As more and more economists are realizing with regard to eastern Europe, shocks may actually accentuate poor economic performance rather than improve it (Hare, 1991). In relation to Northern Ireland, cutting public expenditure, which would result in a significant drop in living standards, appears a fairly precarious route to take in light of the political turmoil there. Thus because of its inexact diagnosis of the problem and its rather dubious prescription, the 'crowding out' thesis cannot be regarded as a satisfactory analysis of the role of the public sector in the Northern Ireland economy.

Nevertheless, the large public sector in the province has produced a number of negative spillover effects. First of all the large fiscal transfer from London to the province creates a 'soft' budget constraint. The concept of a soft budget, first used to highlight the shortcomings of the command economies of eastern Europe, occurs when the strict relationship between income and expenditure has been relaxed (Kornai 1990). Consider the 'Kind Auntie' syndrome; if an individual has a weekly income of £100 but actually spends £140 then a large gap exists between earnings and expenditure. Under normal conditions pressure would very quickly emerge via the bank manager, or other creditors, not only to balance incomings and outgoings, but also to reduce expenditure below income for a given period so as to pay off accumulated debts. This scenario is called the 'hard' budget constraint.

Now consider that the individual has a kind auntie who writes cheques every week for £40 to cover the gap between income and expenditure. Certainly the auntie's intervention ensures that equilibrium is maintained, but it also has the effect of shifting the person's expenditure curve outwards to the extent that a more or less permanent gap between income and expenditure becomes an unquestioned part of routine. This situation is called the 'soft' budget constraint. As a result of the presence of a soft budget constraint, asymmetric information and incentive structures emerge in the local economy. Perhaps the most systemic manifestation of this case in Northern Ireland is that although the underlying economy is quite poor, people do not perceive there to be any deep-seated or intractable problems because the fiscal transfer ensures a disproportionately high standard of living relative to economic performance. In other words the subvention 'decouples' income from the underlying economic structure. Other distortions emerge from the presence of a soft budget constraint. For instance, since public sector employment is more secure and as lucrative as private sector jobs, people's strategic calculations about career paths invariably lead them into the public sector, thereby depriving the market sector of many dynamic individuals. All in all, the soft budget tends to deform and dehydrate entrepreneurial activity in the economy.

As well as having economy-wide effects, the soft budget constraint also impacts on the tradeable sector in the province. By introducing a battery of financial incentives to encourage private sector activity in the province the government has unwittingly created a range of soft subsidies which have been exploited by the government. Take for instance the operation of the Selective Financial Assistance (SFA) scheme. In an effort to increase jobs in the private sector, SFA money is given to firms that suggest they will be able to create a specific number of jobs through a particular commercial project or initiative. Recent studies have shown this scheme not to be working very successfully. In particular, a Northern Ireland Economic Council report finds that a large discrepancy exists between the jobs promoted figure – that is the number of jobs that firms suggest will be created, which determines the amount of grant assistance given to the firm – and the actual jobs created. In a five-year period between 1982 and 1988 grants were given to private sector companies to promote 23,000 jobs, yet only 10,000 jobs actually materialized (NIEC 1990).

To expect a 100 per cent attainment ratio would be unrealistic given market uncertainties and fluctuations faced by business; but an attainment ratio of 40.5 per cent is too low and suggests that enterprises in the province may be using the scheme as an extra source of liquidity to increase profit levels or maintain a more lubricant cash-flow system or whatever. Thus the scheme seems to be used by firms as a route to obtain soft subsidies. Now it needs emphasizing that the SFA is but one element of the incentive package for industry in the province. Estimates suggest that local industry is five times more subsidized than its counterparts in any other region of the UK (Hamilton 1989). Overall, the effect of this kind of feather-bedding is to undermine the horizontal relationship between the firm and the market by creating a kind of vertical maternalistic relationship between the enterprise and government agencies. More concretely, rather than attempting to increase revenue through market transactions, enterprises have the easy option of relying on grants and other forms of financial help from the public sector. Put simply, the existence of extensive subsidies has created a climate of dependency and has sapped the competitive vigour of many firms.

A Circular Flow of Income in the Non-Tradeable Sector

Another result of the large public sector is the development of a vibrant personal service sector. Whereas manufacturing jobs contracted by 17 per cent between 1981 and 1984, over the same decade employment rose by 27 per cent in Retail Distribution, 56 per cent in hotels and catering and 24 per cent in recreation and other cultural services. To a large extent, it is public sector wage levels that sustain demand for such service sector activity. As a result, a circular flow of income has opened up in the non-tradeable sector in the province. At one level this circular flow of income is not a problem since it is the source of much needed economic activity. However, there are negative implications from this situation in that a large proportion of output in Northern Ireland takes the form of 'experience goods' rather than 'search goods', which influences the competitive dynamics inside the economy (Sapir 1991).

'Search goods' are normally associated with tradeable activity. For firms in tradeable activity to be successful, particularly in a small economy, involves searching out markets in other economies. This imperative affects the entire corporate profile and strategy of such firms. They have to be aware of market developments, the strategies of competitors, and latest production techniques as well as having high-quality marketing departments and so on. In other words, 'search goods' oblige firms to be outward looking and dynamic to secure potential markets. By contrast, with 'experience goods' it is almost as if the market finds the goods. 'Experience goods' are usually found in the non-tradeable sector. For the most part, such activity is consumed at the point of contact between buyer and seller and hence confine competition to the local area. To be successful experience goods need to establish a reputation amongst local consumers with regard to quality, liability and so on: thus competition is localized and for the most part unaffected by external market developments.

Overall, reliance on experience goods has profound implications for the dynamics of an economy. If a firm producing tradeable goods closes, local jobs are destroyed and the possibility of bringing income into the economy through exports is lost. On the other hand, closure of firms in the non-tradeable sector will simply result in a shift of production to other local firms. Thus the direct effects of the closure of a factory producing tradeable goods on the number of jobs is immediate. Indirect employment reductions invariably follow in supplier firms, and some expenditures are diverted out of the region. The same dynamic does not arise in the non-tradeable sector. Whatever the level of local efficiency relative to foreign producers of non-tradeable goods, the local producers are insulated from the disciplinary effects of more efficient production elsewhere. Regional forms of competition predominates as non-tradeable firms vie with each other for business. Thus local hairdressers, plumbers and restaurants may be inefficient by international standards but whatever the costs of production, they will not be collectively shut down. With experience regarding goods dominating the economy, a Gresham's law effect appears to be at play in that regional forms of competition in the non-tradeable sector are squeezing out competitive dynamics associated with tradeable activity.

Most of the above shortcomings arise as a result of a large subvention being required from Whitehall to finance the gap between income and expenditure in the province. But it is not being argued here that to obtain improved industrial performance the fiscal transfer should be cut off and Northern Ireland be forced to live within its means. Such a hard policy, which is similar to the strategies being pursued in many east European countries, would be inappropriate given the presence of internal communal violence and the question marks about the efficacy of such a policy course (Landesmann and Szekely 1991). What needs to be done is for the province's financial link with Britain to be reformed and reconstructed so that Treasury money can operate as a lifeline to the region without smothering competitive dynamics (Teague 1991).

The Role of Peripherality

Often the drawbacks associated with geographical peripherality are put down to higher transport costs. Products of firms located in relatively isolated areas are usually regarded as being more expensive since they have further to travel to main market centres. A number of recent studies, however, have argued that this distance factor only slightly affects the price of tradeable goods leaving Northern Ireland: the inference could be drawn that no significant costs arise from the province's peripheral position (Hitchens and Birnie 1989b). Such an inference is quite erroneous, for even accepting the argument about transport costs – which can be questioned – a number of other economic disadvantages still arise from peripherality which can influence the creation of agglomeration economies. In the first place, the operation of the province's local labour market is to some extent influenced by the relative isolation of the region.

Consider the stylization between local labour markets situated in or near relatively prosperous regions and local labour markets in relatively isolated and economically depressed regions. In the former situation, the external flexibility of labour tends to rise: potentially firms can face high turnover rates since workers can move from one employer to another to advance their career paths. The alternative scenario relates to peripheral labour markets. Here, in the relative absence of other employment opportunities, workers tend to remain with the same employer, so the external labour market is less fluid. In essence, the labour market operates as a 'captive' market for local employers. These contrasting external labour markets heavily influence the type of internal labour markets developed by employers in the two regions. Where the external labour market is flexible, pressure is generated for the firm to develop sophisticated internal labour markets in an effort to retain staff. Conversely, in the situation where turnover rates are low, firms will tend to invest less in training and skill development as employers gravitate towards cost rather than commitment orientated internal labour markets. Thus market pressures encouraging firms to adopt advanced work organizations are not as strong in peripheral areas as they are in more central locations. As a result, the labour market will more likely influence firms to pursue strategies based on skill and product quality in the centre than in the periphery.

In Northern Ireland turnover rates are fairly low. The local Labour Relations Agency suggests the stability ratio – the ratio of the current number of employees with more than one year's service to the average of the number of employers at present and one year ago – is about 87 per cent for Northern Ireland enterprises. Thus most employers experience an annual turnover rate of just 13 per cent – a much lower rate than for other more central regions. Evidence suggests that these low turnover rates reflect the absence of alternative job opportunities rather than the existence of advanced internal labour markets. A number of surveys show that training provision in firms in the region is exceptionally low. Lundy (1990) suggests that few firms are introducing new human resource management techniques. Hitchens, Birnie and Wagner (1991) found that many firms in the province suffer from poor production and logistical planning and have weak organizational structures. Together, this evidence convincingly suggests that too few firms are adopting advanced forms of work organization to capture competitive gains. Thus, as a result of the province's location, there is a relative absence of labour market pressures that encourage the adoption of commitment enhancing employee relations strategies.

High transaction costs can also arise from peripherality. In standard accounts of market efficiency full information is assumed, thus no deep-seated distinction is seen to exist between central and isolated regions. However, it is increasingly being emphasized in economic theory that full information is an unrealistic assumption. Most market situations are characterized by the very limited information available to agents about the transactions that are open to them. In other words, most markets are decentralized where it is difficult and costly for potential sellers and buyers to meet each other. Thus a defining feature of decentralized markets are high transaction costs. To circumvent this problem and reduce uncertainty, suppliers and customers will try to establish long-term relationships in which a given exchange is repeated many times. In many instances these long-term relations are normally based on established social relations. The social links involved are of many kinds – formal and informal associations, ties of culture in particular – but they are all influenced by history and tradition, usually in a national or local context.

Now the ability to forge these long-term relationships are greater in regions close to centres of economic activity. In other words, geographical proximity creates advantages in terms of information flows and externality effects. As a result, peripheral regions face higher transaction costs than do more economically central areas (Geroski 1989). Because of the lack of long-term relationships, a misallocation of resources can occur in markets. In particular, to benefit from R&D activity and so on, firms will likely have to undertake investment that will benefit other firms through spillover effects without the latter having to pay. Thus being unable to completely internalize all the benefits of their actions, firms are unlikely to undertake as much investment as they ought. Moreover, with the presence of imperfect information and thus uncertainty in peripheral regions, decisions about whether to bear risk, and how much, become problematic. In such a situation, the moral hazard problem arises since there is a limit to which individuals can be protected from risk without dulling incentives. Accordingly, the tendency will be for attitudes to risk bearing to adversely affect investment decisions. All in all, peripherality establishes considerable barriers in the way of market access and competitiveness.

Low Skills Equilibrium and Negative Enterprise Calculation

With the withdrawal of large branch plants from the province and the lack of innovative high tech enterprises amongst indigenous industry, Northern Ireland's manufacturing activity is now more or less confined to low-skill, low-technology sectors. As a result, industry has settled at a low-skill equilibrium point. Because firms are operating in market segments where little premium is placed on the skill level of the workforce, few incentives exist to develop comprehensive training programmes. Furthermore, in the absence of any widespread firm level training, enterprises become more and more embedded in low-technology operations, thereby further increasing the gulf between themselves and more highly productive enterprises. Moreover, a 'low-skills equilibrium' reduces the absorptive capacity of many enterprises (Finegold and Soskice 1988). Many firms in low-grade manufacturing have neither the organizational ecology nor the skill competency amongst the workforce or management to successfully exploit commercial opportunities offered by the diffusion of new technological equipment. After a time a weak and low-tech manufacturing sector can have an ossification effect, trapping firms within a certain production trajectory, and making it increasingly difficult to catch up with more economically advanced regions.

In these circumstances, it is hardly surprising that negative enterprise calculations tend to predominate. Harris (1988) suggests that technological innovation in Northern Ireland has been relatively low. He highlights that the number of innovations recorded at the Science Research Unit at the University of Sussex from Northern Ireland is lower than other regions in the UK. Using shift-share techniques he argues that this situation cannot be attributed to 'structural' effects but to the activity of enterprises. Harrison and Hart (1990) argue that disproportionately few enterprises engage in R&D activity. Other direct evidence exists suggesting the prevalence of negative enterprise calculations. Gudgin *et al.* (1990) show that Northern Ireland has consistently been the region with the lowest value added per employee, averaging 13 per cent below the national average in the 1980s. Moreover, they argue that despite having the lowest wage levels of any UK region, Northern Ireland has the highest ratio of wages to value added averaging 6 per cent above the UK average.

Another weakness is that Northern Ireland manufacturing employs a proportionately low level of professional staff in such areas as design and marketing which are essential for producing and selling competitively. In Great Britain 13 per cent of all employees were in such occupations, whereas in Northern Ireland the corresponding figure is 4.7 per cent – by far the lowest level of any UK region. In a number of studies Hitchens and O'Farrell (1987) examined small firm competitiveness and performance in Northern Ireland, South Wales, South East of England and the mid-West of Ireland. They found that in comparison with their British and Irish counterparts, Northern Ireland enterprises produced poorer-quality products and were not price competitive. Another range of studies by Hitchens and Birnie (1989a) highlight that a chronic productivity problem exists in the province's manufacturing sector. By using the match plant technique, they found that Northern Ireland firms hugely under-performed relative to similar companies in Great Britain and Germany. The catalogue of evidence indicating widespread and deep-seated negative enterprise calculations is overwhelming.

A Brittle Commercial Infrastructure

In comparison with other disadvantaged regions in the European Community, Northern Ireland is endowed with a relatively advanced physical infrastructure. A modern and extensive road network links all parts of the province with the key points of economic and commercial life. The telecommunications network is a sophisticated state-of-the-art facility. The local universities and other institutions provide a range of new technological services for local business. Modern banking and financial institutions as well as a range of wider business services are also easily accessible. Thus, Northern Ireland's physical and parts of its commercial infrastructures broadly resemble those that exist in the more prosperous parts of the EC. Perhaps some of the local commercial and business organizations do not perform as active a role in the local economy as their counterparts would in other European regions. Thus whereas the German Chamber of Commerce plays an important role in co-ordinating employer pay policy (Soskice 1990), the equivalent body in Northern Ireland has virtually no direct role in business life. A host of 'umbrella' business organizations exist in Italy, promoting training, collaborative activity and so on, but such functional bodies are virtually absent from the province. But even without these business agencies, Northern Ireland's commercial infrastructure seems fairly advanced, being able to comprehensively furnish the needs of local enterprises.

Yet in reality this commercial infrastructure appears to operate suboptimally. For the most part, this under-performance can be attributed to the political and social exoskeleton surrounding business activity in the province. Probably the most distinctive feature of this exoskeleton is the continuing political violence. Whilst perhaps not as intense as sometimes made out in the international press, the violence is sufficiently prevalent as to undermine business activity. First of all, it effectively stops any significant level of foreign investment coming to the province. A related factor is that people with high levels of business or professional expertise from other parts of the UK are extremely reluctant to take a post in the region. The corollary, of course, is that the more energetic and able people in the province have a tendency to leave for a better and more peaceful life elsewhere. Moreover, business life is routinely disrupted as a result of terrorist incidents, which makes basic commercial tasks difficult to undertake. All in all, political instability tends to make businesses reluctant to undertake significant investments or developmental work which would enhance performance.

The sectarian divisions in the province, which have a strong spatial dimension, further distort the local commercial infrastructure. In a recent survey the Fair Employment Agency (1990) found that on an occupational basis the proportion of Catholics and Protestants in employment broadly reflected the respective size of the two communities in the province. But the study also found that a good many enterprises consisted of Catholic-only or Protestant-only employees. This finding suggests that a certain amount of clustering of firms on a religious basis is a characteristic of the industrial structure in the region. Now this situation poses a major conundrum for local economic makers: if they attempt to obtain dynamic gains through agglomeration effects then they may actually be reinforcing or even building new sectarian arrangements in the economy. At a more immediate and frightening level, attempting to create networks between firms which contain mostly Catholic and Protestant employees may actually expose workers in mono-religious enterprises to terrorist attack (since the increased communication flows between the enterprise may result in information falling into the wrong hands). Thus the economic idea of improving local industry through the creation of external economies of scale may be in collision with the political objective of reducing sectarian tensions in the region.

Sectarianism affects the commercial infrastructure in other ways. Allegations about discriminatory practices have persisted since the formation of Northern Ireland. Without entering the debate about the extent and nature of labour market discrimination (see Chambers and Smith 1990), it can be suggested this controversy has sullied the norms and conventions that govern business and economic life. The basic idea is that no society can regulate its action without norms and codes, since these ensure social relations cease to be a series of reciprocal actions subject to uncertainty and constant negotiation. From this point of view, the economic success of countries like West Germany and Japan or regions like Northern Italy lies partly in the rich and dense social networks and norms which underpin business activity (Thompson et al. 1991). But in Northern Ireland, the issue of discrimination has turned the system of rules and conventions governing the world of work into a contested terrain. As a result, those rules which encourage and sustain competitiveness and good business performance become distorted and disfigured as a result of the preoccupation with religious allocation of jobs and work tasks. Sectarianism and competitivity are uncomfortable bedfellows.

Even in the absence of the discrimination or sectarian question, it is doubtful whether the norms that have triggered economic innovation in certain regions would emerge easily in Northern Ireland. As emphasised by Sabel *et al.* (1989), crucial to the emergence of these norms are bargains struck between trade unions and management. But neither the local trade union or employer organizations appear capable of constructing such deals. Organized labour is in a sort of regional limbo, being neither integrated properly into the British nor Irish labour movements. Although this gives it considerable autonomy, the result has been fragmentation and dithering rather than the development of a constructive policy vision with regard to industry and employment. Similarly, the employers' organizations lack cohesion and a clearly formulated view on their role in industrial and business development. While a number of forums exist to bring trade unions and management together, little of any significance emerges from these bodies. More or less bereft of any policy vision in favour of industrial renewal, both sides of industry are preoccupied with their routine concerns or with lobbying government for more money.

In addition to these peculiar factors inhibiting the creation of norms and conventions conducive to agglomeration economies, the province suffers from the same difficulties as other regions which were dominated by traditional industries. Like Northern Ireland, many of these regions have suffered stark deindustrialization. As a result, once thriving and dynamic locations are now virtual wastelands. Because communities in these regions were locked into skill patterns and work ethics which are now outmoded, the process of regeneration has proven very difficult. In not a few instances, commercial and entrepreneurial drive has atrophied and these regions exhibit such characteristics as long-term unemployment, high levels of poverty and social disorder. In other words, because of its association with the Fordist production trajectory, Northern Ireland, like other parts of the UK – for example the North East – are not favoured sites for new post-Fordist commercial activity.

All in all every tier of the governance structure in the province malfunctions in one way or other. As a result, a mendicant entrepreneurial culture has become embedded within the province with the bulk of economic activity being dependent on public money. Furthermore, contagious conventions and norms now rule the economy, producing perverse effects. Thus in the labour market high unemployment co-exists alongside high income inequality whilst the tradeable sector suffers from low productivity and from poor-quality performance despite receiving government finance. A number of initiatives are already in place to address these shortcomings. Existing grant provision is being overhauled to make it more effective. More careful planning is being introduced into public schemes for industry. All these changes will improve the present situation, but it is questionable whether these essentially piecemeal and selective reforms will be enough to redress the current systemic distortions. Perhaps more far-reaching institutional changes are required which aim at building a more robust and benign governance structure.

CONCLUSIONS

A number of conclusions arise from this review. First of all, policy makers, trade unions and employers must realise that the Fordist mass production era has gone. The quest for vertically integrated enterprises, creating internal economies of scale, belongs to a bygone industrial era. In a situation of diversity of demand, it is inimical to strive for long production runs of specific product variants. Of course, Northern Ireland has never had the market size to capture such internal economies of scale effects. But the important point to realise is that it was enterprises pursuing such a commercial logic that gave rise to the branch plant establishments that came to the province in the

1960s. This type of inward investment project is not now on offer on the same magnitude. Of course, regions can pick up an investment project here or there for cost or strategic reasons, but increasingly what determines the scale and nature of inward investment is the type of indigenous industries and economic governance structure in place in the respective region.

Thus, even if Northern Ireland wants to pursue an economic development strategy through promoting inward investment, it must establish a vibrant governance structure for the local economy. But, the analysis above suggests that the present governance arrangements in the province are deeply faulty. Now this argument throws into question whether improved competitiveness can be obtained by simply recasting the current system or certain other grants programmes. Perhaps deep-seated and more far reaching changes are needed before we can align Northern Ireland's governance structure to the productive structure of the twenty-first century. In particular, rather than seeing competitiveness being achieved through small-scale adjustments, it may be more profitable to regard it as a more fundamental project to uproot and reorganize existing economic policy functions.

For instance, it may be worthwhile to explore the positive possibilities of a regional industrial relations system. Currently, Northern Ireland's industrial relations system is probably best described as having a half in and half out relationship with the rest of the UK industrial relations system. A completely autonomous regional industrial relations system may open up a range of positive benefits. First of all, it could possibly create bargains that address the fact that Northern Ireland comes bottom in a rank correlation exercise that assesses the relationship between high unemployment and low income in the objective 1 regions of the European Community. (In other words, Northern Ireland registered high unemployment alongside high income.) At a more speculative level, a regional industrial relations system may encourage local trade unions and employers to make agreements with regard to the new emerging industrial relations agenda. More specifically, rather than seeing collective bargaining being about the conclusion of wage deals, the trade union and employers may forge productivity coalitions. At the heart of such coalitions could be a trade-off between trade unions accepting flexible work practices, in return for employers developing more sophisticated human resource management strategies. More important than any formal agreements reached between the social partners, would be the informal trust and mutuality created between both sides of industry. It is the intangible attributes deriving from management/labour deals that are a key source of a positive governance structure.

As well as institutional change, there may be scope to assess whether positive networks between firms can be established. For example, it may be worthwhile investigating what type of sub-contracting links the big firms, such as Desmond's or Shorts, have with local small firms. Alternatively, it may be useful to examine local sectors where no large firms prevail, to see if some degree of networking could not be introduced. (In creating such networks, the role of government policy, particularly procurement policy, could very well be instrumental.) The key message is to seek out those industrial sectors where the commercial infrastructure could be improved by government intervention. The risk of market failure is too great for the province to accept a limited role for public institutions.

But probably the key area for intervention is the sphere of enterprise calculation. Much research on Northern Ireland industry suggests that most firms pursue a negative enterprise calculation. Thus, rather than giving grants to improve the marketing function or the training function, government policy must attempt to encourage new organization *systems* that integrate in a positive way the marketing, training and financial aspects of firms. If Northern Ireland wants to succeed in the next decade then it must have entrepreneurs who take a longer-term view of commercial life.

Finally, there is little value in pursuing any type of new industrial policy which only focuses on one particular issue or variable in isolation. Perhaps the key message from other studies of regional industrial development is the importance of leverage and co-ordination. Leverage means that public policies are targeted on those spots that will yield the greatest return whilst co-ordination infers that all aspects of policy must dovetail. Getting Northern Ireland out of the economic morass is going to be difficult, but without a radical departure it is certainly not going to happen.

REFERENCES

Amin, A. (1989), 'Flexible' Specialisation and Small Firms in Italy: Myths and Realities, *Antipode*, Vol. 21, No. 1, pp. 13–34.

Aoki, M. (1988), *Information, Incentives and Bargaining in the Japanese Economy*, CUP, Cambridge.

Armstrong, H. and Taylor, J. (1985), *Regional Economics and Policy*, Philip Allen, Oxford.
Atkinson, J., (1986), 'Employment Flexibility and Internal and External Labour Markets, R. Dahnendorf *et al.* (eds), *New Forms of Work and Activity*, Dublin, European Foundation for the Improvement of Living and Working Conditions.
Bacon, R. and Eltis, W.,(1978), *Britain's Economic Problem, Too Few Producers*, Macmillan, London.
Beckerman, W. (1986), 'How Large a Public Sector', *Oxford Review of Economic Policy*, Vol. 2, No. 2, pp. 7-25.
Best, M. (1989), *The New Competition*, Polity Press, London.
Borooah, V.K. and McGregor, P. (1989), *Inequality and Poverty in Northern Ireland*, Stockholm, Trade Union Institute for Economic Research.
Borooah, V.K. and McGregor, P. (1991), 'Poverty and the Distribution of Income in Northern Ireland', *The Economic and Social Review*, Vol. 22, No. 2, pp. 81–101.
Boyer, R. and Petit, P. (1989), 'Cumulative Causation Revisited', CEPREMAP, mimeo.
Brusco, S. (1982), 'The Emilian model: productive decentralisation and social integration', *Cambridge Journal of Economics* 6.
Buiges, P. and Jacquemin, A.,(1989), 'Strategies of Firms and Structural Environments in the Large Internal Market', *Journal of Common Market Studies*, **28**, 1.
Calmfors, L. and Driffell, J. (1988), Centralisation of Wage Bargaining, *Economic Policy*.
Canning, D., Moore, B. and Rhodes, J. (1987), 'Economic Growth in Northern Ireland: Problems and Potential', in Teague, P., *Beyond the Rhetoric: Politics, the Economy and Social Policy in W. Ireland*, Lawrence and Wishart, London.
Chambers, D. and Smith, D. (1990) *Inequality in Northern Ireland*, Clarendon Press, Oxford.
Connolly, M., (1992), *Privatisations in the N. Ireland Economy*, Department of Public Administration, mimeograph, University of Ulster.
Donaghu and Barff (1990), 'Nike just did it: international subcontracting and flexibility in athletic footwear production', *Regional Studies*, Vol. 24, No. 9, pp. 537–553.
Fair Employment Commission (1991), *A Profile of the Workforce in W. Ireland*, Research Report No. 1, Fair Employment Commission, Belfast.
Finegold, D. and Sockice, D.,(1988), 'The Failure of Training in Britain: Analysis and Prescription', Oxford Review of Economic Policy, Vol. 24, No. 5, pp. 383–393.
Fothergill, S. and Guy, N. (1990), *Retreat from the Regions, Corporate Change and the Closure of Factors*, Kingsley, London.
Freeman, C. (1987), *Technology Policy and Economic Performance*, London Printer.
Freeman, C. (1989), *The Economics of Technical Change*, London Printer.
Friedman, D. (1988), *The Misunderstood Miracle: Industrial Development and Political Change in Japan*, Cornell University Press, Ithaca, W.Y.
Gaffikin, F. and Morrissey, M. (1990), *N. Ireland: The Thatcher Years*, Zed Books, London.
Geroski, P. (1989), *1992 and European Industrial Structure in the Twenty-First Century*, Centre for Business Strategy, London Business School, Working Paper, No. 55.
Glyn, A. (1990), *Wage Formation, Patterns of Consumption and Levels of Employment*, mimeo, University of Oxford.

Gordon, R. (1990), 'What Is New Keynesian Economics?', *Journal of Economic Perspectives*, XXVIII, 3.

Gudgin, G. (1991), *Managerial Competences and Northern Ireland Companies*, Northern Ireland Research Centre, mimeograph.

Gudgin, G. and Murphy, T. (1992), 'The Labour Market Context for Fair Employment' in T. Cradden and P. Teague (eds), Labour Market Discrimination and Fair Employment in N. Ireland, special edition of the *International Journal of Manpower*.

Gudgin, G. and Roper, P. (1990), *The Northern Ireland Economy*, Northern Ireland Economic Research Centre, Belfast.

Gudgin, G., Roper, S. and Hart, M. (1990), *Annual Review and Forecast*, Northern Ireland Economic Research Centre, Belfast.

Hamilton, D. (1989), Industrial Development Policy in Northern Ireland – an Evaluation of the IDB, the *Economic and Social Review*, Vol. 22, No. 1, pp.65–80.

Hare, P. (1991), Industrial Reform in the Socialist Countries: Hungary', in I. Jefferies (ed.), *Industrial Reform in the Socialist Countries*, Oxford University Press, Oxford.

Harris, R. (1988), Technical Change and Regional Development in the UK, *Regional Studies*, Vol. 21, No. 5, pp. 361–74.

Harris, R.D. (1987), 'The Role of Manufacturing in Regional Growth', *Regional Studies*, Vol. 21, pp. 301–322.

Harrison, B. (1989), 'The Big Firms are Coming Out of the Corner, Department of Regional and Urban Planning', M.I.T., mimeo.

Harrison, B. (1992), Industrial Districts: Old Wine in New Bottles?, *Regional Studies*, 25, 5.

Harrison R. and Hart, M. (1990), 'Nature and Extent of Innovative Activity in the Peripheral Economy', *Regional Studies*, Vol. 24, No. 5, pp. 383-394.

Hirst, P. and Zeitlin, J., (1991), 'Flexible Specialisation versus post-Fordism', *Economy and Society*, Vol. 20, No. 1, pp. 1–57.

Hitchens, D. and Birnie, E.,(1989), 'Productivity Levels in Northern Ireland Manufacturing Industry : A Companion with Great Britain', *Regional Studies*, Vol. 23, No. 5, pp. 447–454.

Hitchens, D. and Birnie, E. (1989), 'Economic Development in Northern Ireland: Has Pathfinder lost its way?' *Regional Studies*, Vol. 23, No. 5, pp. 477–483.

Hitchens, D. and O'Farrell, P. (1987) 'The Comparative Performance of Small Manufacturing Firms in Northern Ireland and South-East England', *Regional Studies*, Vol. 21, pp. 543–553.

Hitchens, D., Wagner, K., Birnie., D. (1988), 'Northern Ireland Manufacturing Productivity compared with West Germany – a Matched Plant comparison', NIERC report no. 2, Belfast.

Hitchens, D., Wagner, K., Birnie, D. (1990), *Closing the Productivity Gap*, Avebury, Aldershot.

Hudson, J. (1990), *Ruining a Region: Industrial Restructuring in the North-East of England*, Harvester Wheatsheaf, London.

Jones, H. (1975), 'Consumer Behaviour' in D. Morris (ed.) *The Economic System in the U.K.*, Oxford University Press, Oxford.

Kaldor, N. (1963), *Causes of the Slow Rate of Economic Growth in the U.K.*, Cambridge University Press, Cambridge.

Kornai, J. (1990), *Vision and Reality, Markets and State*, Harvester Wheatsheaf, London.

Landesmann, M. and Szekely, I. (1991), *Industrial Restructuring and the Reorientation of Trade in Czechoslovakia, Hungary and Poland*, London, CEPR Discussion Paper No. 546.

Lane, C. (1991), Industrial Reorganisation In Europe, *Work, Employment and Society*, Vol. 5, No. 4, pp. 515–539.

Lawson, A., (ed.), (1985), *Organised Interests and the State: Studies in Meso Corporatism*, Sage, London.

Lipietz, A. (1990), *Pour Eviter l'Europe à deux vitesses*, Cepremap, Paris.

Lipietz, A. (1991), *The regions which win*, CEPREMAP, mimeograph, Paris.

Locke, R. (1990), 'The Resurgence of the Local Union: Industrial Restructuring and Industrial Relations in Italy', *Politics and Society*, Vol. 18, No. 3, pp. 347–381.

Lundy, O. (1990) *Strategic Human Resource Management and Enterprise in N. Ireland*, unpublished Ph.D., Queen's University Belfast, Belfast.

Mankin, N. and Romer, D. (eds) (1990), *New Keynesian Economics*, (two volumes), M.I.T. Press, London.

Maurice, M., Sellier, M. and Silvestre, J-J (1984), *The Social Foundations of Industrial Power*, M.I.T. Press, London.

McCormack, B. (1991), *Unemployment and the Unemployment Puzzle*, Employment Institute, London.

Muelbauer, S. (1986), Productivity and Competitiveness in British Manufacturing, *Oxford Review of Economic Policy*, **2**, 3.

Murray, F. (1985), Flexible Specialisation in the Third Italy, *Capital and Class*, 33 Winter.

Murray, R. (1985), 'Bennetton Britain', *Marxism Today*, November.

NIEC, (1990), *The Private Sector in the Northern Ireland Economy*, Belfast, Northern Ireland Economic Council.

Piore, M., (1980), 'Economic Fluctuation, Job Security and Labour Market Duality in Italy, France and the United States', *Politics and Society*, Vol. 9, No. 4, pp. 379–409.

Piore, M. and Sabel, C. (1984), *The Second Industrial Divide*, Basic Books, New York.

Roper, S. (1991), 'Soft Subsidies and Corporate Profitability in the Northern Ireland Economy', Northern Ireland Research Centre, mimeograph.

Rowthorn, R.E. (1987), 'Northern Ireland: An Economy in Crisis', in P. Teague, *Beyond the Rhetoric: Politics, the Economy and Social Policy*, Lawrence and Wishart, London.

Rowthorn, R.E., (1990), *Social Corporatism and Labour Market Performance*, mimeo, Department of Applied Economics, University of Cambridge.

Sabel, C. (1989), Flexible Specialisation and Regional Development, in Hirst, P. and Zetlin, J., (eds), *Reversing Industrial Decline*, Berg Press, London.

Sabel, C., Herringel, G., Deeq, R. and Kazis, R. (1989), 'Regional prosperities compared: Massachusetts and Baden Wurthenberg in the 1980s' *Economy and Society*, Vol. 18, No. 4, pp. 374–405.

Sapir, A. (1991), *The Structure of Services in Europe: A Conceptual Framework*, London, CEPR Discussion Paper, No. 498.

Saxenian, A. (1989), 'The Cheshire Cat's grin : innovation, regional development and the Cambridge case', *Economy and Society*, Vol. 18, No. 4, pp. 448–478.

Schumpter, J. (1942), *Capitalism, Socialism and Democracy*, Harper & Row, p. 237, New York.

Scott, M. and Storper, M. (1989), *The Capitalist Imperative*, Basil Blackwell, Oxford.

Simpson, J. (1985), 'Must There Be Any Good News About The Economy', *Fortnight*, No. 228, November.

Soskice, D., (1990), 'Wage Determination: The Changing Role of Institutions in Advanced Industrialised Countries', *Oxford Review of Economic Policy*, Vol. 6, No. 4, Winter 1990.

Storper, M. and Harrison, B., *Flexibility, Hierarchy and Regional Development: the Changing Structure of Industrial Production Systems and their Forms of Governance*, Working Paper 0903, School of Architecture and Urban Planning, University of California, Los Angeles.

Storper, M. and Walker, R. (1989), 'The Geographical Organization of Production Systems', *Space and Society*, **6**, 3.

Streeck, W., (1990), *The Social Foundations for Diversified Quality Productivity*, mimeo, Report of Sociology, University of Wisconsin, Maddison.

Teague, P. (1987a), 'Multinational companies in the N. Ireland Economy', in *Beyond the Rhetoric: Politics, the Economy and Social Policy*, Paul Teague (ed.), Lawrence and Wishart, London.

Teague, P. (1987b), 'Fatal Flaws, Clutching at Straws', *Fortnight*, No 225, November.

Teague, P. (1987c), 'Towards a New Economic Policy', *Fortnight*, No 258, January.

Teague, P. (1991), 'Routes to Employment and the Job Crisis in N. Ireland', University of Ulster, mimeograph.

Teague, P. (1992), 'The Potential and Limits of North-South Economic Co-operation' in P. Teague and B. Walker (eds), *The Economies of Ireland*, Institute of Irish Studies, Queen's University Belfast, Belfast.

Teague, P. (1992b), *Governance Structures and Economic Performance*, Department of Applied Economics, mimeograph, University of Ulster.

Teece, O.,(1980), The Economics of Scope and the Scope of the Enterprise, *Journal of Economic Behaviour and Organisation*, **23**, 1.

Thirwall, A. (1991), *European Monetary Union and the Balance of Payments Problem*, mimeo, Department of Economics, University of Kent.

Thompson, G., Frances, J., Levacic, R. and Mitchell, J. (1991), *Markets, Hierarchies and Networks*, Sage, London.

Williams, J., Williams, K. and Haslam, J. (1983), *Why are the British bad at manufacturing?* Routledge, London.

Zysman, J. and Cohen, S. (1987), *Manufacturing Matters*, Basic Books, New York.

4
THE PUBLIC SECTOR AND THE ECONOMY

Michael Smyth

INTRODUCTION

While the scale of public sector activity has grown significantly across industrialized economies over the past forty years, its relative importance in the Northern Ireland economy is virtually unparalleled. To some extent, this is due to the abnormal political and security situation which prevails in Northern Ireland, but it has also come about because of a complex series of institutional arrangements, which have evolved since the creation of a devolved structure of government in the province in 1921. Conventional approaches to the role of the state emphasize the distributional, allocative efficiency and stabilizing functions of this activity, but the public sector in Northern Ireland does not appear to embrace all three functions. Although evidence suggests that the large public sector has ensured stabilization, it can also be argued that it has produced negative spillover effects which together have compromised its allocative efficiency and distributional roles. This chapter sets out to examine the nature of public sector activity in Northern Ireland. First it traces the evolution of both the revenue and expenditure sides of the public sector balance sheet. Then changes in the structure of the Northern Ireland public sector are examined against the allocative, distributional and stabilization criteria. Finally an attempt is made to assess the overall impact of public sector activity in the N. Ireland economy.

HISTORICAL CONTEXT

In terms of both its political and financial status within the United Kingdom, Northern Ireland has always been and remains anomalous.

From 1920 until 1972, Northern Ireland had its own political institutions and some limited control over its public finances. Under the terms of the 1920 legislation, it was envisaged that Northern Ireland would be a self-financing region with a variable surplus which would be available through an Imperial Contribution. With regard to the division of powers, the Government of Ireland Act 1920 empowered the devolved parliament of Northern Ireland (Stormont) to make laws in matters relating only to Northern Ireland subject to certain restrictions. Thus, the main areas of regional economic, social and cultural affairs were to be controlled by Stormont, but Crown affairs, the armed forces, foreign policy, the postal services, customs and excise, income tax and profits tax were chief among the matters which were to be the responsibility of Westminster. Stormont was not empowered to impose any general taxes on capital, but could grant relief from income tax and surtax, though only if funded from the Northern Ireland Exchequer. Stormont was also given power to collect some transferred taxes such as motor vehicle tax and death duties. After making the Imperial Contribution, the revenues from the transferred taxes and so-called 'reserved taxes' (levied throughout the United Kingdom at unified rates), was to be used to fund Northern Ireland expenditure. Limited powers of borrowing for capital expenditure were also available to the Stormont government.

It became clear very quickly that the financial arrangements under the 1920 Act were inadequate. Throughout the 1920s a series of special arrangements gradually altered the basis upon which Northern Ireland's public finances were calculated. Yet Northern Ireland was chronically underfunded vis-a-vis Great Britain over the period 1921–1939, despite additional finance being made available. This raised the question of the extent to which public provision in the province should shadow that existing in the rest of the UK. In 1938, the Treasury settled this matter by declaring that the principle of parity should govern public expenditure in N. Ireland. However it was not until after the war that a concerted effort was made to bring Stormont expenditure up to levels close to parity of services with Great Britain. To operationalize the principle of parity of services a number of changes were introduced to the management of public finances in the province. For the first time the Northern Ireland budget was to be vetted by the Treasury. Large items of new expenditure (for example those costing over £50,000) required Treasury approval before being undertaken. A Stormont budget would continue to be prepared along the lines set out under the 1920 Act, but any gap between current revenue and expenditure would be now funded by transfers from Westminster. Through the 1950s, 1960s and early 1970s these new transfers increased both in scale and in financial weight. By 1971–1972, total transfers from Westminster amounted to £105 million, or 18 per cent of total Northern Ireland public spending.[1] On the surface, the gradual build-up of extra revenues from the United Kingdom Exchequer appeared to confirm that parity was being achieved and that expenditure levels were responsive to economic and social need. Simpson (1980), however, argues that on a per capita basis, spending levels in Northern Ireland were below the national average until the late 1960s; and that if adjusted for need, were less than the required levels until the mid-1970s.

The 1973 Constitution Act changed the method of presentation of Northern Ireland's finances. The Imperial Contribution disappeared, and the formality of matching expenditures or revenues by means of a range of special transfers came to an end. Most of these special forms of assistance were replaced by a general grant-in-aid from the Secretary of State for Northern Ireland to the Northern Ireland Consolidated Fund. It is the retention of a separate Consolidated Fund which enables the identification of most of the transfers between the national and regional exchequers. Northern Ireland thus still retains a system of public finance which is unique among the four home countries.

THE STRUCTURE OF THE NORTHERN IRELAND PUBLIC SECTOR

The institutional setting of the region's public sector also has several unique features. Central government comprises the Northern Ireland Office, headed by a Secretary of State of Cabinet rank, with Northern Ireland spending departments and non-departmental bodies under their responsibility. While Scotland and Wales also have Secretaries of State and spending departments, many of their functions are carried out by regional branches of central government departments. Northern Ireland departments, on the other hand, correspond closely to the functions performed under the devolved Stormont system and comprise the following sectors: agriculture, economic development, education, environmental services, finance and health and social services (including the administration of social security). Many other UK central government departments are active in the provision of services in Northern Ireland, for example, the Lord Chancellor's Office (legal services); the Inland Revenue; Customs and Excise; the Ministry of

Agriculture, Fisheries and Food and the Ministry of Defence (the army presence).

Northern Ireland also has an unusual system of local government in which the twenty-six district councils' powers are limited to the provision of leisure services, local environmental services, small-scale local economic development and the setting of district domestic rates. Specialist services such as health, education and housing are provided by statutory agencies which operate under the aegis of the corresponding Northern Ireland department. Thus, there are four Area Health and Social Services Boards (DSS), five Education and Library Boards (DENI) and the Northern Ireland Housing Executive, which is a publicly-owned corporation operating within the remit of the Northern Ireland Department of the Environment (DOE). Similar types of agencies also operate industrial development policy (the Industrial Development Board (IDB) and the Local Enterprise Development Unit (LEDU)), under the control of the Department of Economic Development.

The other element of the public sector, namely the public corporations, is very small in Northern Ireland and in recent years it has contracted even further as a result of privatization. Over the next two years, other substantial sell-offs of the remainder of the region's electricity industry, the water service and the main airport will leave only the Post Office, Northern Ireland Railways, Ulsterbus and some port facilities in public ownership.

By far the most striking feature of public sector activity in Northern Ireland since 1973 has been the growth of public sector employment. During the 1950s and 1960s, when there was a relative under-provision of public services, public sector jobs averaged between 15 and 25 per cent of total employment, at the time a much lower proportion than in Great Britain. The early years of the 1970s saw a spectacular rise in public sector employment; between 1970 and 1974 employment in public sector organizations grew by nearly 40 per cent and between 1974 and 1979 by a further 25 per cent, by far the most rapid growth occurring in the security, prison, education and health services as shown in Table 4.1. The security and prison service growth reflects the underlying political realities of Northern Ireland. Growth in the social provision such as education and health can be explained in terms of a similar expansion in the rest of the United Kingdom and a 'catching-up' effect. Additionally, as civil unrest effectively cut off the flow of international manufacturing investment to Northern Ireland, successive Westminster governments have used public expenditure to increase jobs in the non-tradeable sector to compensate for the fall in employment in the tradeable sector. Between 1970 and 1992, the proportion of total employment in the public sector rose from just under 25 per cent to around 39 per cent. But as the agricultural and construction sectors of the economy heavily depend upon public expenditures it is likely that over half of all employment in the region is directly determined by state expenditures.[2] Within the public sector in Northern Ireland there has been a massive build-up of employment in police and security-related activities as shown in Table 4.1 in response to the continuing political turmoil. Employment in the 'social services' has made the biggest contribution to the absolute level of employment, reflecting under the parity principle Northern Ireland's greater relative need arising from demographic differences and other social concerns.[3]

Table 4.1 Public sector employment in Northern Ireland, 1974, 1988 and 1992 (June of each year)

	1974	1988	1992	Average annual % change
NI Central Government of which:	42,253	48,526	49,337	0.9
Police & Prison Services	9.114	19.206	19,977	4.5
NI Departments	33,139	29,320	29,860	-0.6
Bodies under the aegis of NI Central Government of which:	88,853	120,908	117,395	1.6
Health & Social Services	44,731	63,842	61,000	1.7
Education Services	40,244	54,508	54,615	1.7
UK Central Government	8,583	6,176	6,248	-1.7
Local Government	7,424	10,346	9,325	1.3
Public Corporations of which:	25,956	20,330	18,827	-1.8
NI based	15,798	15,590	14,156	-0.6
UK based	10,158	4,740	4,671	-4.2
Total of which:	173,069	206,286	201,132	0.8
Males	89,649	90,779	85,206	-0.3
Females	83,240	115,507	115,926	1.8
% of total employment	35.9	41.5	38.9	0.4

Source: Department of Economic Development

One of the most notable features of the expansion of public sector employment in Northern Ireland has been the growth of female jobs. Table 4.1 shows that while overall public sector employment grew by around 28,000 between 1974 and 1992, male employment declined by more than 4,000 while female employment rose by over 32,000 during the same period. Education and health-related services absorbed most of this additional female employment. The same sectors also account for most of the part-time employment growth during the 1970s and early 1980s.

THE ALLOCATION OF PUBLIC EXPENDITURE IN THE UNITED KINGDOM

Although the 1973 Constitution Act greatly simplified the presentation of the ever increasing transfers from the Treasury to the province, precise allocative mechanisms to determine Northern Ireland's entitlement were not put in place during the 1973–1979 period. As a result actual resource decisions appear to have been made on a fairly ad hoc basis. The upsurge in terrorist violence prompted increased expenditures on law and order, but it was undoubtedly the case that the civil unrest also highlighted the need for additional resources in the fields of housing, environmental services and health. Between 1973 and 1976 large increases in socially orientated services were funded via large transfers from central government: total Northern Ireland expenditure grew by nearly a third between the 1972/1973 and 1975/1976 financial years. Hewitt (1991) argues that the massive growth in the volume of public spending in Northern Ireland, in the years immediately following the start of Direct Rule, conforms to the 'displacement hypothesis'. The essence of this hypothesis is that public expenditure is, by necessity, driven up during wars, crises and national emergencies and that taxpayers' resistance to the inevitably greater burden is correspondingly weaker. If this argument is correct, then the resistance of taxpayers in Great Britain to the funding of Northern Ireland's 1992/1993 revenue shortfall of just under £3 billion, is by now wafer thin.

Certainly, there is ample evidence to illustrate the stabilization effects of the rapidly expanding state sector. Following the quadrupling of world oil prices by OPEC in 1973 and the miners' strike and three-day week of 1973/1974, the United Kingdom economy, along with all the other OECD economies, plummeted into a sharp recession in 1974/1975. However, as Table 4.2 shows, the Northern

Ireland economy grew strongly over the entire turbulent period, almost entirely because of the injection of substantial additional public (capital) expenditures.

By the end of the 1970s, the growth of the Northern Ireland public sector eased as the gap narrowed between living standards in the province and the rest of the UK. At this time the Treasury began to reassess the whole basis of public expenditure allocation among the four home countries. The result of this exercise which was a background analysis to the proposals for devolved administration in Scotland and Wales, was that greater structure was introduced into the public finance system.

Table 4.2 Public expenditure in Northern Ireland by programme 1968/69 – 1991/92 (£ million)

	1968/69	1978/79	1988/89	1991/92
Agriculture	39	94	144	141
Trade, industry, energy and employment	65	278	377	482
Transport	24	100	106	163
Housing	32	184	334	201
Environmental services	16	91	252	137
Law and order	11	209	637	800
Education	61	340	852	1,158
Health and social services	54	314	879	1,073
Social Security	98	497	1,568	1,217
Other public services	10	25	46	71
Total public expenditure	410	2,132	5,196	5,443
Capital expenditure as % of total	22	14	10	12

Source: Northern Ireland Abstract of Statistics, Financial Statement.

Public expenditure started to be allocated along the following lines. A UK-wide annual Public Expenditure Survey (PES), which determines the overall national spending total and then the individual programme totals, viewed Northern Ireland as an expenditure block (except for social security). Within this block, total expenditures for individual programmes are determined by the application of what has come to be known as the Barnett formula. This rather simple formula allocated increments in spending in England (the base country) to the other home countries, roughly in proportion to the population in, respectively, Scotland, Wales and Northern Ireland. In principle, as Northern Ireland has about 2.75 per-cent of the United Kingdom population, for every additional £85 spent on, say, housing in England, Scotland would undertake an extra £10, Wales an extra £5 and Northern Ireland an extra £2.75 on the same programme (since together England's £85, Scotland's £10 and Wales £5 makes the GB total £100, N. Ireland will receive £2.75). The attractions of the Barnett formula have hitherto been that it was extremely straightforward and it relieved the Treasury of having to conduct regular assessment needs of different parts of the UK. However, it is a fairly rigid formula and is open to abuse. In the past, the Scottish, Welsh and Northern Ireland Secretaries of State have all successfully been able to argue for additional programme expenditures in response to differential local needs. Of course by receiving such top-ups the principle of parity was being breached with the result of Scotland, Wales and Northern Ireland (the so-called Celtic fringe) receiving more generous public financing than England. These issues have given rise to considerable debate over the past twenty years about the equity implications of the Barnett formula.

Table 4.3 Territorial analysis of identifiable public expenditure per capita, 1983/84 – 1990/91 (£ per head) and relative to UK

	England	Scotland	Wales	Northern Ireland	United Kingdom
1983/84	1,643 (96)	2,096 (122)	1,863 (109)	2,452 (143)	1,717 (100)
1984/85	1,755 (96)	2,207 (121)	1,938 (106)	2,613 (143)	1,829 (100)
1985/86	1,843 (96)	2,340 (122)	2,039 (106)	2,770 (144)	1,924 (100)
1986/87	1,955 (96)	2,516 (123)	2,247 (110)	2,938 (144)	2,047 (100)
1987/88	2,023 (95)	2,622 (124)	2,335 (110)	3,110 (147)	2,122 (100)
1988/89	2,119 (95)	2,748 (123)	2,487 (111)	3,540 (159)	2,232 (100)
1989/90	2,338 (95)	2,957 (121)	2,680 (109)	3,714 (152)	2,448 (100)
1990/91	2,586 (96)	3,196 (119)	2,964 (110)	3,842 (143)	2,694 (100)

Source: Hansard, 25 October 1988, Statistical Supplement to the 1991 Autumn Statement, cm 1920.

Overall it can be suggested that the abuses of the Barnett principle have been infrequent and that for the most part public expenditure has been on the basis of need. But the actual measurement of the need of different parts of the UK has been a matter of some dispute. In 1976/77 the Treasury attempted to evaluate relative need by two different methods in a report known as the Needs Assessment Study. On the one hand, by assembling an elaborate framework of objective factors which were considered to be the main quantifiable variables which could be used to assess whether expenditure levels reflected genuine need. On the other hand, a straightforward rather basic method was used to conduct the same exercise. Table 4.4 compares the two estimates of relative need between England, Scotland, Wales and Northern Ireland. Whereas Row A gives the estimates calculated by the sophisticated method, Row B shows the figures obtained by the journeyman method. A comparison of the two shows that the results are remarkably similar suggesting that immense detail or sophistication is not required to assess whether relative need exists or not.

Table 4.4 Needs assessment results 1976/77 – total public expenditure

	England	Scotland	Wales	Northern Ireland
A (all objective factors)	100	116	109	131
B (only major factors)	100	115	108	130

Other attempts to compare levels of public expenditure in Northern Ireland with Great Britain have tended to suggest that cyclically, actual spending in Northern Ireland has sometimes lagged behind expenditure to meet expected need. Canning, Moore and Rhodes (1987) view the rapid growth of public spending and employment during the 1970s as essentially a catching-up process.[6] On the other hand, a series of unique social, demographic and economic trends in Northern Ireland are cited by the Northern Ireland Economic Council (1981) as explaining most of the difference in regional/national expenditure patterns. In particular, migration, different systems of land tenure, higher proportions of young dependents, the relative importance of agriculture and the special policing needs of Northern Ireland are regarded as explaining the actual spending gap with Great Britain.[7] Heald (1992) examines the mechanics of expenditure allocations on a population basis and suggests that there is no overfunding in Scotland, Wales and N. Ireland and that public finance is given on the basis of need. Borooah and Smyth (1992) propose a model which embodies the parity principle in its long-run behaviour while at the same time permitting short-run deviations in annual spending away from the long-run proportionality implied by parity. They estimate the model for seven spending programmes between 1973 and 1990 and the results are set out in Table 4.5, together with the original Needs Assessment calculated coefficients for 1976/1977. If expenditure growth rates for the programmes are set at their 1973–1990 average, Northern Ireland per capita expenditure was higher than the English equivalent in four categories – for Health Services it was 19 per cent higher, for Other Environmental Services 16 per cent higher, for Agriculture 15 per cent higher and for Education 14 per cent higher. Scotland enjoyed a premium over England with respect to Agriculture, Education, Health Services and Other Environmental Services and Wales, with respect to Housing, Education, Health Services and Other Environmental Services. Comparison of the long-run proportionality coefficients in Table 4.5 with the 1976/1977 Needs Assessment estimations is fraught with problems so the figures are interpreted with some caution. All the countries appear to be underfunded relative to England with respect to Roads and Transport, Housing, Education and Other Environmental Services. The degree of underfunding varied across programmes and countries. In Education, the greatest shortfall (in terms of a percentage points difference between the long-run proportionality coefficients and those based on ones) was for Northern Ireland. For Housing, again it was Northern Ireland. For other Environmental Services it was for Wales, followed by Scotland and Northern Ireland. The only area of overfunding that this study identified was Health Services in which, for both Scotland and Northern Ireland, there was a small percentage points excess.

THE REVENUE SIDE

The existence of separate public sector revenue accounts for Northern Ireland is unique among the home countries and is one of several legacies from the period of devolved government in the province. While the presentational structure of the Revenue Account is straightforward, the precise calculation of some parts of the revenue balance sheet remains unclear. There are two broad divisions namely, revenues generated in or attributable to Northern Ireland and payments from the national exchequer into the local exchequer. Table 4.6 details the

Table 4.5 Estimated long-run coefficients of proportionality (assuming average rate of growth of public expenditure)

		Northern Ireland	Scotland	Wales
Roads & transport	1979–90	0.8788	0.9533	0.9534
	1974–79	0.8228	0.8540	0.8647
	1989–90	0.9310	1.0500	1.0386
Needs assessment		(1.55)	(1.44)	(1.31)
Trade, industry,	1974–90	1.7109	0.8692	0.7662
energy &	1974–79	0.2798	0.5297	0.3792
employment	1979–90	1.1194	1.1061	1.0791
Agriculture, forestry	1974–90	1.1538	1.0675	0.9743
& fishing	1974–79	1.2056	1.0919	1.0003
	1979–90	1.1910	1.0851	0.9930
Housing	1974–90	0.9207	0.8357	1.0154
	1974–79	1.0887	1.0102	1.0219
	1979–90	0.8344	0.7477	1.0116
Needs asessment		(1.59)	(1.30)	(1.07)
Education	1974–90	1.1387	1.1498	1.0312
	1974–79	1.1530	1.1615	1.0388
	1979–90	1.1391	1.1501	1.0314
Needs assessment		(1.29)	(1.07)	(1.04)
Health & personal	1974–90	1.1892	1.1770	1.0447
social services	1974–79	1.1971	1.1775	1.0458
	1979–90	1.1849	1.1763	1.0443
Needs assessment		(1.071)	(1.071)	(1.0610)
Other environmental	1974–90	1.1592	1.1492	1.2265
services	1974–79	0.9749	0.9916	1.1050
	1979–90	1.1554	1.1462	1.2241
Needs assessment		(1.29)	(1.33)	(1.42)
Total public	1974–90	1.0978	1.0560	1.0367
expenditure	1974–79	1.0158	0.9872	0.9631
	1974–90	1.1446	1.0949	1.0786

Source: Borooah and Smyth (1992)

Table 4.6 Northern Ireland government current revenue (£ million at current prices) 1979/80 – 1992/93

	1979/80	1987/88	1992/93*
Revenue generated in Northern Ireland:			
NI net attributed share of UK taxes	1,021.7	2,154.8	3,092.8
National Insurance contributions	270.9	504.0	777.5
Rates	109.4	251.3	230.0
Other revenues	160.3	345.6	292.8
Sub-total	1,562.3	3,255.7	4,392.6
NI Generated revenues as % of total revenue	69.8	75.8	69.9
Transfers from the UK government:			
Grant in aid	590.0	855.0	1,710.0
National Insurance Fund 'Top-up'	73.8	155.0	180.0
Refund of VAT	11.7	30.8	—
Total current revenue	2,237.8	4,296.5	6,282.6
UK Transfers as % of total revenue	30.2	24.2	30.1

Note: * Estimated out-turn.

Source: Financial Statement

presentation of revenues for 1979/1980, 1987/1988 and 1992/1993. The local share of the proceeds of nationally levied taxes, minus the local cost of collection and the local portion of the national contribution to the EC, constitutes the tax revenue element of regional revenue. The rates comprise a regional rate to contribute to the cost of services, provided by central government in Northern Ireland and a district rate to offset the cost of services provided by local district councils. Northern Ireland's attributed share of United Kingdom taxes is calculated in different ways for different types of tax. There are some additional revenues in each year deriving from land annuities, interest on advances, repayments of loans and other miscellaneous receipts. The figures in Table 4.6 show clearly the cyclical sensitivity of the UK transfers to Northern Ireland with the ability of the local economy to generate more of its own revenues during the upsurge and less during times of recession. Over the years since direct rule came into effect, surplus current revenues have been used to fund capital projects in Northern Ireland, thereby keeping public sector borrowing at a low level. The availability of large transfers from the national exchequer to Northern Ireland have led to rather simplistic conclusions about the value and status of Northern Ireland within the United Kingdom.[8] Some of these issues are assessed in the final section of this chapter.

Table 4.7 The Northern Ireland subvention 1966/67 – 1992/93 (£ million at current prices)

	1966/67	1973/74	1977/78	1984/85	1992/93
Social Services Agreement	10	31	—	—	—
Health Services Agreement	—	15	—	—	—
Regional Employment Premium	—	8	11	—	—
Agricultural Remoteness Grant	2	2	—	—	—
MAFF expenditure in NI	25	25	27	53	96
National Insurance transfers	15	30	59	95	180
Grant in Aid	—	175	432	905	1,710
Northern Ireland Office	—	—	175	401	857
VAT refunds	—	1	7	25	—
Total	52	287	711	1,479	2,843

Sources: Hewitt (1990); Northern Ireland Annual Abstract of Statistics; NI Financial Statement 1992/93

Table 4.7 attempts to calculate the total scale of United Kingdom transfers to Northern Ireland, the so-called 'subvention'. The total national contribution to Northern Ireland has changed both in form and in substance over the past quarter of a century. In addition to the transfers outlined in Table 4.6, Table 4.7 details expenditure by the Northern Ireland Office on law and order and local expenditure by the Ministry of Agriculture, Fisheries and Food. The lack of transparency in the Northern Ireland public accounts does not permit the disclosure of two further transfer items – the extra cost of the army presence in

Northern Ireland, which is borne by the Ministry of Defence and the cost of the courts service, which is covered by the Lord Chancellor's Department. But for 1992/1993, these are estimated to total £300 million. As a result the full subvention for the current year is approximately £3,143 million or £2,000 per head of population in Northern Ireland.

THE ISSUES

Within a unified state where parity of public services throughout the regions is a firm policy commitment, fiscal transfers from the centre to the periphery are often used to ensure the provision of services when local revenues prove insufficient. On a much larger scale, the creation of an economic and monetary union within the EC will necessitate similar fiscal transfers from Brussels. Indeed, the main purpose of the present Community Support Framework (CSF) or the Structural Funds which operates such transfers is to help reduce the peripherality and permit the economic convergence of lagging (poorer) regions (such as Northern Ireland and the Republic of Ireland).

In recent years, the debate about the size, growth and impact of the public sector in Northern Ireland has grown significantly. Canning, Moore and Rhodes (1987) assert that the growth of public services during the 1970s was probably not part of an overall coherent economic strategy but nevertheless prevented the collapse of the Northern Ireland economy. Hewitt (1991) in his analysis of public sector activity in Northern Ireland highlights the stabilizing properties of public expenditure in the region and implicity argues Northern Ireland's case for differentially higher levels of spending on the grounds of relative need. He also runs through a familiar litany of the negative effects of a large public sector on the rest of the regional economy, but concluded that little empirical evidence has been produced of their relative importance.

What are the key issues arising from the development, size, structure, micro- and macro-economic impact of the public sector in Northern Ireland? For the sake of simplicity and convenience, the important effects can be divided into two groups – those which may be deemed beneficial and those which may be termed detrimental. Overall the detrimental effects roughly *outnumber* the beneficial effects by two to one, though in terms of relative weight and importance the argument seems more finely balanced.

Table 4.8 Output and expenditure in Northern Ireland, 1970-90 (£m at current prices)

	1970	1979	1984	1990
Domestic output:				
Transportable goods	360	992	1,391	2,116
General government	137	890	1,639	3,045
Other non-government	413	1,647	2,513	4,660
(A) Gross domestic product	910	3,529	5,543	9,821
Domestic expenditure:				
Consumer's expenditure	616	2,578	3,818	8,085
General government final consumption	153	1,041	1,977	2,823*
Gross domestic capital formation	299	1,121	1,296	1,289
(B) Total domestic expenditure	1,068	4,740	7,091	12,197
(C) Balance of trade (=A-B)	-158	-1,211	-1,548	-2,376
c.f. Official subvention	89	1,059	1,533	2,320*

Note: * estimated

Source: Rowthorn (1987); Financial Statement

Turning to the negative spillover effects first, many of the arguments which follow are closely inter-related but it is felt that they should be given separate assessments. The inexorable rise in the level of transfers from Westminster to Stormont, while explicable in terms of additional security costs and higher relative need, as argued earlier, has an unfortunate counterpart in the regional accounts, namely a rapidly growing balance of payments deficit. Despite inadequate visible trade data, Rowthorn (1987) has estimated the Northern Ireland balance of payments position within a simple regional accounts framework. Table 4.8 replicates Rowthorn's calculations for 1990, the latest year for which the necessary date is available. The Northern Ireland trade deficit is the gap between domestic output and domestic expenditure and over the 1970–1990 period this deficit has been financed by fiscal transfers from Westminster and Brussels. When inward investment was still being attracted to Northern Inland, the capital flows financed the deficit on trade in goods and services. During the 1970s the payments deficit worsened as the capital inflow from inward investment fell away, creating a 'financing problem'. The gap, of course, has been filled by financial assistance from Britain. Rowthorn asserts that the trade deficit, particularly in what he terms transportable goods, (mostly manufactured goods) is indicative of prodigal behaviour or overspending and that if Northern Ireland were forced to balance domestic income and expenditure, living standards would have to fall to 60 per cent of present levels.

The fact that public sector borrowing in Northern Ireland has been kept low by using surplus current revenue to fund much of the region's capital programmes represents the public finance counterpart to the balance of payments deficit. For Northern Ireland, there is no real pain resulting from running a persistent payments deficit of around 25 per cent of GDP. With a fixed exchange rate, the bulk of the fiscal transfers from Westminster bolster living standards and shore up incomes. This point is discussed in more detail below. By not having to make difficult choices about taxation and expenditure adjustments in order to live within its means, the Northern Ireland economy operates with what has been termed a 'soft' budget constraint. Consider the following analogy. If an individual has a weekly income of £100 but actually spends £140 per week, then a large gap exists between earnings and expenditure. Under normal conditions, pressure would very quickly mount via bank managers and other creditors not only to balance incomings and outgoings but also to reduce expenditure below income for a given period so as to pay off accumulated debts. This scenario is termed the 'hard' budget constraint.

Now consider the case of the individual with a kind aunt who writes a cheque for £40 every week to cover the shortfall between income and expenditure. In this instance, an external agent or institution ensures that equilibrium is maintained. When the individual comes to expect such external financial assistance, a softening of the budget constraint has occurred. The person's subjective expectations about expenditure limits shifts and a more or less permanent gap between income and expenditure becomes an unquestioning part of daily routine. By funding the deficit between income and expenditure, the United Kingdom government is in effect Northern Ireland's kind aunt. A comparison of Northern Ireland's budgetary arrangements with those of the Republic highlights the real financial advantages which direct rule has brought to the region. Even at its current modest level of around 2.5 per cent of GNP the Republic's Exchequer Borrowing Requirement (EBR) imposes very severe limits on Irish economic policymaking. For Northern Ireland a recurring deficit of the order of

25 per cent of GDP implies no significant pressure to alter behaviour or to make difficult resource allocation decisions. The 'real' effects of this fiscal divergence between the two Irish economies are to be seen in the rate of development and current state of the physical infrastructures North and South. While major improvements have been made, in recent years, to the telecommunications and rail networks in the Republic, the road network remains very poor in comparison with the Northern Ireland road system. Differences in the rates and incidence of most forms of taxation between Northern Ireland and the Republic are the other telling effects of 'soft' and 'hard' budget constraints. Higher excise duties and indirect taxes in the Republic during the latter half of the 1980s led to the phenomenon of 'cross-border' shopping. Consumer prices in the Republic were pushed up to over 20 per cent higher than prices in Northern Ireland by 1987. The study by Fitzgerald, Quinn, Whelan and Williams (1988) found that, of the 23 per cent North/South differential in consumer prices, 16 per cent was due to higher indirect taxes in the Republic. The need for tax revenues to hold the EBR to sustainable levels forced taxation up to very high levels and in the case of cross-border shopping caused the outflow of between IR£150 and IR£200 million per annum at its peak, a sum equivalent to around 2 per cent of consumers' expenditure in the Republic.

As public services in Northern Ireland expanded rapidly during the 1970s and 1980s, there was a parallel growth in private services, particularly consumer services. Rapid growth of public sector employment, strong linkages between government and the construction sector and the evolution of a complex structure of financial support to agriculture and manufacturing industry, together with personal transfers on a very large scale, have produced what is termed a 'circular flow' of expenditures between the public sector and the private service sector. Manufacturing industry operates at arms length from this circular flow and is isolated. The circular flow accounts for the relatively flourishing retailing and distributive sectors and the large financial services industry and, together with the relatively low cost of housing, explains much of the conspicuous consumption which has become a feature of high street commercial life in Northern Ireland. The effect of this process has been to encourage the emergence of experience goods (consumer goods) rather than search goods for export markets. Employment patterns changed during the 1970s and 1980s as inward investment declined and public services expanded. Female activity rates increased and as already shown, female employment in the public sector soared. Borooah and McGregor (1989) report that Northern Ireland has the highest proportion of two income families in the United Kingdom as well as the highest unemployment and dependency rates. They find that one of the main causes of relative income inequality in Northern Ireland is the uneven distribution of employment associated with the two-income family group. While not all of the two-income families are employed in the public sector, a significant proportion have at least one salary earner in a public sector job. The existence of such inequality in income distribution is perpetuated to an extent by a quasi-dual economy. With 38 per cent of employees employed in the public sector at national rates of pay and 15 per cent of the working population unemployed, the gap between the haves and have-nots is very wide indeed.

Undoubtedly the most beneficial effect of high levels of public expenditure in Northern Ireland is stabilization of the regional economy. It was pointed out earlier that expansion of the state sector during the 1970s prevented economic collapse in the face of civil unrest. The scale and structure of the Northern Ireland public expenditure system mean that it primarily stabilizes incomes through its effects on employment. Since the mid-1980s there has been a policy of partnership between the public and private sectors in terms of the regeneration of Northern Ireland's two largest cities, Belfast and Londonderry. This has produced a significant number of large property developments, the expansion of retail activity and a hefty increase in office space. Needless to say the construction industry benefited considerably from this policy. The unwritten policy underlying much of the extension of the public sector in Northern Ireland for many years has been twofold: firstly to maintain the economic status quo as far as possible, to hold the economy together while, secondly, efforts continue to find a political accommodation acceptable to all parties. An earlier version of this policy was the 'hearts and minds' approach which was aimed at trying expanding the Northern Ireland economy, to provide employment opportunities and higher living standards in order to undermine the economic rationale for terrorism. Increasingly the authorities are moving to the position where they see a political agreement as the precursor of economic development in Northern Ireland. Historically, the period of most rapid economic and industrial growth occurred in the 1960s prompted by large-scale inward investment. Inward investment remains a necessary condition for future economic development and realistically can only be promoted under a stable political system. Expansion of the public sector in Northern Ireland has been a surrogate for autonomous growth, a buttress against political instability and remains the dominant feature of the region's economy.

NOTES

1. Simpson, J.V., 'The Finances of the Public Sector in Northern Ireland 1968-78', *Journal of the Statistical and Social Inquiry Society of Ireland*, Vol.XXIV, Part II, 1979/80, p.102.
2. Simpson, op. cit., pp.102ff.
3. Rowthorn (1988) argues that, given the elaborate structure of state aid to manufacturing industry in Northern Ireland – inward investment, employment subsidies, soft loans, grants, etc. – most jobs in manufacturing receive some form of public support. The true size of the state therefore is consistently underestimated.
4. See Hewitt (1990) for a comprehensive review of the structure of public sector employment in NI.
5. See O'Dowd (1987) for a much fuller discussion of spatial, sectoral and employment change in the NI public sector.
6. Canning, Moore and Rhodes (1987) point out that in 1981/82 for instance, total 'needs expected' expenditure *exceeded* actual spending by £84 million (2.3 per cent). By 1984/85 actual spending exceeded expected expenditure by roughly the same amount.
7. Hewitt (1990) op. cit. updates the NIEC calculations of adjusted needs and his estimates confirm the Canning *et. al.* (1987) finding of relative underfunding in 1981/82. His results are as follows: (GB = 100)

	Unadjusted	Adjusted
1980/81	130.3	101.6
1981//82	113.6	98.4
1982/83	135.8	99.5
1983/84	137.8	101.1
1984/85	137.9	100.6
1985/86	141.9	101.7

8. Perhaps the most memorable was the then Prime Minister Harold Wilson's quip that Northern Ireland was populated by 'spongers'.
9. Canning, Moore and Rhodes (1987), op. cit., p. 193.

REFERENCES

Borooah, V.K. and McGregor, P. (1989) 'Inequality and Poverty in Northern Ireland', Trade Union Institute for Economic Research, Working Paper No. 67, Stockholm.

Borooah, V.K. and Smyth, M. (1992) 'The Allocation of Public Expenditure Between the Countries of the United Kingdom: An Application of the Error Correction Mechanism', paper presented at the European Public Choice Conference, Linz.

Canning, D., Moore, B. and Rhodes, J. (1987) 'Economic Growth in Northern Ireland: Problems and Prospects', in Teague, P. (ed.) *Beyond the Rhetoric: Politics, the Economy and Social Policy in Northern Ireland*, Lawrence and Wishart, London.

Fitzgerald, J.D., Quinn, T.P., Whelan, B.J. and Williams, J.A. (1988), An Analysis of Cross-Border Shopping, *ESRI*, 137, Dublin.

Green, A.J. (1979) 'Devolution and Public Finance: Stormont from 1921 to 1972', *Studies in Public Policy* No. 48, University of Strathclyde.

Heald, D.A. (1992) 'Formula-based Territorial Public Expenditure in the United Kingdom', *Aberdeen Papers in Accountancy, Finance and Management* No. 7.

Hewitt, V.N. (1991) 'The Public Sector' in Harris, R., Jefferson, C. and Spencer, J., The Northern Ireland Economy – a Comparative Study in the Economic Development of a Peripheral Region, Longman, London.

H.M. Treasury (1979) 'Needs Assessment Study – Report', The Report of an Interdepartmental Study coordinated by H.M. Treasury on the relative public expenditure needs in England, Scotland, Wales and Northern Ireland, HMSO, London.

Lawrence, R.J. (1965) *The Government of Northern Ireland: Public Finance and Public Services*, Oxford University Press, Oxford.

Northern Ireland Economic Council (1981) 'Public Expenditure Comparison Between Northern Ireland and Great Britain', Report No. P8, January.

Hewitt, V.N. (1991) 'The Public Sector', in Harris, R., Jefferson, C. and Spencer, J., *The Northern Ireland Economy: A Comparative Study in the Economic Development of a Peripheral Region*, Longman.

O'Dowd, L. (1987) 'Trends and Potential of the Service Sector in Northern Ireland', in Teague, P. (ed.) *Beyond the Rhetoric: Politics, the Economy and Social Policy in Northern Ireland*, Lawrence and Wishart, London.

Rowthorn, R. (1987 'Northern Ireland: An Economy in Crisis', in Teague, P. (ed.), *Beyond the Rhetoric: Politics , the Economy and Social Policy in Northern Ireland*, Lawrence and Wishart, London.

Rowthorn, R. and Wayne, N. (1988) *Northern Ireland: the Political Economy of Conflict*, Polity Press, Cambridge.

Short, J. (1981) *Public Expenditure and Taxation in the UK Regions*, Gower, Farnborough.

Short, J. and Nicholas, D.J. (1981) *Money Flows in the UK Region*, Gower, Farnborough.

Simpson, J.V. (1980) 'The Finances of the Public Sector in Northern Ireland: 1968-78', *Journal of the Statistical and Social Inquiry Society of Ireland*, Vol. XXIV, Part II, 99–118.

5
Discrimination and Fair Employment in Northern Ireland

Paul Teague

Ever since the formation of Northern Ireland, there have been claims of widespread discrimination against Roman Catholics. Unsurprisingly, this is a highly contested and sensitive issue in Northern Ireland. Disputes rage about whether discrimination ever occurred, whether it has ceased, and if Catholics did encounter disadvantage, how systematic was this treatment. Yet for all that has been written few of the analyses have made direct use of the economics and related literature on discrimination and labour market segmentation. This is surprising since these writings are insightful and sophisticated and have improved understanding of the dynamics which gave rise to and sustained labour market disadvantage elsewhere, particularly in the USA. Of course, this wider theorizing has influenced the debate in Northern Ireland about discrimination, but only in an imprecise and opaque way.

Thus a glaring lacuna exists in the investigations of labour market discrimination in the province, and to some extent this is reflected in the somewhat stale and repetitive nature of the current debate. In this chapter, little attempt is made to counteract this shortcoming – for example, by recasting existing studies so that they take account of discrimination and segmentation theory. Rather, the more limited objective is pursued of highlighting various strands of this literature to increase awareness and to indicate how it could be used in the local debate about unequal treatment in the labour market. The chapter is organized as follows. The first section critically assesses the mainstream economic writings on discrimination. Then the theoretical underpinnings of segmentation theory are outlined. The next section assesses the various influences and processes that give rise to segmentation tendencies in the labour market. Finally, the chapter suggests ways in which these approaches could be used to reveal weaknesses and strengths in the current exchanges on Catholic labour market disadvantage in Northern Ireland.

THE UTILITY PREFERENCE VIEW

In mainstream economics discrimination is said to exist when individuals who are comparable in respect of education, skills and productive potential receive unequal rewards. In other words, personal characteristics not immediately relevant to the transaction shape its outcome. Becker (1957) was probably the first conventional economist to seriously investigate why discriminatory practices emerge in labour markets. Initially, Becker attributed discrimination to the personal tastes of labour market participants. In particular, he suggested that some employers would have preferences for certain groups over others -men over women, whites over blacks – which could result in unequal treatment in the labour market. However, the act of discrimination would incur a cost or disutility. Since an employer may have a taste for only a certain type of worker, it is highly probable that the most skilled and productive workers may not be recruited. By maximizing the utility involved in having only employees of a certain type, the employer sacrifices the ability to maximize profits. Thus discrimination involves a pecuniary cost to employers and the most extensive the discrimination the higher the cost. Now because non-discriminating employers also exist in the same product market, who do not incur such costs, the discriminating employers are placed at a competitive disadvantage against such rivals. As a result, sooner or later the more efficient non-discriminatory employers drive the discriminatory employers out of business. In other words market dynamics will eliminate prejudice from the labour market.

A good many criticisms have been launched against this line of reasoning. Madden (1973) shows that Becker's model contains a number of mathematical errors. Thurow (1969) argues that far from incurring costs, discrimination may yield considerable economic advantages. More specifically, discrimination is not about the utility preference of individual employers but represents the exploitation of certain groups with little economic or political power. Arrow (1973) challenges Becker's assumption that the market will drive out discriminatory employers by suggesting that foregone profits can be treated as consumption expenditure which is not in conflict with Walrasian equilibrium models that allow for long-run wage differentials stemming from employer preferences. Dex (1986) takes issue with Becker for *assuming* that discrimination exists, thereby treating as a black box the processes and mechanisms that generate discriminatory practices. From a public policy standpoint, many regarded Becker's conclusions as unpalatable. For instance, if discrimination occurred in an imperfect market setting then from a Becker standpoint the answer may simply be to promote open competition. All in all, because of its many shortcomings, few now attempt to explain sex, racial or religious discrimination by the utility preferences of employers and it has not been used in any guise in the debate about alleged discrimination of Catholics in Northern Ireland.

THE HUMAN CAPITAL APPROACH

A more robust view of discrimination from the mainstream economics perspective is the human capital school, also pioneered by Becker (1964). At root, the human capital approach suggests that a strong and systematic relationship exists between education and personal economic success. But rather different explanations are put forward for sex and racial under-performance. With regard to racial discrimination, the human capital school contends that earnings differentials between black and white men, for instance, result from corresponding differentials between the two groups in both the quantity and quality of their education. Thus to reduce black/white earnings differentials, the educational attainment of blacks has to improve relative to whites. The human capital story for sex discrimination, or perhaps more precisely, the gender earnings differential, is a little different. Accordingly to this account, men and women have different utility functions which result in women getting paid less than men. In other words, the gender earnings differential mostly stems from women's own choices. More specifically, women tend not to pursue education courses, particularly in scientific and technical fields, that yield a high return. In addition, they are more likely to choose jobs with a high starting salary but which involve little on-the-job training and offer little career progression. Furthermore, since women expect to leave the labour force intermittently to have children they select occupations that carry few penalties for such withdrawals. Yet another factor seen as accounting for women's lower earnings is their higher quit rates.

Empirical work, mostly in the United States, has been carried out on the arguments of the human capital school. With regard to black/white male earnings differentials there is agreement that the gap has narrowed, but disagreement exists about whether the human capital hypothesis best explains the convergence. While one group of studies supports the human capital argument, other empirical work claims that wider institutional variables, such as the presence of fair employment legislation, offer a better explanation for the convergence (see Smith 1984 and Smith and Welch 1988). The econometric exercises with regard to gender wage differentials have not proved conclusive, so controversies rage in this area too. For instance, Polachek (1987) and England (1988) *et al.* have had an exchange about whether women select jobs with high starting salaries but which hold out few long-term prospects. Osterman (1982) contests the argument that women's lower earnings are partly caused by high quit rates by suggesting that it is the other way around, with low-paid work inducing high turnover among women. Although the male/female wage gap has narrowed in the past several decades it has proved impossible, given the lack of reliable data, to attribute the reduced differential to changes in educational attainment or to changes in the return to educational attainment. As a result, the empirical studies on this issue tend to reach the cautious conclusion that whilst the human capital school has a role in explaining the narrowing differentials between the sexes it does not represent the whole story.

With regard to the debate in N. Ireland about discrimination, the human capital thesis has not been used explicitly. But it has implicitly influenced discussion on the matter. A common explanation for Protestant over-representation in employment and in better jobs is that they have more appropriate education and qualifications than Catholics. Cormack and Osborne (1983 and 1985) are perhaps the strongest exponents of this thesis. In support of it, a number of studies have shown that fewer Catholics than would be expected obtained 'O' and 'A' level qualifications, especially before the mid-1970s. Since then the situation has improved but a gap still remains between the 'actual' and 'expected' qualification levels of Catholics. Cormack and Osborne attribute this gap to fewer Catholics attending grammar schools than Protestants. In addition, the same authors (1990) suggest that the greater proportionate numbers of Protestants at the higher tiers of the labour market can be partly explained by Protestant schools specializing more in scientific and technical subjects than Catholic schools, where there is more interest in the humanities. Thus Cormack and Osborne among others are suggesting that the different employment fortunes of Catholics and Protestants are mainly determined by the different education and training profiles of the two communities.

Superficially this argument has appeal, but it is open to the general criticisms that have been levied at this approach. In human capital theory the connection between education and earnings is made by arguing that the more knowledgeable or skilled the worker, the better will be his or her productivity performance. But there is some question as to whether such a direct link can be made. One argument, known as the screening hypothesis, accepts that a positive association exists between education and earnings, but suggests that it is not because additional education yields higher productivity but that employers use additional or certain types of education as a 'screen' to hire certain types of workers. A related argument, usually referred to as the theory of statistical discrimination, is that employers recruit in a world of uncertainty and limited information, and thus cannot make accurate calculations about the productive potential of prospective employees. In such circumstances if employers believe that a certain group of workers are less productive (in the long run) than other groups, their tendency is for these 'alleged' inferior groups to be more or less excluded from certain occupations.

The credentialist view championed by Thurow (1975) represents a further line of attack against the human capital school. Thurow argues that it is the job tasks allocated to the worker and not his or her educational attainment that determines productivity performance. In other words, earning differentials between groups arise not out of differing educational attainment but because of how employers structure and allocate jobs. A similar view is put forward by the internal labour market theories (see Doeringer and Piere 1971). According to this point of view, a set of administrative rules and procedures govern a firm's internal labour market which result in specific wage contours and job clusters arising within the organization. These arrangements give the employer considerable power in allocating jobs and determining promotion decisions which may have little to do with educational levels or productivity performance of the workers concerned. Recent theorizing on efficiency wages can also be evoked to challenge the human capital theory (Solow 1990). In particular, the efficiency wage view – that employers set wages above the market rates for reasons other than to reward high productivity performance – undermines the human capital thesis that a strong connection exists between experience and productivity and productivity and earnings.

Clearly these varied criticisms take issue with different aspects of human capital theory. But they share the common attribute of rejecting the idea that differential experiences in the labour market with regard to earnings and jobs can be mainly explained by the individual characteristics of workers. High transactions costs, limited information, the actions of employer to structure employment and the presence of other labour market institutions, are all seen as working against a purely supply-side explanation of unequal labour market outcomes.

Some of these criticisms have relevance to the human capital type arguments made about supposed discrimination in N. Ireland. First of all, it is quite wrong for Cormack and Osborne as well as other analysts to draw human-capital type conclusions from studies which do not connect actual labour market performance with actual levels of training or education. Here it is important to note the screening hypothesis. In the absence of concrete information about training, earnings and productivity performance, some N. Ireland employers may have a preference for Protestant employees since they believe that Protestant schools produce better-trained pupils. In other words, the screen potential recruits to overcome the adverse selection problem of not having information about who they are employing. But once screening practices are seen to be at play, a pandora's box is opened about the assumptions and even prejudices which might be influencing employer decisions. Even a slight departure from the human capital view invariably leads any analysis into the untidy world of social process and dynamics that might cause and sustain labour market discrimination.

SEGMENTATION THEORY: SOME BASIC PREMISES

Scepticism about the orthodox human capital account of discrimination led to alternative accounts of disadvantage in the labour market which to a greater or lesser extent fall under the heading of segmentation theory. At the core of segmentation theory is the idea that labour markets do not work perfectly in the standard neoclassical sense, but contain discrete segments. This is not a particularly new observation ,since in the last century John Stuart Mill talked about 'non-competing groups' in the labour market which inhibited less advantaged workers from moving to more rewarding areas of the employment structure (1985). But the modern segmentation literature really emerged in the late 1960s, and since then a huge list of publications has appeared on the subject. One of the pioneers of the modern literature was Piore (1976), who suggested that the labour market was bifurcated into primary and secondary sectors. Jobs in the primary sector were characterized by relatively high wages, job security and good working conditions, whereas employment in the secondary market was mostly precarious, low paid and with poor working conditions. This observation gave rise to the theory of dual labour markets. However, since that earlier theorizing it has become accepted that dividing the labour market into two neat categories is too restrictive.

Nevertheless segmentation theory still holds that a substantial distribution of labour market outcomes occurs across workers. McNabb and Ryan (1990) suggest that three features underpin and differentiate this approach. In the first place, the labour market contains processes that generate economic inequality, and is not a reflector of different endowments people bring to it. Secondly, wage and job structures do not solely arise from the dynamics of the market for labour, but are influenced by a variety of factors such as demand variability in the product market, the role of labour market institutions such as trade unions, the type of technology in use and wider societal pressures. Thirdly, tastes, preferences, public policy and so on, which are treated as exogenous in the human capital model, are regarded as endogenous in the segmentation model. Thus the predominance of youths and (married) females in lower-paid jobs is not seen as resulting from pre-given attributes and attitudes they bring to the labour market but rather by the (subordinate) positions they hold within the family and society. In other words, segmentation theory suggests that far from being governed by the laws of competition, the labour market is highly structured and this results in certain groups being more likely to be over-represented in certain types of jobs.

POSITIVE FEEDBACK AND DIVERGENT DEVELOPMENT

Exactly why segmentation tendencies emerge in the labour market is a matter of some dispute. Victorisz and Harrison (1973) provide a systemic view of the process. Departing somewhat from the neoclassical paradigm, they develop a feedback model of the labour market. Feedback is regarded as a relatively closed cycle of causation in complex systems whose parts are dynamically interconnected. In relation to the labour market, an example of a feedback cycle is where wages are initially high, which encourages firms to substitute capital for labour, thereby reducing the demand for labour and thus putting downward pressure on wages. This sequence is seen as an instance of negative feedback since the outcome of the process is opposite to the original state of affairs. In many ways, the negative feedback scenario correlates with the equilibration assumptions of standard neoclassical models. However, Victorisz and Harrison suggest that positive feedback mechanisms are also in play which induce cycles that leave unchanged, and sometimes even reinforce, the initial situation. Figure 5.1 gives two examples of positive feedback.

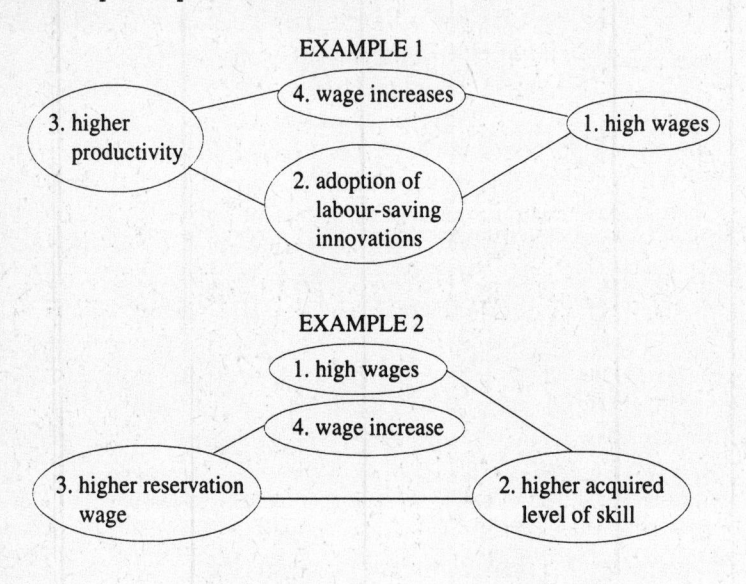

EXAMPLE 1

- 3. higher productivity
- 4. wage increases
- 2. adoption of labour-saving innovations
- 1. high wages

EXAMPLE 2

- 1. high wages
- 4. wage increase
- 3. higher reservation wage
- 2. higher acquired level of skill

Figure 5.1 Positive feedback mechanisms

In the first example in Figure 5.1, the positive feedback procedure works as follows. The presence of high wages encourages the enterprise to introduce best practice technology (1->2) in a way not to alter the capital/labour mix in a static production function, but in a way that increases productivity and leads to innovations (2->3). A variant of the efficiency wage hypothesis underpins the causation from 3 to 4. In effort to sustain high productivity levels through discouraging shirking, retaining key employees, sharing rents or whatever, the enterprise increases wage levels. As a result, the high wage cycle continues. A similar type process is at work in example 2. In this example labour-saving technological innovations substitute both capital goods and higher skills for less skilled labour. Since skilled workers have a higher reservation wage (the level of wage below which a person is unwilling to work) the firm has to increase wages.

Essentially Victorisz and Harrison argue that both positive and negative feedback dynamics exist in the labour market. Positive feedback is a benign story about the linkages between technical change, good productivity performance and high skill and wage levels. In contrast, negative feedback is a malign scenario where a vicious circle exists between low wages, persistent labour-intensive production techniques and poor productivity performance. As a result of the simultaneous presence of these dynamics, a process of divergent development opens up in the labour market, causing discrete segments to emerge. Since it is assumed that mobility is low between the high-productivity and low-productivity segments, the labour market becomes more or less bifurcated into good and bad jobs.

Rather than highlighting labour market discrimination as such, the 'positive' and 'negative' feedback mechanisms developed by Victorisz and Harrison to suggest why some economies become bifurcated into good and bad jobs, with little mobility between the two sectors, could be used to show how obtaining a religiously balanced employment structure in the province is going to be extremely difficult. In particular, as well as having high unemployment, job creation in Northern Ireland occurs along highly dualist lines. On the one hand, many jobs created are low paid, low skilled and precarious – in sectors such as retailing and distribution. On the other hand, a good many relatively secure and well-paid jobs are created in the public sector. With this tendency for jobs to be created either at the lower or higher ends of the labour market, attempts to achieve a more religiously balanced workforce in the province will face major difficulties.

EMPIRICAL STUDIES ON THE SEGMENTATION HYPOTHESIS

This view that the labour market contains centrifugal pressures which causes bounded submarkets to emerge, distinguished both by industry and occupation, encouraged numerous empirical tests on the segmentation hypothesis. The early studies tended to focus on three issues in particular: (i) the existence of distinct labour segments; (ii) differing behavioural patterns within each segment; and (iii) restrictions on mobility between segments (see Rumberger and Carnoy 1980). Overall, these studies were inconclusive, neither fully endorsing or rejecting the segmentation argument. However, they were heavily criticized for using inappropriate data, particularly on the grounds of truncation or selection biases (which tended to increase the co-efficient of segmentation variables and lower the co-efficient of non segmentation variables) and for imprecise theorizing about the problem (Reich 1984).

These criticisms prompted a new and more sophisticated batch of studies on segmentation. Using a variety of statistical techniques, this generation of research attempted to establish whether a dual industrial structure existed, and what its relationship was with unequal labour market outcomes. This empirical work was more proficient than its predecessors, even if it was more restrictive and static. Most of these studies concluded that industrial and labour market variables were positively correlated. But much of this statistical work took place in the absence of a fully developed theoretical framework. As a result, key questions remained unanswered about the nature and scope of duality and segmentation in the labour market. The upshot was that these quantitative investigations could simultaneously conclude that the US industrial structure contained two, three, six and sixteen segments (Buchelle 1989).

With these various generations of empirical studies containing so many blemishes, segmentation labour market (SLM) theory was criticized for being 'sketchy, vague and diverse, if not internally conflicting' (Cain, 1976, p. 1217). Certainly the credibility of SLM theory as an alternative to traditional competitive labour market theories was severely undermined due to these contradictory empirical findings. To some extent, these criticisms halted the empirical search for discrete industrial and occupational segments, although some quantitative work in this tradition has continued.

Perhaps the study by Smith for the Policy Studies Institute (1987) is the best non-orthodox empirical investigation into labour market discrimination in N. Ireland. Smith's methodology was to attempt to quantify how much discrimination there had been against Catholics by controlling in a regression equation for the factors that had been identified by other studies to explain poor Catholic labour market performance. Thus he controlled for location, class and family size, differential labour markets, differential educational qualifications and different age structure. If these factors together were able to explain Catholic advantage, then the equation should have had no shift effect or only a very small one. But Smith's regression exercises using the Continuous Household Survey found a large shift effect; in other words, some other factor or factors beyond the five built into the model were also at play in causing Catholics to have a worse labour market performance than Protestants. Smith concluded, therefore, that much of the shift effect captures discrimination against the minority community. As a result, this study is perhaps the one that comes closest to suggesting that discrimination against Catholics was extreme and virtually systematic.

Because of this controversial conclusion, Smith's work has come in for considerable criticism. Like many non-orthodox studies into labour market disadvantage in the USA, the empirical methodology was called into question. For instance, some argue that his control variables were incomplete. Thus, SACHR (1987) proposes that a dummy should have been inserted into the equation to control for the dynamic of the black economy. Wilson (1989) suggests that the fact that security force employment is virtually entirely Protestant (given Catholic reluctance to join the Royal Ulster Constabulary and the Ulster Defence Regiment) will have distorted the results of the regression by inflating the residual. Another discrepancy found was that the 'chill factor', which refers to the reluctance of members of one community to take a job in a location dominated by the other community, was left out of the model. Yet a further line of attack was that Smith's model itself was relatively unsophisticated, by treating the labour market as being made up of a *stock* of jobs. If he had rather treated the labour market as a *flow* phenomenon, he would have captured a more dynamic picture about Catholic unemployment and other labour market disadvantage. Most of these criticisms have some validity, which suggests that Smith's conclusion was much too bold. At the same time, Smith's exercise cannot be rejected entirely since it does represent the most elaborate attempt so far to quantify how much discrimination has occurred in Northern Ireland.

PRODUCTIVE STRUCTURE AND SEGMENTATION TENDENCIES: (1) FORDISM

In recent years, qualitative and sociological investigations have dominated segmentation-type studies. One important line of enquiry has been the role of productive structures in segmenting labour markets. Closely associated with this view are writers from the French regulationist school. They suggest that the Fordist production system underpinning the golden age of economic growth gave rise to a distinctive form of segmentation (see Boyer 1973). A key dynamic of the Fordist era was the growth of large vertically integrated enterprises, exploiting economies of scale. Within these enterprises, the work process was organized in a highly hierarchial way. Because of the specialization of productive tasks, there occurred a vertical differentiation of the job structure. Moreover, individual employees were closely supervised and monitored through a range of techniques such as time and motion studies. This type of work organization was a form of Taylorism, so named after the founder of 'scientific management', Frederick Taylor.

Thus employment and career progression within the characteristic Fordist factory was organized on a rigid vertical ranking system (Aglietta 1979). Work tasks associated with the bottom rung were invariably routine and standardised. Further up the ladder, the worker gained supervisory and production planning functions, as well as greater control over the setting up and maintenance of machines. As a rule, promotion of workers meant that they became more and more involved in the process of supervision and control of less skilled and less qualified manpower. Thus there was a tendency for bipolar job structures to emerge in the Fordist factory involving those engaged in relatively menial and rudimentary tasks and those responsible for monitoring and supervising such activity. During the 1950s and 1960s, this process resulted in large numbers of 'marginal workers' being recruited into unskilled industrial jobs throughout western Europe. Thus Sengenberger (1982) shows how German companies resolved their labour scarcity problems by bringing Turkish and other foreign workers into the German labour market with the status of 'guest workers'. Gallie (1983) highlights that French employers acted in a similar way, resulting in a huge traffic of labour from Algeria and other north African countries to France. In Britain, workers from former colonies were mass recruited for standardized and routine tasks. Overall the evidence suggests that Taylorism created a tendency towards 'enterprise-centred' labour market segmentation.

Berger and Piore (1980) argued that in addition to the 'Taylorist effect', bifurcation tendencies arose out of attempts by large firms to hedge against uncertainty. Under their stylization, the period of intensive growth resulted in large-scale enterprises catering to predictable and more or less stable product markets. However, in addition to this stable component of demand there were also volatile and cyclical markets. To service this fluctuating portion of demand, large enterprises tended to develop sub-contractual relationships with small firms. When demand was buoyant in these fluctuating markets, work was passed on to the small firms, but when times were bad many of these enterprises were squeezed as orders dried up. In other words, to reduce uncertainty the large firm created a web of commercial networks which could be activated at peak demand periods and stood down in a recession. Meantime the large-scale enterprises continued to serve stable markets, allowing steady state profits. As a result of this commercial behaviour, the economy was divided into two main sectors: a stable core where employment was fairly continuous, if not always rewarding, and a periphery where unpredictably and precariousness ruled both product and labour markets.

SEGMENTATION AND REGIONAL ECONOMIC SYSTEMS

But Fordism is not the only productive system giving rise to segmenation dynamics. A popular theme in regional studies at the moment is the idea of spatially concentrated forms of commercial activity. These geographically-based economic systems can take a number of forms. In some instances they may involve one or two big employers or industries dominating the local economy. Examples of this type of spatial system in the past were those localities reliant on industries such as shipbuilding, coal or steel. Current examples are more likely to lie in some aspect of the financial or services industries, like Atlanta in the USA, or Cite Scientique outside Paris. Other cases are reminiscent of Marshall's idea of industrial districts, where clusters of inter-related firms produce a range of goods and services for a limited number of markets. Northern Italy and Baden Württenburg in Germany are widely regarded as the supreme examples of such commercial arrangements.

Although somewhat distinctive, these various forms of spatial economic systems share the common objective of attempting to capture external economies of scale. A number of economic benefits arise from the presence of external economies of scale: the existence of external commercial institutions sensitive to the needs of local business; the right type of human capital and skill base; and commercial and market know-how that lowers transaction costs. Now the cohesion and efficacy of these geographically defined productive systems do not arise spontaneously. Rather they emerge and are sustained by the social ties and traditions of the particular locality. These social institutions and norms operate to supplement the normal competitive rules governing business behaviour. Thus regionally-based economic activity is held together by a subtle blend of co-operation and competition between firms.

Doeringer *et al* suggest that in some cases the presence of social institutions and norms in regional economic zones compromises, if not totally replaces, the textbook competitive employment system (1986). In their study of different fishing ports in Massachusetts they found kinship rather than competitive employment arrangements. Essentially their argument is that in kinship employment systems external non-market conventions govern the labour market rather than the price dynamic. Clearly this process works in highly distinctive ways and in line with the prevailing political and cultural traditions of an area.

But one arrangement seen as cutting across different experiences is the 'extended internal labour market'. For the most part, the extended internal labour market (EILM) is about employers using informal linkages with outside communities as recruitment channels. Manwaring (1981) suggests that an EILM can take a number of forms. Whereas in areas of high social stability, the EILM can either be structured or unstructured, locations with low social cohesion invariably produce unstable EILMs. A defining feature of a structured EILM is that the enterprise's recruitment is embedded within a local community. People from the locality establish a queue for a job in the enterprise and when a job becomes available it is filled from this waiting list. Personnel management (if it exists at all) plays only a passive role, since it merely manages the process. The outside queue and the enterprise are connected by a variety of social and personal links – key workers already inside the plant, for instance, may act as information linkages between prospective employees and management.

The unstructured EILM is a much looser arrangement in which queues for jobs are not established in the local community and where the personnel manager exercises considerable discretion over the recruitment procedure. Nevertheless people from the firm's vicinity are taken on in large numbers and usually represent the majority of the workforce. Normally unstructured labour markets arise where a large firm which offers higher wages and job security dominates the local economy. In this situation, there is always a high level of demand by local workers for jobs in the enterprise, and with a greater pool of applicants for vacancies management can afford to pick and choose. The unstable EILM often emerges in areas such as greenfield sites or new towns, where there are no firmly rooted social traditions. In these locations, employers cannot maximize the benefits from an EILM such as using it as a screening device or as a method to save on recruitment costs. Nevertheless, the employers are eager to form an

EILM of sorts since it is seen as a route to creating a loyal and stable workforce.

Extended internal labour markets are usually beneficial to both managers and workers. For employees an EILM means that members of a social network or community can gain access to a stable job and income and enjoy social relations at the workplace. On the other hand, the EILM reduces the moral hazard problem for employers when recruiting. Problems of screening and shirking are lessened as individual recruits are aware that proper behaviour is required if the EILM is not to be undermined. Moreover, the EILM is a useful device to improve the tacit skills necessary for the production process. Whilst an EILM may be self-servicing to both employers and employees in the local area, it also, to some extent, closes the labour market since job opportunities are monopolized by erecting social barriers to entry. In societies where a high degree of social fluidity exists such a dynamic is not a problem. But where a society is segregated either by race or religion, an extended internal labour market may result in one group having preferential employment treatment over another.

In addition to the extended internal labour market, regional economic systems can spawn other non-competitive employment arrangements. Surveys of industrial districts around northern Italy suggest that a key in their success is structured employment relations which creates a system of non-competing groups (see Pyke, ed., 1990). Thus in detailing the success of the knitwear industry in the Madeira Province of Italy, Solinas (1987) suggests that much of it depends on a hierarchial employment system. At the top of the hierarchy are the artisans or craft workers who perform the most skilled and intricate tasks in the production system; in the middle there is an amalgam of skilled workers – technicians, specialists in certain functions and so on; and at the bottom there are groups of semi-skilled and unskilled workers who perform menial jobs, perhaps even on an occasional or infrequent basis. As a result of this employment system, the local knitwear industry is able to combine quality production with a high degree of flexibility. But since little mobility exists between the different tiers of the employment structure, segmentation tendencies arise whereby some groups in the locality are more or less permanently trapped in bad jobs whilst others enjoy stable high-skilled and high-income work.

The notions of the extended internal labour market and kinship networks may be used to investigate instances of local employment systems in the province. Thus for instance Harland and Wolff, the shipbuilding company and Short Bros, the aircraft manufacturer, which have traditionally been large Protestant employers, are frequently held up as examples of a grand conspiracy against Catholics. But it could be argued that these enterprises were at the centre of highly formal and rigid extended internal labour markets. In the past most employees were drawn from the surrounding East Belfast area, which is socially very stable and cohesive. All the features of an extended internal labour market were present; recruitment was normally conducted on a word of mouth basis with existing employees – normally a shop steward – acting as guarantor for the good behaviour and conduct of new recruits.

Other regions in the UK and elsewhere, particularly if they were reliant on traditional heavy industries such as shipbuilding, steel or coal, displayed similar features. Most studies of these areas suggest that extended internal labour markets developed autonomously and were built into the social fabric of the local community. As a result their operation became an unquestioned part of daily routine. Thus the view that the extended internal labour market in East Belfast was engineered and continually manipulated to maintain the dominance of one religious group over another is probably misleading. When presented with the accusation that Catholics were discriminated against in the labour market, many Protestant employers and workers vehemently deny being involved in such practices, and in all likelihood they were not – at least in any direct sense.

Certainly the extended internal labour markets worked to the disadvantage of Catholics, and certainly government passivity in the face of such disadvantage can be called into question. But it is likely that this unfair treatment owes more to the social processes operating in the labour market than to any deliberate discriminatory action. In a similar way, social processes may best account for other apparently sectarian features of Northern Ireland's employment structure. A recent Fair Employment Commission (1990) report revealed that a large number of private sector enterprises employ people from one religious group only. Almost certainly, this employment segregation is the outcome of the province being subdivided into pockets of Catholic-only and Protestant-only areas. Firms in such locations mainly employ people from the local catchment areas, which virtually ensures that the workforce is of the same religion. Rather than being manipulated to exclude a particular religion, this social dynamic reflects the kinship employment systems found by Doeringer *et al.* in Massachusetts. In other words, it could be argued that the strong sectarian tinge to some aspects of the province's labour market is the result of local (mainly rural) communities creating kinship employment networks.

THE ROLE OF ECONOMIC AGENTS IN THE SEGMENTATION PROCESS

So far the argument is that labour market segmentation has its origins in a range of productive and institutional dynamics. But economic agents have also considerable freedom to organize an industry or to structure labour markets from which can emerge good and bad jobs and unequal access to employment opportunities.

For instance, employers within a specific industrial sector or segment can establish an employment system which gives rise to bifurcation tendencies. Perhaps the most notorious example of this type of action has been building employers who have succeeded in institutionalizing casualization and sub-contracting in the construction industry. The building trade is shot through with precariousness. Unpredictability and uncertainty arise from the tendering system, since firms are unsure whether or not they will win contracts. Moreover, construction work is highly seasonal in character with much of the work being done in the summer months. Furthermore, because production occurs on scattered and transitory building sites the industry suffers from a high degree of fragmentation.

In the face of these unstable conditions, employers found it costly and inefficient to maintain a direct labour force. As a result, wholesale casualization and sub-contracting arrangements were introduced into the industry which meant a massive hollowing out of building firms. Now the typical large building firm has a streamline core of administrative and technical staff with other employment contracts based on casual or sub-contracting terms. Thus any construction project involves 'buying in' technical, legal and managerial skills; subcontracting the actual building to teams of bricklayers, carpenters and so on; and hiring unskilled labour on a team basis. Because of these changes, casualization has replaced stability as the main characteristic of the construction industry. And as Bluestone (1971) shows casualization tends to envelope large groups of the workforce into low-skilled and low-paid jobs.

As well as employers, trade unions have the capacity to trigger or embed segmentation tendencies. Rubery (1978) argues that by bargaining over wage levels, terms and conditions of work, and production and technological systems, trade unions have contributed to the formation of structured labour markets. In particular, in defending and promoting the interests of workers, trade unions in many industries have initiated and entrenched demarcation lines, accelerated the moves towards internal labour markets, maintained skill differentials between occupations and so on. The basic thesis is that trade union have been able to influence the work patterns of employees in primary sector industries to the relative exclusion of those in secondary and precarious sectors. As a result, they have contributed to a gap opening up between core and periphery workers. And since the majority of their members are in the primary sector they are unable to effectively challenge this gap, since to do so would be against the direct interests of their constituents. Thus, indirectly at least, worker organization though the exercise of institutional power contributes to the rise and continuation of segmentation tendencies in the labour market.

No satisfactory study has been made on how labour market institutions may have affected discriminatory practices. Andrew Boyd's *Have the Trade Unions Failed the North* (1985) appears a step in the right direction, but it is replete with assumptions about the purpose of trade unions and the relationship between trade unions and politics which most serious scholars of industrial relations would, quite frankly, find amazing. The portrayal of trade unions is one of being compliant dupes or even active agents in the British/Loyalist domination of 'the Six Counties'. By his account, the extent to which trade unions exacerbated sectarian divisions at the workplace, by helping to structure labour markets, was driven by the entirely malign purpose of wanting to exclude Catholics. A subtler account would have recognized that trade union action to defend demarcations and such like was not peculiar to Northern Ireland, but was prevalent across industrialized countries. As a result, where such action occurred in the Province, to the benefit of Protestants at the expense of Catholics, it may have arisen from processes endogenous to certain kinds of labour markets. It would be going too far to say that there was no sectarian tinge to Northern Ireland's employment structure; but a more convincing assertion would be that there was a symbiosis of certain universalistic segmentation influences and certain societal influences – between, for example, aspects of local Protestant culture and standard trade union practice. Moreover, such a fusion is likely to have arisen autonomously rather than through deliberate, conscious action.

Of course it is conceivable that labour market actors may structure the employment relationship in a way that promotes fair employment. This is particularly true for large firms or organizations which have the capacity to establish internal labour markets. Through such arrangements rules and systems can be put in place to marginalize discriminatory practice and promotes equal treatment. For example, more professional recruitment and selection procedures may be introduced, as well as sophisticated job evaluation schemes to encourage fair employment practice. In addition, promotion arrangements can be more effectively monitored for any basis. Because nearly 40 per cent of total employment in N. Ireland is in large public sector organizations there appears considerable scope for such internal organizational initiatives. Public sector organizations are devising some type of schemes in this mould. Thus for example the Civil Service, after amending their human resource management policies to encourage non-discriminatory work practices, are now setting targets for the religious composition of top executive and managerial posts. Other parts of the public service, for example, district councils, are actively taking steps to address possible religious imbalances in their workforces. All in all, this move towards structuring internal labour markets to promote fair employment will become more pronounced.

THE FEEDBACK PROCESS IN LABOUR MARKET SEGMENTATION

Although revealing dynamics behind labour market segmentation, the discussion above has not fully addressed the question why specific employment groups are persistently found in certain occupations. Various studies emphasize the role of social processes and customs in limiting movement between good and bad jobs in the labour market (see Loveridge and Mok 1984 and Craig *et al.* 1982). In the first place, people in skilled and unskilled jobs obtain different work routines and habits. Those in precarious employment, performing low-grade and mundane tasks, tend not to be committed to their enterprise. As a result, turnover is relatively high in such segments, and people accept that regular spells on the dole queue are part of routine. In contrast, skilled employees tend to have a more structured and diligent attitude to work. Because they are able to perform more interesting and demanding tasks, with greater degrees of autonomy, skilled workers have a preference for a stable employment routine. This preference is reinforced by a number of devices such as training programmes, which as well as increasing the human capital of the workers also increase the sense of attachment they have to the enterprise.

Differential work habits and routines give rise to different expectations about the opportunities and rewards offered by the world of work. For the most part, fringe workers have a low evaluation of the returns of work, largely seeing it as the only way of avoiding acute financial hardship. On the other hand, people in better jobs have a more positive assessment of the benefits from employment; for as well as performing relatively rewarding job tasks, they regard work as a route to a modestly prosperous lifestyle. These different expectations about the rewards of employment help generate a process of self-selection in the labour market. At the lower end of the labour market, people with a low evaluation of work opportunities or rewards come to regard a whole range of jobs as being outside their reach. And because they believe that they do not have the skills or competences to operate in the upper tiers of the labour market, they tend to shun training programmes and other initiatives to increase their human capital. As a result, they assign themselves more or less permanently to jobs that require low skills and pay low wages.

The flip side of this scenario is that skilled workers will tend to avoid precarious forms of employment, given the stigma or loss of skill such a move would involve. Such a strategy has led to an increase in what is called 'wait' or 'search' unemployment, which suggests that skilled workers tend to stay on the dole queue rather than take a low-skill job, since this might jeopardize the possibility of moving back into the core of the labour market. In essence the argument is that any type of employment creates socialization processes which mould the behaviour and motivation of individuals.

Piore (1975) argues that these social feedback mechanisms take on an added dimension if certain groups who are confined to the bottom end of the labour market also constitute residential clusters. Attempting to capture the experience of black ghettos and immigrant communities in the USA, he suggests that in such situations community norms emerge which reinforce individual work habits, thus further undermining the possibility of mobility from bad to good jobs. In her studies of a number of Irish immigrant communities in Australia, Leven-Teacey gives an insight into the dynamic of such a norm in a relatively homogeneous community (1988). This study highlighted how people with few skills mostly bypassed the formal labour market and attempted to secure employment through informal methods such as personal contact. Thus rather than regarding levels of human capital as the best method of securing a job, the prevailing opinion was that 'luck', especially with regard to who you knew, was the key to success.

But the thesis that community norms can act as a barrier to mobility between different labour market segments should not be taken too far. For a variety of reasons, people do escape ghetto life and enter jobs at the higher end of the labour market. Moreover, some people in low-grade occupations make tremendous efforts not to recycle the work habits and norms associated with their work amongst friends and family networks. Instead they inculcate the importance of education and training. Thus the social feedback mechanisms Piore talks about are not so encompassing that they place a straitjacket on the lives and choices of individuals. Nevertheless as witnessed by a host of research studies these mechanisms are clearly at play and they do influence people's outlook and behaviour and constrain opportunities.

This line of argument has been under-developed in the local debate on Catholic disadvantage. As a result, many investigations into the subject are unconvincing. For instance Compton (1985) offers an essentially demographic account to explain why Catholics have fared badly, particularly with regard to unemployment rates. In particular, Compton argues that because Catholics have a higher birth rate than Protestants, a higher proportion of them enter the labour market relative to their share in the total working population. As a result, the minority community is more likely to experience higher unemployment. Normally this argument is supplemented by suggesting that since Catholic workers have lower qualifications, they tend to work in sectors which have undergone large contractions and live in unemployment black spots, and so on. The message from this line of analysis is clear enough. Catholics are themselves to blame for poor labour market performance.

To a large extent, this argument reflects studies in the USA twenty years ago suggesting that black under-performance in the labour market could be explained by factors endogenous to the black community – and argument which Piore, for example, sets out to challenge. Compton, however, in developing his thesis apparently feels no obligation to deal with the counter-arguments raised by the social feedback literature. Unsurprisingly, therefore, he fails to address fairly basic yet crucial explanations. For instance, he fails to question why Catholics were crowded into sectors more vulnerable to unemployment shocks, or why Catholics were located in sub-regions with poor employment opportunities. In other words, he virtually takes as given certain economic and social characteristics of the two Communities without questioning whether these features were the outcome of discriminatory dynamics.

Perhaps one of the most disappointing aspects of the debate on employment discrimination in Northern Ireland is the relative absence of studies of how labour market institutions may have caused or accentuated this problem. Probably the best anslysis in this broad social freeback tradition is Howe's (1989) study of work habits and attitudes to employment in two housing estates in the Belfast area. He found that in the face of high unemployment in the formal labour market, many Catholics turned to the black economy as a route to earn income. Furthermore, he discovered that many of those in formal employment were confined to a relatively limited range of occupations – construction for men and retailing and low-level jobs in the public sector for women. To a large extent, Howe's findings coincide with similar investigations elsewhere: that fairly homogeneous racial or religious communities develop distinct work habits and norms. These conventions can lead to the creation of fairly dense employment networks outside the offical labour market and to processes which perpetuate certain employment patterns and characteristics.

SOCIETAL EFFECTS

Finally the extent or prevalence of labour market segmentation varies across societies according to the political regime in place (Rosenberg 1980). At one extreme, governments deliberately segment or bifuricate the employment system for malign racial or religious motives. The apartheid policies of the South African government provide the most notorious case of this type of behaviour. But such full-blown public policies to segment the labour market along racial lines are very much the exception. However, governments and public institutions can indirectly cause or accentuate segmentation tendencies. For instance during the 1950s and 1960s many West European countries contributed to the marginalization of many migrant workers by granting them only guest worker status. And of course when the economic downturn came in the 1970s these workers were the most immediately and disproportionately affected group. In other words, governments rather cynically created rules so that foreign workers would operate as shock absorbers for the indigenous labour force.

Governments can also give an indirect fillip to segmentation influences if they have a loose legal framework for industrial relations. In the 1980s, it became popular to attribute high unemployment to rigidities in the labour markets. Excessive government intervention and too much trade union power were widely seen as the causes of these sclerotic tendencies. To counteract these rigidities a good many governments – with Britain going further than most – introduced a series of measures to reduce their legal and policy interventions in the labour market. As a result, many long-standing social provisions and workers' rights were streamlined. Now since it became easier for employers to recruit part-time and temporary workers as well as to dismiss existing employers, a number of studies concluded that polarization pressures in the labour market were heightened. The distinction between core and periphery workers became highly fashionable. Thus by affording little protection to vulnerable groups in the labour market, governments could be accentuating segmentation and discriminatory employment practices.

Of course if governments pursue public policies prohibiting employment discrimination or promoting equal opportunities, they can reduce segmentation and discriminatory dynamics in labour markets. Thus a general consensus has emerged that the programmes introduced in the United States to tackle the problem of discrimination against blacks in the labour market have produced positive results. Likewise, the anti-discrimination drive in certain Canadian provinces has also been regarded as a success. To a much lesser extent, policies introduced to improve the position of women in the labour market are seen as going some way to improving sex equality at work.

The politics literature on discrimination in N. Ireland is quite extensive. For the most part, this literature has focused on whether or not discrimination has been systematic. Debate on this issue oscillates between two wide extremes. At one end, there is the claim that Northern Ireland was constructed as a 'Protestant state for a Protestant people', which has resulted inevitably in endemic discrimination against Catholics. The incident most commonly wheeled out in support of this view was a speech in 1933 by Basil Brooke, who was later to be Prime Minister for Northern Ireland for twenty years, urging Unionists 'wherever possible, to employ good Protestant lads and lassies' (Farrell 1980). At the other end of the spectrum is the view held by militant Unionists that no discrimination has taken place, and that claims of unfair treatment are simple mischief-making on the part of Catholics. In this account, Catholic over-representation in the unemployment figures and at the lower ends of the labour market can best be explained by the work habits and attitudes within that community. To be fair, few Protestants actually hold such a fundamentalist outlook. As a result, softer and subtler explanations are offered to account for the gap between Protestant and Catholic labour market performance. One argument is that the extent to which the minority community was discriminated against can be explained by it having no loyalty to Northern Ireland, which caused Protestant employers to be cautious and 'safe' in their recruitment. Another view is that discrimination has been practised by both Protestant and Catholic employers and that to focus simply on the former is an impartial and one-sided view of the situation.

No conclusive answer has emerged to the question about whether discrimination was systematic. But it does seem excessive to attribute all actions of discrimination to government action. As stressed throughout this chapter, unequal performance in the labour market can arise from a range of influences that are more or less autonomous from the political system. Thus to explain Catholic disadvantage in the labour market in terms of the actions of the British government or Unionist politicians is inexact and partial.

Equally unconvincing is the contrasting argument most forcibly made by Hewitt (1983) that Catholic grievances about unfair treatment have more to do with the contested constitutional status of Northern Ireland than with any 'exclusionist' practices within the labour market. In particular, he suggests that Catholic complaints about discrimination have the primary purpose of adding backbone to the nationalist campaign for Irish unification. However, there are good grounds for questioning this argument. In the first place, opinion poll data consistently show that whilst an overwhelming majority of Catholics believe that discrimination has taken place against the minority community in the job market, less than half are in favour of a united Ireland. Thus the evidence suggests that most Catholics do not make any automatic connection between job discrimination and the national question.

Moreover, if one were to pursue Hewitt's logic, then the solution to the Northern Ireland problem would be to copper-fasten its union with the rest of the United Kingdom – by measures as the Republic of Ireland removing its constitutional claim over the Province. If such things were done, Catholic dissatisfaction with the political system would evaporate, as would complaints about discrimination and unequal treatment. In the light of twenty years of violence, this outlook appears rather simplistic, if not downright naive.

Certainly, there has been an interaction between Catholic grievance against discrimination and nationalist politics, but perhaps not in the way suggested by Hewitt. Initially, at least, it is plausible to argue that Catholic complaints about discrimination were genuinely felt; they were a real source of grievance and not part of some conspiracy to bolster the nationalist cause. In other words, the question of discrimination was a democratic issue, separate from republican/nationalist politics. However, since the beginning of the present troubles, militant nationalists have succeeded in incorporating these democratic concerns with their campaign for Irish unity. This is particularly true of Sinn Fein in the early to mid-1980s. A consistent theme in its political statements remains that Catholic disadvantage will only be effectively addressed when there is a *nationalist* solution to the Northern Ireland problem. But it was not inevitable that militant nationalists would be able to capture the discrimination issue to their advantage. Their ability to do so largely stems from the failure of the British government's earlier measures to make any substantial impact on Catholic disadvantage. Had these measures been effective, a wedge could well have been driven between that dimension of the problem and the nationalist dimension.

The 1976 Fair Employment Act did, of course, outlaw discrimination, but the Fair Employment Agency it set up to promote equal treatment in the province was a relatively powerless body. These legal and institutional arrangements were also similar to provisions then existing in Britain to address racial discrimination. But, given the turbulences of Northern Ireland politics at the time, and the imperative to marginalize the Provisional Sinn Fein and the IRA, a much more far-reaching initiative was perhaps needed. Whether or not the British government was bogged down with security matters and other similar concerns, a golden opportunity to capture the democratic terrain for itself was missed. The passing of a new and stronger Fair Employment Act in 1989 can be seen as belated recognition that it should have been more purposeful on the matter sooner, and the new Act certainly represents a more concerted drive to promote fair employment in the province. Indeed, Northern Ireland now has what is probably the most extensive anti-discrimination legislation in western Europe, if not the western world.

What prompted the British government to adopt a more resolute approach is a matter of some dispute. The generous assessment is that it took on board the various research studies that were emerging which showed that Catholic disadvantage in the labour market had persisted during the 1970s and 1980s. A less benign view is that the government was simply responding to internal and external political pressures. Externally, as a result of the success of the MacBride Principles campaign, mounted in the USA to highlight alleged discrimination in

Northern Ireland, the government's image with regard to its administration of the province was considerably, if somewhat unfairly, tarnished. Internally it had to do something to check the political advances of Sinn Fein and to promote the fortunes of 'constitutional' nationalists. Whether as a result of political exigencies or enlightened policy making, however, the British government is now promoting a democratic agenda for Northern Ireland.

Whether it will be successful in this project is, unfortunately, open to question. Prevailing labour market conditions could not be more inhospitable. Catholics are approximately two and a half times more likely to be unemployed than Protestants and any drive to lessen Catholic disadvantage within the labour market must attempt to reduce this ratio. However, in the context of high overall unemployment, it is difficult to see how this can be done without *increasing* Protestant unemployment. With no change in total employment, equalization of unemployment rates in the two communities would require the transfer of 50,000 or even more jobs from Protestants to Catholics. Furthermore, with labour market turnover low, at least as regards more secure jobs, it is going to be difficult to change the religious complexion of the workforce in the immediate future. Thus the co-existence of a public policy on discrimination which is strongly interventionist and a labour market resistant to equity pressures may well result in serious political and economic tensions. Whether these will be strong enough to undermine the government's project, it is too early to say.

CONCLUSIONS

The above survey has attempted no more than to highlight the main features of labour market discrimination and segmentation theory and to show how it might be applied to the N. Ireland debate on the issue. Perhaps the key lesson to be drawn from the theoretical literature is that simplistic or one-sided views about any alleged labour market discrimination in N. Ireland must be treated with extreme caution. Invariably such arguments underestimate the complex range of influences that give rise to and sustain unequal treatment in the labour market. Unfortunately even though the debate about religious discrimination in N. Ireland has been going on for over twenty years, most of the studies are narrow and relatively unsophisticated. As a result, crude assertions and explanations that cannot be substantiated continue to dominate the debate. Greater use of some of the theories presented in this chapter may add much needed subtlety and precision to an otherwise now sterile debate.

REFERENCES

Aglietta, M. (1979) *A Theory of Capital Accumulation*, New Left Books, London.

Arrow, K. (1973) 'The Theory of Discrimination', in Ashenfelter, O. and Rees, A. (ed.), *Discrimination in Labour Markets*, Princeton University Press, Princeton, New Jersey.

Aunger, E. (1975) 'Religion and occupational class in Northern Ireland', *Economic and Social Review*, 7, 1, pp. 1–18.

Becker, G. (1957) *The Economics of Discrimination*, University of Chicago Press, Chicago, Illinois.

Becker, G. (1964) *Human Capital: A Theoretical and Empirical Analysis*, National Bureau of Economic Research, New York.

Berg, I. (1981) (ed.) *Sociological Perspectives on Labour Markets*, Academic Press, London.

Berger, S. and Piore, M. (1980) *Dualism and Discontinuity in Industrial Societies*, Cambridge University Press, Cambridge.

Bluestone, B. (1971) 'The characteristics of marginal industries', in Gordon, D. (ed.), *Problems in Political Economy*, D C Heath, Lexington, Massachusetts.

Boyd, A. (1985) *Have the Trade Unions Failed the North?*, Mercier Press, Dublin.

Boyer, R. (1973) 'Productivity and employment structures in France', mimeo, Cepremap, Paris.

Boyer, R. (1979) 'Rapport Salarial et analyses en termes de regulation. Une mise en rapport avec les théories de la segmentation du marché du travail', *Economic Applique*, No. 7, pp. 179–202.

Buchelle, R. (1989) 'Economic Dualism and Employment Stability', *Industrial Relations*, Vol. 22, No. 3, pp. 410–18.

Cain, C. (1976) 'The Challenge of Segmented Labour Market Theories to Orthodox Theories: A Survey', *Journal of Economic Literature*, Vol. 14, No. 4, pp. 1215–71.

Compton, P. (1985) 'An Evaluation of the Changing Religious Composition of the Population in Northern Ireland', *Economic and Social Review*, 16, 3, pp. 201–224.

Cormack, R. and Osborne, R. (1985) 'Employment and Discrimination in Northern Ireland', *Policy Studies*, 9, 3.

Cormack, R. and Osborne, R. (1990) 'Employment Equity in Canada and Fair Employment in Northern Ireland', *British Journal of Canadian Studies*, 4, 2, pp. 33–54.

Cormack, R. and Osborne, R. (eds) (1991), *Discrimination and Public Policy in Northern Ireland*, Clarendon Press, Oxford.

Cormack, R. and Osborne, R. (eds) (1983) *Religion, Education and Employment in Northern Ireland*, Appletree Press, Belfast.

Craig, C. *et al.* (1982), *Labour Market Structure, Industrial Organisation and Low Pay*, Cambridge University Press, Cambridge.

Dex, S. (1986) *The Costs of Discrimination: A review of the literature*, London Home Office, Research and Planning Unit.

Dex, S. (1987) *Women's Occupational Mobility: A Lifetime Perspective*, Macmillan, London.

Doeringer, P. and Piore, M. (1971) *Internal Labour Markets and Manpower Analysis*, Heath, Lexington, Massachusetts.

Doeringer, P. et al., (1986) 'Capitalism and Kinship: Do Institutions Matter in the Labour Market? *Industrial and Labour Relations Review*, Vol. 40, No. 1, pp. 48–61.

Edwards, R. (1979) *Contested Terrain, The Transformation of the Workplace in the Twentieth Century*, Basic Books, New York.

England, P. (1988) *et al.*, 'Explaining Occupational Sex Segregation and Wages: Findings from a Model with Fixed Effects', *American Sociological Review*, Vol. 111, pp. 544–558.

Eversley, D. (1989) *Religion and Employment in Northern Ireland*, Sage, London.

Eversley, D. (1991) 'Demography and Unemployment in Northern Ireland' in R. Cormack and R. Osborne (eds) *Discrimination and Public Policy in Northern Ireland*, Clarendon Press, Oxford.

Farrell, M. (1980) *Northern Ireland: The Orange State*, Pluto, London.

Gallie, D. (1983) *In Search of the New Working Class*, Routledge, London.

Hewitt, C. (1983) 'Discrimination in Northern Ireland', *British Journal of Sociology*, 34, 3, pp. 446–451.

Hewitt, C. (1985), 'Catholic Grievance and Violence in Northern Ireland', *British Journal of Sociology*, 36, 1, pp. 102–105.

Howe, L. (1989), 'Unemployment: Doing the Double and Labour Markets in Belfast', in C. Curtin and T. Wilson (eds), *Ireland From Below: Social Change and Local Communities*, Galway University Press, Galway.

Kuasi Fosu, A. (1990) 'Occupational Mobility of Black Women 1958–81', *Industrial and Labour Relations Review*, Vol. 45, No. 2, pp. 281–298.

Leven-Treacey, C. (1988) 'Labour Market Segmentation and Diverging Migrant Incomes', *Australia and New Zealand Journal of Sociology*, Vol. 17 No. 2, pp. 21–30.

Loveridge, R. and Mok, A. (1984) 'Theoretical Approaches to Segmented Labour Markets', *International Journal of Social Economics*, Vol. 7, No. 5, pp. 376–411.

McNabb, R. and Ryan, P. (1990) 'Segmented Labour Market' in Sapsford, D. and Tzannato, S. *Current Issues in Labour Economics*, Macmillan, London.

Madden, J. (1973) *The Economics of Sex Discrimination*, D C Heath, Lexington, Massachusetts.

Manwaring, T. (1981) 'The Extended Internal Labour Market', *Cambridge Journal of Economics*, Vol. 5, pp. 327–351.

Mill, J.S. (1985) *Principles of Political Economy*, Appleton, New York.

Osterman, P. (1982) 'Affirmative Action and Opportunity: A Study of Female Quit Rates', *Review of Economics and Statistics*, Vol. XIV, pp. 604–612.

Piore, M. (1975) 'Notes for a Theory of Labour Market Segmentation', in Edwards, R. *et al.* (eds), *Labour Market Segmentation*, D C Heath, Lexington, Massachusetts.

Piore, M. (1976) 'The Dual Labour Market: Theory and Applications' in Barringer, R. and Beer, S. H. (eds), *The State and the Poor*, Winthrop, Cambridge, Massachusetts.

Piore, M. (1985) *Birds of Passage*, MIT Press, Cambridge, Massachusetts.

Polachek, S. (1987) 'Occupational Segregation and the Gender Wage Gap', *Population Research and Policy Review*, Vol. VI, 47–67.

Pyke, F. (ed.) (1990), *Industrial Diversity and Interfirm Cooperation in Italy*, International Labour Organisation, Geneva.

Pyke, F. *et al.* (1990) *Industrial Districts and Inter-Firm Co-operation in Italy*, International Institute for Labour Studies, Geneva.

Reich, M. (1984) 'Segmented Labour: Time Series Hypothesis and Evidence', *Cambridge Journal of Economics*, Vol. 18, No. 1, pp. 63–8.

Rosenberg, S. (1980) *The State and the Labour Market*, Plenum Press, London.

Rubery, J., (1978) 'Structural Labour Markets, worker organisation and low pay', *Cambridge Journal of Economics*, Vol. 2, March, pp. 38–53.

Rumberger, R. and Carnoy, M. (1980) 'Segmentation in the US Labour Market: Its effects on the Mobility of Whites and Blacks', *Cambridge Journal of Economics*, Vol. 4, pp. 117–32.

SACHR (Standing Advisory Committee on Human Rights) (1987), *Religious and Political Discrimination and Equality of Opportunity in Northern Ireland*, Cm 237, HMSO, London.

Salais, R. and Thevenot, L. (eds), (1987) *Le travail, marchés, règles et conventions*, Economica, Paris.

Sengenberger, W. (1982) 'Labour Market Segmentation and the Business Cycle', in Wilkinson, F. (ed.), *Labour Market Segmentation and Orthodoxy*, Academic Press, London.

Smith, D. (1987) *Equality and Inequality in Northern Ireland*, PSI Occasional Paper No. 39, Policy Studies Institute, London.

Smith, D. (1988) 'Policy and Research: Employment Discrimination in Northern Ireland', *Policy Studies*, 9, 1, pp. 41–57.

Smith, J. (1984) 'Race and Human Capital', *American Economic Review*, Vol. 4, XXVI, December, pp. 685–698.

Smith, J.P. and Welch, F., (1988) 'Racial Discrimination: A Human Capital Perspective', in Magnum, G. and Philips, P. (eds), *Three Worlds of Labour Economics*, Sharpe, Armonk, New York.

Solinas, G. (1987) 'Labour Market Segmentation and Workers' Careers: The Case of the Italian Knitwear Industry', in Tarling, R. (ed.), *Flexibility in Labour Markets*, Academic Press, London.

Solow, R. (1990) *The Labour Market as a Social Institution*, Basil Blackwell, Oxford.

Thurow, L. (1969) *Poverty and Discrimination*, Brookings Institution, Washington DC.

Thurow, L. (1975) *Generating Inequality*, Basic Books, New York.

Victorisz, T. and Harrison, B. (1973) 'Labour Market Segmentation: Positive Feedback and Divergent', *American Economic Review*, Papers and Proceedings, May, pp. 366–83.

Whyte, J. (1990) *Interpreting Northern Ireland*, Clarendon Press, Oxford.

Wilson, T. (1989) *Ulster Conflict and Consent*, Basil Blackwell, Oxford.

6
WOMEN IN THE NORTHERN IRELAND LABOUR MARKET

Norma Heaton, Gillian Robinson and Celia Davies

INTRODUCTION

Increased participation by women in the labour market is a key trend in western industrialized countries, though there remain unresolved debates as to its nature and causes (Beechey and Perkins, 1987). This development is confusing, because women's participation rates have risen at the same time as the economies of the advanced industrialized countries have been undergoing substantial changes (Jenson, 1988). Whilst the growing importance of the service sector has resulted in more jobs in areas where women have traditionally worked, economic restructuring has had negative effects for those workers who were lowest paid and least covered by legislative protection. Women are often over-represented in such groups. In Britain, there has been extensive research into women's work experiences (e.g. Joshi, 1989 and Martin and Roberts, 1984) and exploration of the growth of part-time work and its effects on job segregation (for example, Robinson, 1988). However, Northern Ireland has rarely, if ever, featured in the debates and research.

As Davies (1991) has argued, economic and social policy in Northern Ireland has been predominantly concerned with inequalities between the Catholic and Protestant 'communities' and often only between Catholic men and Protestant men. Inequalities between women and men either in terms of religion or more generally have been given much less priority. Indeed, it was still possible in the early 1980s to justify the exclusion of women from employment analyses on the grounds of 'the importance of the male in Northern Ireland society'

(Aunger, 1983). More recently, Smith and Chambers (1991) chose to analyse only men in in their explanation of the unemployment gap between Catholics and Protestants.

Research into women's employment in Northern Ireland has been carried out by relatively few people. The analyses of Trewsdale and Trainor (1979, 1981, 1983) and Trewsdale (1987, 1990) concentrated for the most part on comparing the characteristics of the female labour force in Northern Ireland with those of the Republic of Ireland and Great Britain. More recently McWilliams (1991) has highlighted similarities and differences between employment opportunities of Protestant and Catholic women.

This chapter makes comparisons between women in Northern Ireland and Great Britain, and also examines the labour market position of Catholic and Protestant women in Northern Ireland. The Northern Ireland Labour Force Survey for 1991 is the main data source, but the analysis also draws on the findings of the Women's Working Lives Survey (Kremer and Montgomery, 1993).

The first section examines the extent to which women participate in the labour market in Northern Ireland, the influence of children on women's employment status, and the hours worked by women. In the next section, the focus is more on the quality of participation in terms of the occupations in which women are employed and the hours they work. Although we know that the growth in female employment has been largely associated with an increase in part-time jobs (see for example Northern Ireland Economic Council, 1992) very little is known about the quality of these jobs. For instance, one of the major data sources of employment in Northern Ireland, the Fair Employment Commission annual census, omits employees who work for less than sixteen hours, thereby restricting analysis of Catholic and Protestant women's job levels to employees with at least some statutory employment rights. As a result, the status of women working part-time, in terms of the proportion engaged in low-paid, low-security jobs, and the amount in higher paid employment with better conditions remains a blur. The third section concentrates on the labour market experience of Protestant and Catholic women. Finally, we discuss the issues raised and implications for future research.

THE EXTENT OF PARTICIPATION

According to the Labour Force Survey data, women in 1991 comprised 43 per cent of all people of working age in employment (see

Table 6.1 below). This is exactly the same proportion which is found in Great Britain in that year (*Employment Gazette*, 1992) and certainly destroys the myth of 'the male breadwinner' in Northern Ireland once and for all. Moreover, this figure of 43 per cent is very similar or even higher than that found in other industrialized countries. Windsor (1990) shows that in Australia women also comprise 43 per cent of the workforce, while within the EEC only Denmark has a higher share of women in employment (Commission of The European Communities, 1992).

Table 6.1 shows the breakdown of people of working age in employment, in Great Britain and Northern Ireland, based on their own assessment of whether they worked full-time or part-time. The figures include self-employed people, who accounted for 6 per cent of working women and 20 per cent of working men in Northern Ireland.

Table 6.1 People of working age in employment (1991)

	Northern Ireland			Great Britain		
	Full-time	Part-time	Total	Full-time	Part-time	Total
Men	55	2	57	54	3	57
Women	28	15	43	25	18	43
Total	83	17	100	79	21	100

Source: Labour Force Surveys Northern Ireland and Great Britain

Notes: These figures exclude those who did not say whether they worked full-time or part-time.

Whilst useful, the table does not tell the whole story, particularly with regard to the division between full-time and part-time work. As noted in the Northern Ireland Economic Council Report (1992) on Part-Time Working, the definition of part-time work varies. In particular, the Census of Employment data defines as part-time anyone working for thirty hours a week or less, while for the Labour Force Survey, workers themselves make an assessment as to whether they are full-time or part-time. This creates difficulties if attempts are made to cross reference from one source to the next. In assessing themselves, some people will regard anything less than thirty-eight hours a week as part-time – this might, for example, constitute a four- as opposed to a five-day week. In general, the Census of Employment, which counts jobs rather than people, reports more part-time workers than the Labour Force Survey. Thus, in 1989, 25 per cent of workers in Northern Ireland were classified as part-time in the Census of Employment, compared to just under 20 per cent in the Labour Force Survey (NIEC,1992).

Overall, the figures suggest that approximately 66 per cent of working women in Northern Ireland were in full-time employment, compared to 58 per cent in Great Britain. However, a more accurate picture can be obtained by examining actual hours worked. Table 6.2 shows the proportion of women working over thirty hours, between sixteen and thirty hours, and less than sixteen hours. This last division is important since only those employees who work for sixteen hours or more are entitled to the same statutory employment rights as full-time employees. These include access to pension provision, maternity leave, sick pay and holiday entitlement. The table shows that 15 per cent of women in Northern Ireland worked less than sixteen hours a week in 1991, and as a result fell below the plinth of rights automatically enjoyed by other workers, while the corresponding figure in Great Britain was higher, at 18 per cent.

Table 6.2. Usual weekly hours of women of working age, 1991 (per cent)

	Northern Ireland	Great Britain
0–15	15	18
16–30	24	24
31 or more	61	58

Source: Labour Force Surveys, Northern Ireland and Great Britain

These figures confirm that part-time work is an integral dimension to the labour market position of women. Around two in five women in Northern Ireland work less than thirty hours a week: the proportion is slightly higher in Great Britain. Moreover, more than one in seven women in Northern Ireland work in the 'precarious' less than sixteen hours category, where only those employed for more than eight hours a week, and with five or more years service have the same statutory rights as a full-time employee.

Far from being a minority of workers, women in Northern Ireland may well gradually move into a position where they make up the majority of employees (Morrissey, 1991). This possibility is not always fully realized as women in the local economy have lower economic activity rates, compared to those in Great Britain: in 1991, as Table 6.3 shows, the respective figures were 62 per cent in Northern Ireland and 71 per cent in Great Britain. A large part of the explanation for this differential is the higher unemployment in Northern Ireland. Thus for instance the economic activity rates for men in Northern Ireland are also lower than those of their counterparts in Great Britain – 85 per cent, compared to 88 per cent. If the economy in Northern Ireland were to improve, the numbers and proportion of women working would probably increase further.

At the same time, there are some important differences in the pattern of participation of women in Northern Ireland and Great Britain. Conventionally, a key influence on women's participation in the labour market is seen to be their need to care for their children. In particular, in Great Britain it is the age of the youngest child that is regarded as a major determinant of women's employment status (Martin and Roberts, 1984). Table 6.3 shows the employment levels of economically active women in Northern Ireland and Great Britain by age of youngest dependent child.

Table 6.3 Women's economic activity rates, by age of youngest dependent child, 1991 (per cent)

	Northern Ireland		Great Britain	
	All	In employment	All	In employment
Women aged 16–59	62	57	71	66
With youngest dependent child aged:				
0–4	55	49	49	43
5–10	56	51	72	67
11–15	56	52	78	74
Without dependent children	69	63	77	72

Source: Labour Force Surveys, Northern Ireland and Great Britain

Note: In the Labour Force Survey, people are counted as economically active if they are either (a) in employment or (b) they are unemployed but available to start work in the following fortnight, and had looked for work at some time in the previous four weeks or were waiting to start a job already obtained.

The table shows that the economic activity rate of women in Northern Ireland was lower than that of their counterparts in Great

Britain whether they had dependent children or not. It also confirms a trend of increasing participation in the labour market of women with pre-school children, which is a move away from the general view of this matter. As Cohen (1990) has shown, in the United Kingdom as a whole, the proportion of mothers with a child under five in paid employment rose from 29 per cent in 1985 to 37 per cent in 1988. The Labour Force Survey suggests that, in Great Britain in 1991, 43 per cent of women whose youngest child was under five were working, while the proportion in Northern Ireland was even higher, at 49 per cent. In Great Britain, however, levels of economic activity increase rapidly once children reach school-going age, whereas the data here suggest that for women in Northern Ireland levels of economic activity change little with increasing age of dependent children.

But on this last point, it should be noted that the Women's Working Lives Survey (Kremer and Montgomery, 1993) found that, in Northern Ireland, the proportion of women in employment and with dependent children did increase as their youngest child grew older: from 44 per cent when the youngest child was under five, to 57 per cent when the youngest child was aged five to ten, and 61 per cent when the youngest child was aged eleven to fifteen years.

Overall, however, it is clear that, while in Great Britain levels of economic activity increase rapidly once children reach school age, the participation rate of mothers in Northern Ireland does not increase to the same extent. What is not clear is why this should be so. It has been suggested by McWilliams (1991) that it reflects the lower availability of part-time work and also the negative impact of male unemployment on wives' take-up of part-time work (a point to which we return when looking at Catholic and Protestant women at work in Northern Ireland). It is also likely to be a reflection of the poor childcare and after-school facilities in Northern Ireland compared to other parts of the United Kingdom (Cohen, 1990). As Montgomery (1993) points out, 'it is relatively more easy and more common to obtain child-care facilities for pre-school children through the extended family system in Northern Ireland than to make arrangements for children to be collected after school and also cared for during the school holidays'.

None of these explanations has been proven one way or the other. But two factors that certainly have a strong influence on female participation rates are the types of job and hours of work available for women. The next section, therefore, considers the industries and occupations where women are most likely to work, and looks at the hours for which they are employed. In combination, these give an

THE QUALITY OF PARTICIPATION

Table 6.4 gives the industrial breakdown of men's and women's jobs together with the hours worked by women. The standard classifications have not been used here, but instead those divisions where most women work have been highlighted. Details of the divisons used are included in Appendix A, along with a table showing men's and women's work by industrial division within the conventional classification.

The importance of the service sector is clear – only 16 per cent of women were working in non-service areas, compared to 46 per cent of men. More than 20 per cent of working women were employed in distribution, hotels and catering and, of these, only half worked for more than thirty hours a week. In education, too, a high proportion of women worked for less than thirty hours a week. Putting this another way, half of all jobs involving less than sixteen hours a week were found in the distribution, catering, hotels and education divisions

Table 6.4 Industry division of men and women of working age in Northern Ireland, 1991 (per cent)

Industry division	Men	Women	Hours worked by women		
			<16	16–30	over 30
Distribution, hotels, catering and repairs	16	21	21	28	51
Financial services	7	9	10	16	73
Education	5	13	22	35	44
Medical and health	3	14	4	28	68
Other public sector	11	10	9	15	76
Other services	12	17	23	30	47
Non-service industries	46	16	7	1	79
All industries	100	100	15	24	61

Source: Labour Force Survey Northern Ireland

Note: Industrial classifications used are detailed in Appendix A

Table 6.5 shows the occupations held by men and women, and again includes a breakdown of the hours worked by women. The categories have been derived from the standard occupational categories, to illustrate the areas where women actually work. The details are shown in Appendix B, together with a table containing the breakdown with the more usual classification.

Table 6.5 Men's and women's occupations in Northern Ireland, 1991 (per cent)

	Men	Women	Hours worked by women		
			<16	16–30	over 30
Managers and administrators	17	8	3	12	85
Professional occupations	10	10	6	35	59
Associate professional and technical occupations	5	10	6	22	72
Clerical and secretarial occupations	9	25	6	20	74
Craft and related occupations	27	5	3	10	87
Personal services	2	14	20	27	53
Sales occupations	7	23	37	35	28
Plant and machine operatives	14	4	4	10	86
Other occupations	9	1	6	22	72
All occupations	100	100	15	24	61

Source: Labour Force Survey Northern Ireland

Note: the occupational categories were derived from standard occupational classifications – see Appendix B.

Not surprisingly, the pattern of occupations held by men and women is quite different. Clerical, secretarial and sales occupations accounted for almost half of all the jobs held by women in 1991. Approximately one in six working women were employed in the 'personal services' sector, which includes catering, childcare and hairdressing. On the other hand, two out of five working men were involved in a craft or craft-related occupation, or employed as a plant or machine operative. Far more men than women were managers or administrators – 17 per cent compared to 8 per cent.

But what of the hours worked by these men and women? It is widely accepted that female part-time employees are generally engaged in unskilled, low-graded and low-paid jobs, mainly in service industries. We also know that part-time employment is growing, partly in response to employers' desire for increased 'flexiblity' – the use of part-time labour may produce cost advantages for employers in both manufacturing and service industries (Robinson, 1988). Thus as the NIEC (1992) report demonstrates, more than 97 per cent of the increase in female employment in Northern Ireland between 1971 and 1989 was accounted for by part-time jobs. Nevertheless, not all part-time employment is of the low-grade/low-pay type. Some progressive employers (primarily but not exclusively in the public sector) do have provision for part-time employees in higher-status jobs with correspondingly higher pay and better prospects. It is worth noting that 94 per cent of working men were engaged in employment for over thirty hours a week. With regard to women in the better-paid occupations, it is clear that the vast majority of managerial jobs involved working for more than thirty hours a week. The professional occupations (teaching, health and so on) offer more scope for part-time work particularly in the sixteen to thirty hours category. However, in the lower-paid occupations of sales and personal services far more of the jobs involved lower hours, presumably resulting in very low take-home pay. About three-quarters of the clerical and secretarial jobs were in the thirty hours and over category, with very few involving less than sixteen hours.

One of the surprising findings, in view of moves towards greater 'flexibility' was that approximately 86 per cent of female operative jobs were full-time. However, as Horrell and Rubery (1991) have shown, manufacturing establishments have differed from both public and private services in their use of part-time working to extend operating hours, preferring to use voluntary overtime and shiftworking. Horrell and Rubery found that it was the private service sector which was most reliant on part-timers – this is confirmed by the Labour Force Survey data. What we have overall, then, is a picture of a minority of women in Northern Ireland working full-time in high-status, highly-paid jobs. More than a third of working women are employed in personal services and sales where poor-quality part-time work is associated with low weekly hours.

To a large degree then the pattern of employment for women is set by the different combinations of industries, occupations and hours prevailing in the economy. For example, the non-service industries are organized along the lines of a 'male' model of employment, with full-time work very much the norm for men and women. On the other hand, within the service industries, some occupations where women predominate – primarily sales and personal services – are characterized by having many 'small' jobs. At an intermediate level are the jobs in the 'professions' where between a fifth and a third of jobs held by women are part-time, but with over sixteen hours. These different 'terms' of female work raise questions about the way in which jobs are perceived and designed – an issue which is discussed further in the concluding section.

PARTICIPATION OF CATHOLIC AND PROTESTANT WOMEN

Previous research (McWilliams, 1991 and Heaton, 1992) has shown that the level of economic activity for Catholic women is lower than that for Protestant women in Northern Ireland. Analysis of the 1991 Labour Force Survey data confirms this: restricting the analysis to women of working age, 65 per cent of Protestant women were economically active, while the corresponding figure for Catholic women was 56 per cent. Moreover, 12 per cent of Catholic women were unemployed compared to 6 per cent of Protestant women. The previous year's figures were much closer – 7 per cent for Protestant women, and 9 per cent for Catholic women (PPRU,1992). Much is made of the unemployment rate for Catholic men being two and a half times that of Protestant men. Thus, the Standing Advisory Committee on Human Rights has recommended that the Government should set a target for a reduction of this differential to one and a half (Fair Employment Commission, 1991) However, the Labour Force Survey data suggest that the female Catholic/Protestant differential should be regarded as equally important.

McLaughlin (1993) points out that a net flow of women out of employment occurs when their husbands are unemployed, resulting in a polarization between couples where both are unemployed and those where neither are. Using data from the Women's Working Lives Survey, she demonstrates that the discouraging effect of male unemployment on female unemployment was a phenomenon affecting nearly four times as many Catholic women as Protestant women surveyed. In another piece, McLaughlin, Millar and Cooke (1989) found that the wives of unemployed men were deterred from taking up or staying in part-time work by the low amount that they could earn before pound for pound deductions were made from households' unemployment benefit or income support. This may provide part of the explanation for the differences in participation of Catholic and Protestant women in full-time and part-time work. The figures are in Table 6.6.

Table 6.6 Women in employment by age group, religion and work category (Northen Ireland, 1991) (per cent)

Age group	Catholic		Protestant	
	Full-time	Part-time	Full-time	Part-time
16–24	85	15	85	15
25–34	79	21	70	30
35–44	61	39	55	45
45–59	49	51	52	48

Source: Labour Force Survey, Northern Ireland

For the youngest age group, the divisions between full-time work and part-time work were exactly the same for women from the two communities. However, for the next two age groups (25–34 and 35–44) Catholic women were more likely to be in full-time employment than Protestant women. For the oldest age group the situation was reversed, with rather more Catholic women now working part-time.

The quality of participation of Catholic and Protestant women is explored further in Tables 6.7 to 6.10. First, in Tables 6.7 and 6.8, the industry divisions and hours worked are shown. Here, there are some notable differences. There were more Protestant women in both the relatively high paying financial services sector, and the low-paying distribution and hotels industries. On the other hand, a higher proportion of Catholic women were employed in education and also in health-related jobs where the difference is particularly striking – 18 per cent of Catholic women were working in this sector, compared to 11 per cent of Protestant women.

Overall, and contrary to popular opinion, the pattern of 'quality' of participation between women in both communities is not totally clear cut. For when figures for hours worked are examined they show that a higher proportion of Protestant women than Catholic women working for less than 16 hours a week – the figures were 16 per cent for Protestant women and 14 per cent for Catholic women. A higher proportion of Catholic women overall worked for more than thirty hours a week – 64 per cent compared to 58 per cent of Protestant women. This is also true for every division except education. For both Catholic and Protestant women, approximately two-thirds of all jobs involving less than sixteen hours a week were located in three sectors: distribution/hotels, education and other services. However, there were far fewer Catholic women working less than sixteen hours a week in the medical and health category.

Table 6.7 Industry division of Catholic women of working age, by hours of work (Northern Ireland, 1991) (per cent)

Industry division	Proportion of sample	Hours worked <16	16–30	over 30
Distribution, hotels, catering and repairs	19	22	25	53
Financial services	6	2	14	84
Education	15	24	34	42
Medical and health	18	2	25	74
Other public sector	8	13	13	74
Other services	19	18	29	53
Non-service industries	15	7	9	84

Source: Labour Force Survey Northern Ireland

Note: Industrial classifications used are detailed in Appendix B

Table 6.8 Industry division of Protestant women of working age, by hours of work (Northern Ireland, 1991) (per cent)

Industry division	Proportion of sample	Hours worked <16	16–30	over 30
Distribution, hotels, catering and repairs	22	21	32	47
Financial services	10	12	18	70
Education	12	20	36	44
Medical and health	11	7	32	61
Other public sector	12	9	17	74
Other services	17	25	30	45
Non-service industries	17	8	16	76

Source: Labour Force Survey Northern Ireland

Note: Industrial classifications used are detailed in Appendix B

Tables 6.9 and 6.10 show the occupations and hours in which Catholic and Protestant women were working. The overall occupational breakdown is similar for both Catholic and Protestant women

– see the proportions in managerial jobs, and the professional and associate professional occupations, for example. This is very much the pattern identified in previous research. Aunger (1983), for example, has commented on the fact that the division of the educational system into Protestant and Catholic schools creates the need for large numbers of Protestant and Catholic teachers.

The major differences occur in clerical/secretaral jobs, and in sales jobs, where a higher proportion of Protestant than Catholic women work. There are also interesting differences as to the hours worked in the different occupational groupings. Within most of the occupational groupings, Catholic women were more likely than Protestant women to work in excess of thirty hours a week. The most striking example is in the clerical and secretarial occupations, where 81 per cent of Catholic women worked for more than thirty hours a week, compared to 70 per cent of Protestant women.

Over-representation of Protestant women in clerical occupations and sales jobs has been noted in previous research, for example in analysis of census data up to 1981 (Gallagher, 1991). The 1991 data suggest that, overall, the different opportunity structures for Catholic and Protestant women in sales jobs, and in the finance sector, are the most striking examples of continuing inequality. Further, detailed study of individual sectors such as these may be one way forward in the research agenda. Such studies could incorporate, for example, detailed analyses of recruitment and training policies and practices, to shed some light on the disparities between opportunities for Catholic and Protestant women.

CONCLUSION: IMPLICATIONS FOR FUTURE RESEARCH

This chapter has sought to comprehensively explore the true extent of women's contribution to the Northern Ireland labour market and to emphasize that gender is an important principle, both in the contemporary structuring of the labour market and in the opportunities, or lack of them, that it displays. Gender inequality is not of course the only form of inequality in the labour market. Religious disadvantage is another acute aspect of the employment system in Northern Ireland. But research on gender inequality has played an important part in opening up debate about the differences between Protestant and Catholic women. Moreover, from the figures presented in this chapter it is not unreasonable to suggest there might be two rather different

Table 6.9 Occupational classification of Catholic women of working age, by hours of work (Northern Ireland, 1991) (per cent)

	Proportion in sample	Hours worked <16	Hours worked 16–30	Hours worked over 30
Managers and administrators	6	2	14	83
Professional occupations	10	1	38	61
Associate professional and technical occupations	12	2	23	74
Clerical and secretarial occupations	23	5	14	81
Craft and related occupations	7	2	9	89
Personal services	16	19	22	59
Sales occupations	21	40	34	26
Plant and machine operatives	4	0	8	92
Other occupations	1	17	33	50
All occupations	100	14	23	64

Source: Labour Force Survey Northern Ireland

Table 6.10 Occupational classification of Protestant women of working age, by hours of work (Northern Ireland, 1991) (per cent)

	Proportion in sample	Hours worked <16	Hours worked 16–30	Hours worked over 30
Managers and administrators	8	5	12	83
Professional occupations	9	9	32	58
Associate professional and technical occupations	9	8	20	72
Clerical and secretarial occupations	27	7	24	70
Craft and related occupations	5	4	12	84
Personal services	12	8	32	50
Sales occupations	25	36	36	28
Plant and machine operatives	4	7	12	81
Other occupations	1	0	0	100
All occupations	100	16	26	58

Source: Labour Force Survey Northern Ireland

female labour forces, shaped on the one hand by what they have in common as women but also on the other hand by influences related to their respective communities. The clear unemployment differential between women in the two communities, and the way this has been ignored in policy discussion and debate, is the most striking example of this point. Clearly, far more research is needed as to the causes of higher female Catholic unemployment, and ways in which the female Catholic/Protesatnt unemployment differential can be reduced.

Turning to the question of the quality of women's participation in the labour market, we have shown that there is little evidence of 'flexibility' affecting the way jobs are constructed in the non-service industries in Northern Ireland. However, there are very different opportunities for full-time and part-time work, depending on industry and occupation. Beechey and Perkins (1987), in their analysis of part-time jobs, suggested that certain jobs had been constructed as part-time jobs because they were seen as women's jobs. We have shown similarly that, notably in sales and personal services jobs, where women form the majority of the workforce, the predominant model is that of many part-time jobs. On the other hand, where men form a majority of the workforce, such as in manufacturing, the model of full-time work is the norm also for women.

A crucial issue for future research, then, must be the way in which jobs are designed. Australia provides some recent and accessible examples of attempts to transform career structures within occupations. Top down, comprehensive sectoral reviews have been undertaken, resulting in the broadbanding of occupations, the restructuring of jobs, and the redesign of career and training paths. At the same time, local initiatives have complemented these comprehensive schemes. A shop stewards industrial democracy project, for example, carried out a redesign of the the company wages system so that the wages system did not contribute to a widening of pay differentials between skilled and unskilled; that it encouraged all workers to expand their skills and undertake training; and that the company specifically invested in labour by promoting opportunities for the largest occupational group (process workers and machine operators) to upgrade their positions (Windsor, 1990, see also O'Donnell and Hall, 1988. Windsor insists:

> Improving employment opportunities for women needs to go beyond strategies to reshuffle the existing jobs: what must be questioned is the fundamental design of a work process that divides job opportunities into primary positions – offering job security, job satisfaction and favourable pay and conditions – and secondary positions, which are often part-time

or casual, which involve few opportunities for developing, applying or rewarding skill, which have no career prospects and which are highly vulnerable to redundancy in restructuring processes (Windsor, 1990:140).

Finally, we have shown that whilst there are many striking similarities in the pattern of jobs held by Catholic and Protestant women in Northern Ireland, there are some notable disparities. Detailed sectoral reviews must address this issue – as well as that of male/female inequalities – if we are to move forward towards to a fairer division of labour.

ACKNOWLEDGEMENT

This chapter was prepared as a collaborative exercise, under the auspices of the Centre for Research on Women, University of Ulster. We are grateful to the Policy Planning and Research Unit for providing the 1991 Labour Force Survey data on which the analysis is based.

APPENDIX A

Men and women of working age, by industrial division in Northern Ireland, 1991

Industrial division	Women	Men
0 – Agriculture, forestry and fishing	0.8	6.9
1 – Energy and water supply	0.5	1.2
2 – Mineral extraction	0.4	3.0
3 – Metal goods	2.3	9.4
4 – Other manufacturing	11.8	11.9
5 – Construction	0.6	13.4
6 – Hotels, distribution	21.1	15.7
7 – Transport and communication	1.6	6.7
8 – Financial services	8.8	6.6
9 – Other services	52.2	25.2

Revised groupings used in Tables

Industrial division	Industrial code	Revised divisions
0	500–502	Non-service
1	503–514	Non-service
2	515–558	Non-service
3	559–633	Non-service
4	634–724	Non-service
5	725	Non-service
6	726–741	Hotels, distribution
7	742–754	Transport and communication
8	755–774	Financial services
9	775–817 broken into:	
	797-811	Other services
	775-784	Public sector
	785-790	Education
	812-817	Education
	791-796	Medical and other health services

APPENDIX B

Men and women of working age, by standard occupational classification.
Northern Ireland, 1991 (per cent)

SOC	Women	Men
1 – Managers and administrators	7.8	17.4
2 – Professional occupations	9.9	9.8
3 – Associate professional and technical occupations	10.0	5.4
4 – Clerical and secretarial occupations	25.0	8.9
5 – Craft and related occupations	5.3	26.5
6 – Personal and protective service occupations	13.9	4.4
7 – Sales occupations	11.0	5.1
8 – Plant and machine operatives	3.9	14.0
9 – Other occupations	13.2	8.6

Revised groupings used in Tables

Major groups	Minor groups	Revised groups
SOC 1	Remains same	1
SOC 2	Remains same	2
SOC 3	Remains same	3
SOC 4	Remains same	4
SOC 5	Remains same	5
SOC 6	Split into:	
	60-61	6 Security
	62-69	7 Personal
SOC 7	Remains same + 95 (other sales)	8 Sales
SOC 8	Remains same	9
SOC 9	Remains same – 95 (other sales)	10 Other occupations

REFERENCES

Aunger, E. (1983) 'Religion and Class: an Analysis of 1971 Census Data' in Cormack, R. and Osborne, R. *Religion, Education and Employment: Aspects of Equal Opportunities in Northern Ireland*, Appletree Press. Belfast.

Beechey, V. and Perkins, T. (1987) *A Matter of Hours*, Polity Press. Cambridge.

Cohen, B. (1990) *Caring for Children – the 1990 Report*, Family Policies Study Centre. Edinburgh.

Commission of the European Communities (1992) 'Women of Europe: Supplement No 36', CEC.

Davies, C. (1991) 'Reforming the Agenda' in Davies, C. and McLaughlin, E. (eds) *Women, Employment and Social Policy in Northern Ireland: a Problem Postponed?*, Policy Research Institute. Belfast.

Employment Gazette (1992) 'Women and the Labour Market: Results From the 1991 Labour Force Survey' (September), HMSO. London.

Fair Employment Commission (1991) 'A Profile of the Workforce in Northern Ireland – A Summary of the 1990 Monitoring Returns', *Research Report No 1*, FEC, Belfast.

Gallagher, A. (1991) 'Employment, Unemployment and Religion in Northern Ireland', *The Majority Minority Review* No. 2, University of Ulster,. Coleraine.

Heaton, N. (1992) 'Women in Paid Work in Northern Ireland', *International Journal of Manpower* Vol. 13, Nos 6/7.

Horrell, S. and Rubery, J. (1991) 'Gender and Working Time: an Analysis of Employers' Working-Time Policies', *Cambridge Journal of Economics* Vol. 15.

Jenson, J., Hagen, E. and Reddy, C. (eds) (1988) *Feminization of the Labour Force – Paradoxes and Promises*, Polity Press. Cambridge.

Joshi, H. (1989) *The Changing Population of Britain*, Basil Blackwell, London.

Kremer, J. and Montgomery, P. (eds) (1993) *Women's Working Lives*, HMSO, London.

McLaughlin, E. (1993) 'Unemployment' in Kremer, J. and Montgomery, P. (eds) '*Women's Working Lives*', HMSO, Belfast.

McLaughlin, E., Millar, J. and Cooke, K. (1989) *Work and Welfare Benefits*, Avebury, Aldershot.

McWilliams, M. (1991) 'Women's Paid Work and the Sexual Division of Labour' in Davies, C. and McLaughlin, E. (eds) *Women, Employment and Social Policy in Northern Ireland: a Problem Postponed?*, Policy Research Institute.,Belfast.

Martin, J. and Roberts, C. (1984) *Woman and Employment – a Lifetime Perspective*, HMSO, London.

Montgomery, P. (1993) 'Paid and Unpaid Work' in Kremer, J. and Montgomery, P. (eds) *Women's Working Lives*, HMSO. Belfast.

Morrissey, H. (1991) 'Different Shares: Women,Employment and Earnings' in Davies, C. and McLaughlin, E. (eds) *Women, Employment and Social Policy in Northern Ireland: a Problem Postponed?* Policy Research Institute. Belfast.

Northern Ireland Economic Council (1992) 'Part-time Employment in Northern Ireland' Northern Ireland Economic Development Office. Belfast.

O'Donnell, C. and Hall, P. (1988) *Getting Equal*, Allen and Unwin, London.

Policy, Planning and Research Unit (1992) '1991 Labour Force Survey. Religion Report' ,PPRU, Belfast.

Robinson, O. (1988) 'Part-time Employment and Segregation' in Walby, S. (ed.)

Gender Segregation at Work, Open University Press, Milton Keynes.
Smith, D. and Chambers, G. (1991) *Inequality in Northern Ireland,* Clarendon Press, Oxford.
Trewsdale, J. (1987) 'The Aftermath of Recession: Changing Patterns of Female Employment and Unemployment in Northern Ireland', *Womanpower* No. 4, Equal Opportunities Commission for Northern Ireland, Belfast.
Trewsdale, J. (1990) 'Labour Force Characteristics' in Harris, R., Jefferson, C. and Spencer, J. (eds) *The Northern Ireland Economy: a Comparative Study in the Economic Development of a Peripheral Region,* Longman, London.
Trewsdale, J. and Trainor, M. (1979) 'Womanpower No 1: A Statistical Survey of Women and Work in Northern Ireland', Equal Opportunities Commission for Northern Ireland, Belfast.
Trewsdale, J. and Trainor, M. (1981) 'Womanpower No 2: Recent Changes in the Female Labour Market in Northern Ireland', Equal Opportunities Commission for Northern Ireland, Belfast.
Trewsdale, J. and Trainor, M. (1983) 'Womanpower No 3 :The Impact of Recession on Female Employment and Earnings in Northern Ireland', Equal Opportunities Commission for Northern Ireland, Belfast.
Windsor, K. (1990) 'Making Industry Work for Women', in Watson, S. (ed.) *Playing the State: Australian Feminist Interventions,* Verso, London.

7
FOREIGN DIRECT INVESTMENT AND INDUSTRIAL DEVELOPMENT IN NORTHERN IRELAND

Douglas Hamilton

The globalization of production has been a major trend over the last few decades with transnational corporations (TNCs) increasingly operating across national boundaries. While there are significant examples of companies which have operated outside of their own country since at least the beginning of this century, the last ten years have witnessed a substantial increase in this trend. During the 1980s the world economy experienced a huge increase in flows of foreign direct investment (FDI): outflows of FDI from the seven major OECD countries increased almost fourfold between 1980 and 1990 (OECD, 1992), a rate of growth substantially faster than that in GDP, international trade or domestic investment in these economies.

A small, open, peripheral and regional economy such as Northern Ireland has not been immune to these changes in the structure of international production. During the 1960s there was a large inflow of FDI into Northern Ireland and a major plank of industrial policy since 1945 has been the attraction of new investment from outside the region through various and substantial forms of financial and other assistance. However, despite the clear significance of such changes in industrial structure and of policy for industrial development in Northern Ireland over such a long period of time, little research has been carried out which has analysed in any detail the extent and effects of foreign investment on the regional economy.[1] This is surprising, not only because of the importance and high profile which is attached to the attraction of foreign investment in Northern Ireland and the substantial role which it has and continues to play, but also because of the extensive academic and policy debate which has taken place on the costs and benefits of such investment. Over the last forty years or more there have been few, if any, evaluations of the effectiveness of policy towards FDI and little information has been available on what might be regarded as straightforward aspects such as the number of externally-owned firms operating in Northern Ireland.

It is difficult to be clear on the reasons for the relative neglect of FDI in Northern Ireland in terms of research, analysis, monitoring and overall policy evaluation. Negligence and a lack of interest on the part of both researchers and policy makers could be suggested. What is clear is that the role and impact of FDI in Northern Ireland and the public resources that are expended make it imperative that the process of research and analysis is developed. In this context this chapter builds on work recently carried out and published in NIEC (1992).[2]

The first part of the chapter looks at recent trends and characteristics in FDI worldwide and some of the main reasons that have been put forward to explain the phenomenon. This section discusses the various forms which FDI has taken, the origins and destinations of FDI and, importantly, the range of issues that have been raised about the role and impact that FDI may have on recipient economies. The actual contribution which FDI makes in the Northern Ireland economy is then analysed, particularly in terms of the number of plants and employment. Data are presented in terms of country of ownership, industry and spatial distribution within the region. Relevant comparisons are made with the role of FDI in the Republic of Ireland. In the final section recent policy towards FDI in Northern Ireland is assessed. In conclusion a number of suggestions are made on how policy towards FDI should be implemented and how research in this important area could be usefully developed.

THE GLOBALIZATION OF PRODUCTION

To say that transnational corporations and by definition FDI are important components of the world economy is to state the obvious. It is now widely recognized, if only from casual empiricism, that economic organizations span the world and are by no means restricted to their own country of ownership. This is evident from McDonald's US hamburger restaurant in Moscow to the recent huge investments made by the Japanese car manufacturers, Nissan and Toyota, in England. Perhaps less realized is the level of such investment across national boundaries and the extent of involvement of transnational corporations in many countries. 'Foreign owned subsidiaries account for well over 30 per cent of manufacturing turnover in Australia, Belgium, Canada and the Republic of Ireland, 20–30 per cent in Austria, France, Germany, Portugal and the UK and 10–20 per cent in Denmark, Italy, Norway, Sweden, Turkey and the US – but less than 10 per cent in Finland and Japan' (Vickery, 1992, p. 12). In terms of flows of FDI there has been an almost fourfold increase in the level of outflows of FDI from OECD countries from $48.9bn in 1980 to $193.5bn in 1990, although this is estimated to have fallen to $153.7bn in 1991 (OECD, 1992). Moreover it has been estimated that TNCs now account for 70–80 per cent of world trade through intra-firm transactions in countries outside the former centrally planned economies (Cowling, 1990).

In terms of the geographic distribution of FDI flows it is clear that there have been substantial changes during the 1980s. The US and the UK had both the largest level of outflows and inflows in 1980, accounting for 66 per cent of total flows. By 1990 both countries had become net recipients of FDI, rather than net exporters, and their joint share of overall FDI flows had fallen to 39 per cent. This was particularly the case for the US during the second half of the 1980s, although the estimates for 1991 suggest that the US has reverted to being a net exporter of FDI. In terms of outflows of FDI Japan became the principal investing country in 1989 overtaking both the US and the UK. Germany and France have also become major investors of capital abroad but, in contrast to the US and the UK, outflows of FDI far outweigh inflows in these two countries. Although growing, outflows from countries in South East Asia, such as South Korea and Taiwan, are still relatively small. Indeed Julius (1991) has pointed out 'contrary to popular perceptions in the developing world, the bulk of foreign direct investment takes place within the industrialised countries' (p. 15). 'The share of the Third World has dropped to under 20 per cent, despite the rapid in-flow of foreign investment into the Far East and a recent revival in international interest in Latin America' (Vickery, 1992, p. 12). In terms of inflows the US became the main host country for FDI during the 1980s and, in anticipation of the Single European Market, substantial levels of FDI have also come into EC countries.

Major changes have also occurred in the industrial composition of FDI. In line with general structural changes in developed economies during the 1980s, the service sector has grown in importance in terms of FDI, in particular financial and trade-related services. However, transnational manufacturing production continues to lead the globalization process and is still common in high-technology industries such as computers, electronics and chemicals and in assembly industries like cars. In terms of the form FDI takes the traditional type has been branch plants. However, increasingly cross-border mergers, acquisitions and strategic alliances have become more prevalent. In Europe mergers and acquisitions have taken place as companies have restructured as a result of developments in the EC. In addition, strategic alliances have increased in sectors to offset high R&D and manufacturing costs or to gain access to more extensive distribution networks. Moreover, international diversification has been achieved by companies through joint ventures, non-equity investments and technical agreements.

Vickery (1992) has argued that the huge increase in FDI has been motivated by five major objectives:

— to facilitate the penetration of foreign markets such as the US and the EC;
— to take advantage of the opportunities provided by technological change;
— to secure a presence in all the big centres of production and consumption including North America, Europe and the East Asia;
— to keep costs down, in particular those related to labour; and
— to increase global flexibility in production and distribution (p. 12).

In general these objectives suggest that there are particular benefits to be obtained by TNCs in terms of expected returns on FDI which outweigh the risk and uncertainty that is associated with investment outside the domestic economy. Daniel (1991) suggests that 'in a sense, FDI is a product of rent-seeking on a global scale, whether those rents are generated by natural monopolies or regulatory barriers. Less pejoratively, FDI can be viewed as linked to the pattern of trade; it is in fact a substitute for trade where, for some natural, technological or regulatory reason, trade opportunities are restricted' (p. 2). From a Marxist perspective the growth in FDI reflects the evolution of a new international division of labour so that profits or surplus value can be extracted from host countries or regions at the expense of labour and with the associated cost of uneven development.

FDI – GOOD OR BAD?

In the past decade there has been a general liberalization in the approach taken by many countries towards the attraction of transnational corporations. With the exception of certain countries, in particular Japan and to some extent the US, the fear of foreign domination of key domestic sectors has receded causing policy towards FDI to be more welcoming and liberal. This observation is important as it touches upon the extensive debate on the contribution of foreign investment to national economic development.[3]

On the positive side, the main benefit highlighted from the successful attraction of FDI is the possibility of substantial numbers of jobs, both directly in the form of employment in the foreign-owned plant or company and indirectly in terms of the multiplier effects of new investment. Not surprisingly it is this aspect of FDI which has been given most emphasis by development agencies, especially in areas suffering from endemic unemployment such as Northern Ireland. Other claimed benefits associated with FDI are that it can give rise to new capital, industries and skills and, in particular, new technology which otherwise may not have developed. In addition, more efficient management and production techniques may be introduced both directly in foreign-owned companies themselves and indirectly in indigenous companies through positive spillover effects.

On the downside, the claim is that the supposed benefits of FDI simply do not materialize. With regard to employment generation many jobs may be created by the attraction of FDI, but they often last for only short periods of time as companies either contract or close down production as soon as the economic environment worsens, or when the initial benefits of the incentives package ends. Moreover, it is argued that foreign firms mainly create low-quality jobs in terms of both the level of wages and skills. In addition, few positive backward linkages may be developed with local indigenous industry as only a limited degree of local sourcing may be pursued by the foreign firms. In the case of Northern Ireland this has in fact found to be the case (NIEC, 1986).

A further criticism is that foreign-owned plants in peripheral economies tend to undertake little research and development (R&D) activity. Low R&D activity in foreign plants leads to the production of low value-added products and increases their vulnerability to closure since they are not central to the overall performance of the TNC. In Northern Ireland Harris (1991) shows that the externally-owned sector is dominated by relatively unsophisticated and low-grade operations. In the absence of strong regulation foreign-owned plants may also incur certain environmental costs, such as pollution, because of their relatively low degree of allegiance to the particular location. Recent cases in Cork and Derry have highlighted this problem in Ireland.

Yet another possible shortcoming with the operation of foreign-owned companies is that they tend to reinvest only a small proportion of the profits they create in the host economy. Through the process of transfer pricing, which allows externally-owned companies to reduce artificially the value of inputs and increase the value of outputs through intra-firm trading, a high degree of profit repatriation can take place from low tax jurisdictions. In the case of the Republic, for instance, such a process is openly encouraged by the very tax incentives which are used to attract FDI in the first place. Thus in the Republic the level of capital outflow associated with profit repatriation totalled over IR£2bn in 1990, amounting to around 10 per cent of the economy's GNP. Profit repatriation alongside little domestic sourcing highlights the purely asembly nature of much FDI in many peripheral economies. This leads to the importation of a high level of inputs together with a high export propensity. The net effect of this on the host country's balance of payments can be substantial and unclear.[4]

In conclusion the critics of FDI argue that foreign ownership can leave the destiny of an economy, especially a small, regional economy like Northern Ireland, highly sensitive to the fortunes, corporate resource deployment and decision making of a small number of foreign-owned companies whose economic allegiance to the local economy is at best marginal. In other words 'the fundamental issue relates to the assymetry of power between corporation and community, which derives from the transnationality of the corporation – and the international perspective and flexibility which that implies – compared with the locational rigidity of a specific, local regional or national community' (Cowling, 1990, p. 12). In these circumstances it is difficult for governments to ensure that decisions made by TNCs coincide with the interests and priorities of the local economy. In a similar vein to this dependency theory argues that a national or regional economy, which is highly dependent in terms of its economic, political, social and technological inter-relationships on one or a small number of more advanced and more dominant economies, can never, or at least will have severe difficulties in developing successfully to its full potential.[5]

A PROFILE OF FDI IN NORTHERN IRELAND

The only systematic source of information on the role and contribution of FDI in Northern Ireland relates to employment. Inevitably this restricts the scope of the analysis – other important aspects of foreign ownership are output, trade, investment, profitability and capital flows – nevertheless employment is a key variable in terms of policy and general industrial structure. Moreover an employment analysis of foreign-owned companies in Northern Ireland allows comparisons to be made with the Republic[6] for which similar data are available.

Table 7.1 Externally-owned manufacturing plants in Northern Ireland by country of ownership

Country	Number 1973	Number 1986	Number 1990	% of Total 1973	% of Total 1986	% of Total 1990
GB	290	148	121	83	61	58
US	31	37	30	9	15	14
Canada	4	4	4	1	2	2
RoI	15	32	25	4	13	12
Rest of EC	8	16	20	2	7	10
Far East	0	1	4	0	0	2
Other	3	6	3	1	2	1
Total	351	244	207	100	100	100

Sources: NIERC; Northern Ireland Economic Council (NIEC)

Table 7.1 shows that in 1990 there were 207 plants in Northern Ireland which were externally-owned, a decrease of 144 or 41 per cent since 1973.[7] Between 1986 and 1990 the number of externally-owned plants fell by thirty-seven. In terms of the nationality of the externally-owned plants almost 60 per cent were British in 1990, followed by the United States (14 per cent), the Republic (12 per cent) and countries within the EC (10 per cent). Only four plants in 1990 were identified as being owned from the Far East. Looking at the changes over time the most significant trend has been the falling number of British-owned plants, a decrease of 169 or 58 per cent over the period 1973 to 1990. Indeed Table 7.1 shows that 83 per cent of externally-owned plants were British in 1973. The number of US-owned plants reached a peak in 1986 but by 1990 had fallen back to a total of thirty. Likewise the number of plants owned from the Republic doubled between 1973 and 1986, standing at twenty-five in 1990. The biggest increase is seen in plants owned in the EC, especially Germany, the Netherlands and France.

Table 7.2 shows that the 207 externally-owned plants in Northern Ireland in 1990 employed just over 41,000 people. This represents a fall of almost 600 since 1986, but a huge fall of over 46,000 or 53 per cent since 1973. This substantial decline in the overall level of externally-owned employment has led to a significant decrease in the proportion of total manufacturing employment in Northern Ireland accounted for by externally-owned plants – from 53 per cent in 1973 to 39 per cent in 1990. In other words, employment in externally-owned plants fell much more rapidly than the overall level of manufacturing employment in Northern Ireland. Indeed of the decline of almost 60,000 in overall manufacturing employment between 1973 and 1990 almost 80 per cent took place in externally-owned plants. If only employment in non-UK plants is considered then the proportion of overall manufacturing employment accounted for by foreign companies actually increased from 14 per cent in 1973 to 17 per cent in 1990.

Table 7.2 Employment in externally-owned manufacturing plants in Northern Ireland by country of ownership

Country	Employment			% of Total		
	1973	1986	1990	1973	1986	1990
GB	64,445	22,331	23,259	74	54	57
US	17,344	11,654	9,282	20	28	23
Canada	606	808	951	1	2	2
RoI	1,379	3,012	2,718	2	7	7
Rest of EC	2,579	2,875	3,155	3	7	8
Far East	0	13	1,496	0	0	4
Other	1,208	957	224	1	2	1
Total	87,561	41,650	41,085	100	100	100
Percentage*	52.8	39.5	38.6			

Sources: NIERC; NIEC

Note: * Employment in externally-owned plants as a percentage of total manufacturing employment.

In terms of nationality over half of the employment in 1990 was in British plants, followed by the US (23 per cent). The Republic and other EC countries each accounted for around 8 per cent of employment in externally-owned plants. As in the analysis of the number of externally-owned plants, the most significant changes in employment took place in British plants with a decrease of over 41,000 or 64 per cent over the period 1973 to 1990. This compares with a fall in employment in non-UK plants of 23 per cent over the same period. Indeed, British plants accounted for 89 per cent of the fall in externally-owned employment between 1973 and 1990 and 69 per cent of the overall fall in manufacturing employment. US employment also fell steadily over the same period with a decrease of just over 8,000 or 46 per cent and in 1990 accounted for 23 per cent of total employment in externally-owned plants, slightly above the proportion in 1973 but below that in 1986. Although the number of plants owned from the EC (excluding the Republic) rose significantly over the period 1973 to 1990, employment in these plants grew by only 580 reflecting the small size of these plants. Only by 1990 was there any significant employment in Far Eastern plants but this totalled just 1,500.

Table 7.3 shows that of the 41,085 employed in externally-owned plants in 1990 almost 70 per cent were employed in just three industrial groupings, textiles and clothing (34 per cent); electrical and instrument engineering (18 per cent); and food, drink and tobacco (17 per cent). These figures show a high concentration of FDI in the more traditional and declining industries with the exception of electrical and instrument engineering industry. This level of concentration has actually increased over the period 1973 to 1990 from 65 per cent to 69 per cent despite significant falls in employment in externally-owned plants in all of the industrial sectors. Thus employment in externally-owned plants in textiles and clothing fell by over 13,000 (48 per cent), in food, drink and tobacco by over 9,000 (56 per cent) and in electrical and instrument engineering by over 6,000 (45 per cent). A particularly significant and well documented decline in employment (Fothergill and Guy, 1990a) took place with the closure of a number of large externally-owned plants in the chemicals and man-made fibres industry. Between 1973 and 1986 employment in externally-owned plants in this industry declined by almost 9,000 or 80 per cent. Two reasons were found for these plant closures. First, there were general long-term and adverse structural shifts in demand in the industry. Second, the Northern Ireland plants were selected for closure because of the role they played within their respective companies, particularly in terms of their factory size and product range.

Table 7.3 Employment in externally-owned manufacturing plants in Northern Ireland by main industrial sector

SIC	Industry	Employment			% of Total		
		1973	1986	1990	1973	1986	1990
21–24	Mineral products	1,663	991	1,022	2	2	2
25, 26	Chemicals & man-made fibres	11,234	2,281	2,774	13	5	7
31	Metal goods	1,691	723	306	2	2	1
32	Mechanical engineering	4,319	1,884	1,481	5	5	4
33, 34, 37	Electrical & instrument engineering	13,385	5,745	7,329	15	14	18
35, 36	Transport equipment	2,204	2,639	2,027	3	6	5
41, 42	Food, drink & tobacco	16,350	8,358	7,113	19	20	17
43–45	Textiles & clothing	27,212	14,133	14,160	31	34	34
47	Paper, printing & publishing	1,631	1,591	1,486	2	4	4
46, 48, 49	Other manufacturing	7,872	3,305	3,387	9	8	8
	Total	87,561	41,650	41,085	100	100	100

Sources: NIERC; NIEC

In order to assess the importance of FDI across industrial groupings it is important to look at the proportion of employment in each industry accounted for by externally-owned plants. In this respect there are wide differences between industries. The electrical and instrument engineering and chemicals and man-made fibres industrial groupings had 70 per cent or more of their employment in externally-owned plants in 1990. This contrasts with the metal goods; mineral products; and mechanical engineering industries which had significantly lower levels of externally-owned employment. In general those industries which in 1990 had high concentrations of FDI also experienced such shares in 1973. The exception was the food, drink and tobacco industry in which external ownership fell from 64 per cent in 1973 to 37 per cent in 1990.

In terms of nationality there is a high concentration of British ownership in the textiles and clothing industry with British owned plants accounting for 86 per cent of externally-owned employment in this industry. Over 50 per cent of all British owned employment in Northern Ireland was in this industry in 1990. British ownership is also particularly high in the food, drink and tobacco industrial grouping and in electrical and instrument engineering. In 1990 US-owned firms were most heavily concentrated in the chemicals and man-made fibres; electrical and instrument engineering; food, drink and tobacco; and textiles and clothing industrial groupings. Employment in plants owned from the Republic is most prevalent in the electrical and instrument engineering; and food, drink and tobacco industries. Employment in other EC owned plants, especially those from Germany, France and the Netherlands covers a wide range of industrial activities.

THE 'TROUBLES'

An important factor in explaining the performance of foreign-owned companies in Northern Ireland and, in particular, the relative success of the development agencies in attracting new FDI has been the impact of the political situation over the past two decades. Previous studies have argued that the 'troubles' have had a particularly harmful impact by limiting the amount of new FDI coming to Northern Ireland and, to a lesser extent, the level of new investment by existing foreign-owned companies has been lowered. Mergers and takeovers of indigenous industry by foreign-owned companies may also have been reduced. It is commonly agreed that the adverse impact of the 'troubles' was at its height during the 1970s when manufacturing employment was as much as 25,000 below what it would have been, but that during the 1980s employment loss, though still significant, was reduced.[8] Estimates covering both the 1970s and early 1980s attributed job losses in manufacturing due to the 'troubles' in the range 40,000 to 46,000.[9] These estimates suggest, not surprisingly, that Northern Ireland is severely handicapped as a location for FDI by the continuation of the 'troubles'.[10]

In summary there were just over 200 externally-owned plants in 1990 employing 41,000 people, around 39 per cent of total manufacturing employment in Northern Ireland. Since 1973 employment in externally-owned plants fell by over 46,000 or 53 per cent and the number of plants by 41 per cent. This rapid decline, due largely to falls in employment in British owned plants, led to a significant and continuous reduction in the dependence of manufacturing employment on externally-owned plants from over 50 per cent in 1973 to 39 per cent in 1990. The majority of externally-owned employment has been in British plants although this has fallen considerably since 1973. Thirty US-owned plants accounted for 23 per cent of employment in externally-owned plants in 1990. While there has been a general decline in employment across all industrial sectors, most externally-owned employment (34 per cent in 1990) has been in the textiles and clothing industry, a traditional and declining industry, while 18 per cent was in the more modern electrical and instrument engineering industry.

THE REPUBLIC OF IRELAND

In order to assess the level of FDI in Northern Ireland it is particularly appropriate to compare the degree of employment in externally-owned plants with that in the Republic. Like Northern Ireland the Republic has pursued highly active policies towards the attraction of FDI, similar to those pursued by the Industrial Development Board (IDB) and its predecessors, and they are both economies which are peripheral to the major European and international markets.

Table 7.4 Externally-owned manufacturing plants/companies* in Northern Ireland and the Republic of Ireland by country of ownership in 1990

Nationality	Northern Ireland		Republic of Ireland	
	Number	% of Total	Number	% of Total
GB/UK	121	58	357	36
US	30	14	225	23
Canada	4	2	25	3
RoI	25	12	—	—
Rest of EC	20	10	201	20
Far East	4	2	14	1
Other	3	1	164	17
Total	207	100	986	100

Sources: NIERC; NIEC; Department of Industry and Commerce (1990)

Note: * The figures for Northern Ireland refer to the number of plants, while those for the Republic of Ireland refer to companies.

Table 7.4 shows that in 1990 there were just over 980 foreign-owned companies in the Republic of which 36 per cent were UK owned, 23 per cent US owned and 20 per cent owned from countries within the EC.[11] These figures show a lower proportion of British firms in the Republic than in Northern Ireland but a higher proportion of US and EC companies. The more illustrative employment figures for foreign-owned plants/companies in Ireland are shown in Table 7.5. These figures show that in contrast to the data for the number of companies almost half of all foreign-owned employment in the Republic in 1990 was in US owned companies (reflecting their relatively large size), with UK and EC companies accounting for 19 per cent and 15 per cent respectively. The proportions for US- and UK-owned employment are the converse to the situation in Northern Ireland where British employment dominates. In both economies employment in plants/companies from the Far East was relatively low.

Table 7.5 Employment in externally-owned manufacturing plants/companies in Northern Ireland and the Republic of Ireland by country of ownership in 1990

Nationality	Northern Ireland Employment	% of Total	Republic of Ireland Employment	% of Total
GB/UK	23,259	57	16,900	19
US	9,282	23	43,800	48
Canada	951	2	2,800	3
RoI	2,718	7	-	-
Rest of EC	3,155	8	13,900	15
Far East	1,496	4	1,900	2
Other	224	1	11,400	13
Total	41,085	100	90,700	100

Sources: NIERC; NIEC; Department of Industry and Commerce (1990)

Table 7.6 shows that in 1990 the proportion of industrial employment accounted for by foreign-owned plants/companies in the Republic was considerably higher than in Northern Ireland – 45 per cent compared with 39 per cent. Moreover, over the period 1973 to 1990 there was a substantial increase in this proportion in the Republic from 31 per cent in 1973. This contrasts with a falling dependence on employment in externally-owned plants in Northern Ireland from 53 per cent in 1973 to 39 per cent in 1990. These contrasting trends clearly reflect the greater success of the Republic in attracting substantial amounts of FDI compared with Northern Ireland.

Table 7.6 Externally-owned manufacturing employment as a percentage of total manufacturing employment

	1973	1986	1990
Northern Ireland	53	39	39
Republic of Ireland	31	43	45

Sources: NIERC; NIEC; IDA

The information presented in Table 7.7 shows that there are significant differences in the industrial breakdown of foreign-owned employment in Northern Ireland and the Republic. The main differences are that in Northern Ireland there is a much lower concentration of FDI in metals and engineering, 27 per cent compared with 46 per cent in 1990, and a much higher concentration in the textile and clothing industries, 34 per cent compared with 13 per cent in the Republic. The other main difference is that in 1990 Northern Ireland had only half the proportion of employment in the chemicals and man-made fibres industry compared with the Republic.

Table 7.7 Percentage shares of employment in externally-owned manufacturing plants/companies in Northern Ireland and the Republic of Ireland by industrial sector

Industry	Northern Ireland		Republic of Ireland	
	1986	1990	1986	1990
Mineral products	2	2	5	4
Chemicals & man-made fibres	5	7	12	12
Metals & engineering	26	27	42	46
Food, drink & tobacco	20	17	16	14
Textiles & clothing	34	34	15	13
Paper, printing & publishing	4	4	2	2
Other manufacturing	8	8	7	8
Total manufacturing	100	100	100	100

Sources: NIERC; NIEC; IDA

As a proportion of total employment in each industry, FDI in Northern Ireland was more important in the paper, printing and publishing, and food, drink and tobacco industrial groupings than was the case in the Republic in 1990. Both Northern Ireland and the Republic have experienced particularly high degrees of foreign ownership in the chemicals industry, 70 per cent and 75 per cent respectively, but there was a significantly higher level of foreign ownership in the metals and engineering industry in the Republic in 1990 – 59 per cent compared with 35 per cent. By contrast, 52 per cent of employment in the textiles and clothing industry in Northern Ireland was accounted for by externally-owned plants in 1990 compared with just 47 per cent in the Republic. These figures suggest that in general foreign-owned companies in the Republic are associated with the more 'modern' industrial sectors while in Northern Ireland FDI has been largely concentrated in the 'traditional' industries which have been in long-term decline. The duality in the Republic's industrial base between a modern, dynamic and relatively more technologically advanced sector associated with foreign investment and a traditional, declining and relatively low-technology based Irish-owned sector has been highlighted elsewhere.[12]

Much of the information presented above comparing the manufacturing sectors in Northern Ireland and the Republic highlights the contrasting experiences of industrial development in the two parts of Ireland. In Northern Ireland total employment in manufacturing declined by 36 per cent between 1973 and 1990 with an even bigger reduction in employment of 53 per cent experienced in externally-owned plants. In contrast the contraction of the industrial base in the Republic has been mild with total industrial employment declining by just 11 per cent over the period 1973 to 1990, with most of this collapse in employment occurring in Irish companies, although 16,000 jobs were lost in British companies between 1977 and 1990. Foreign-owned companies in the Republic actually increased employment by 27 per cent over this period even allowing for the decline in employment in British companies. This contrasting experience of Irish-and foreign-owned industry in the Republic has been highlighted by a number of commentators (NESC, 1982 more commonly known as the Telesis Report, and O'Malley, 1989) who have suggested that it can to some extent be explained by the strong emphasis of industrial policy since the early 1970s on attracting foreign investment. However, these commentators do not suggest that foreign companies have held back indigenous development, although it is clear that, due to low linkages, branches of transnational corporations have not helped to promote the development of indigenous companies. Rather it is argued that in the absence of effective policy intervention, wider economic factors, in particular the established competitive strengths of transnationals in world export markets, have greatly limited indigenous development.

It also seems likely that the contrasting experiences of the foreign-owned sectors in Northern Ireland and the Republic have been largely due to the adverse effects of the 'troubles'. While employment in British-owned companies has declined substantially in both Northern Ireland and the Republic, employment in other foreign-owned companies has increased in the Republic but fallen in Northern Ireland. Given the comparable incentives packages which have been available for foreign investors since the early 1970s in both parts of Ireland,[13] the 'troubles' would seem to be a major reason for the lack of success in increasing the foreign-owned component of manufacturing employment in Northern Ireland.

In summary the process of de-industrialization experienced in Northern Ireland over the past twenty years, due largely to the fall in employment in externally-owned plants, in particular British plants, contrasts with the late industrialization of the Republic's economy which has been almost exclusively due to the attraction of a large level of FDI. The outcome of these divergent trends has been the evolution of two manufacturing sectors in both parts of Ireland which reflect similar ownership structures in terms of their high dependence on foreign-owned companies, though quite different characteristics in terms of industrial composition (Hamilton, 1993). Not surprisingly a major reason for the contrasting experience of FDI in the two parts of Ireland would seem to be the adverse impact of the political situation in Northern Ireland.

POLICY ASSESSMENT

The attraction of new industry through the use of a wide range of financial and other incentives has been a major strand of industrial policy in Northern Ireland since 1945 when selective financial assistance was first introduced under the Industries Development Act (NI). This policy was further strengthened in 1951 with the introduction of automatic financial assistance for new capital investment. Since that time a wide range of other incentives has been introduced in an attempt to attract foreign investment to Northern Ireland against increasing competition from other development agencies. These incentives, which are also used to develop indigenous industry, include the provision of advance factories, industrial derating, electricity subsidies and various types of grants with specific aims such as the encouragement of research and development (R&D) activity.[14]

Despite the range of these incentives, which is one of the most generous in Europe, only on rare occasions over the last forty years or more has there been any external and published evaluation of the effectiveness of this policy in terms of the impact of FDI on economic development in Northern Ireland. For example, a major review of economic and industrial strategy by Quigley (1976) devoted only a few paragraphs to a discussion of FDI.

Apart from the obvious point about the public accountability of government policy, there are two main reasons why the effectiveness of policy towards the attraction of FDI should be assessed. The first is that research (NIEC, 1990 and Hamilton, 1990) has found that externally-owned plants which received selective financial assistance created only 2,500 jobs or 27 per cent of the total number of jobs created by the IDB between 1982 and 1988 and still in existence at the end of the period. Moreover, US-owned firms created only 440 jobs over the period, less than 10 per cent of the number of jobs which they planned to create. British plants performed little better with just over 1,000 jobs created – only 21 per cent of those planned. For US-owned plants the combination of the poor job creation performance and the magnitude of the public funds necessary to attract them to Northern Ireland meant that the cost-per-job created for these projects was extraordinarily high at over £205,000. Even when one project, Lear Fan, was excluded from the calculation the cost-per-job created fell to £31,000.

Gudgin *et al.* (1989) also questioned the effectiveness of foreign investment policy with its finding that 'in Northern Ireland only 65 firms employing 16,000 people remain to show for all the effort of industrial attraction from 1945 to 1973' and 'only 44 firms employing 6,000 people remained by 1986 in firms attracted into Northern Ireland after 1973' (p. 64). Indeed almost 36,000 jobs were lost over the period 1973 to 1986 in branch plants that had located in Northern Ireland between 1945 and 1973. This was the main explanation given for Northern Ireland's poor performance in terms of industrial employment change compared with the Republic.

A second reason why it is important to assess the effectiveness and cost of foreign investment policy is the lack of change which it has undergone. In April 1990 a major review of industrial development policy culminated in the publication 'Competing in the 1990s' (DED,

1990) and the subsequent operational strategy documents from the development agencies, in particular IDB (1990). With regard to foreign investment the methods proposed in the IDB's 'Forward Strategy' to promote Northern Ireland as the prime European location for manufacturing and tradeable services investment were refinements of existing practices. The only significant change in policy towards foreign investment was a more focused approach on particular industrial sectors, firm type and geographical markets, although much of this change predated the publication of the new strategy. There was no questioning of the long-term effectiveness and cost of foreign investment policy and, most importantly, its role as a key strand in the overall industrial development effort.

Table 7.8 Jobs promoted* in new inward investment projects by the IDB and its predecessors, 1980–81 to 1991–92

Year	Jobs promoted with financial assistance	Jobs promoted without financial assistance**	Total jobs promoted
1980–81	178		178
1981–82	348		348
1982–83	159		159
1983–84	539		539
1984–85	548		548
1985–86	224		224
1986–87	415		415
1987–88	867		867
1988–89	1,856		1,856
1989–90	1,577	400	1,977
1990–91	258	1,036	1,294
1991–92	80	350	430
Total	7,049	1,786	8,835

Source: IDB

Notes:

* Job Promotions refer to the number of jobs which a company plans to create over an agreed number of years.

** The vast majority of jobs promoted without financial assistance were 'back office' or what is now termed 'business support' jobs which the IDB has had the task to attract since 1989. However, more than 300 jobs not financially assisted by the IDB were in the manufacturing sector.

To place the achievements of the IDB's foreign investment policies in context Table 7.8 lists the number of job promotions (jobs which companies plan to create as the result of receiving assistance[15]) of new external investment projects for each of the years 1980–81 through to 1991–92. In total almost 9,000 jobs were promoted over the twelve-year period, an average of just over 700 per annum. Given the level of unemployment in Northern Ireland during the 1980s (an average of around 103,000 over the decade) it is clear that the attraction of new foreign investment projects did not make a significant contribution to resolving the fundamental problem of the economy. While it can be argued that foreign investment projects have a multiplier effect by creating jobs elsewhere in the economy, and in some cases may proceed through subsequent stages of expansion, NIEC (1990), Hamilton (1990) and Gudgin *et al.* (1989) show that job promotion targets are rarely achieved in full. This suggests that closures and contractions are probably more prevalent than the expansion of foreign projects. Certainly insufficient numbers of externally-owned plants are being attracted to Northern Ireland to offset the reductions in employment in existing externally-owned plants.

To make an evaluation of the comparative success of the IDB in attracting new foreign investment projects it is possible to present the number of job approvals by the Industrial Development Authority (IDA) in the Republic for new overseas greenfield projects for each of the years 1980 to 1991. Table 7.9 shows that over the twelve-year period the IDA approved 88,553 jobs in the manufacturing sector, an average of just under 7,400 per annum. If international and financial services are included then just over 102,000 jobs were approved over the twelve-year period. Despite the difficulties involved in making comparisons between the two agencies[16] it is clear that the IDA has been able to attract substantially more jobs from new overseas projects than has the IDB. However, the amount of public resources used to attract this level of FDI has been substantial. The Culliton Report (1992) stated that grants totalling IR £429m (1990 prices) were paid to new foreign start-ups over the period 1981–90 leading to the net creation of 24,000 jobs by the end of 1990. In addition, substantial costs were incurred in the form of tax relief for these projects. It is estimated that in 1991 alone this amounted to IR £600m or more for all industry located in the Republic of which a proportion would be accounted for by new foreign start-ups.

Table 7.9 Jobs approved by the IDA in the RoI in new overseas greenfield projects, 1980 to 1991*

Year	Manufacturing	International and financial services	Total
1980	16,306	849	17,155
1981	11,707	1,464	13,171
1982	10,650	922	11,572
1983	4,930	421	5,351
1984	7,477	914	8,391
1985	5,516	1,000	6,516
1986	6,967	890	7,857
1987	3,617	1,204	4,821
1988	2,738	642	3,380
1989	7,041	2,557	9,598
1990	6,413	1,895	8,308
1991	5,191	727	5,918
Total	88,553	13,485	102,038

Source: IDA

Note: * IDA job approvals are essentially the same as IDB job promotions in that they are the number of jobs which a company plans to create over an agreed period of time as a result of receiving financial assistance. New overseas greenfield projects refer to projects where there was no employment record for the company in the RoI in the previous year. The expansion of existing overseas projects are, therefore, not included.

In Northern Ireland the public cost of promoting jobs in foreign investment projects has also been substantial. The forty-six projects offered assistance by the IDB over the six-year period 1986–87 to 1991–92, and which promised just over 5,000 jobs, were attracted to Northern Ireland at a potential cost of almost £103m (constant 1990–91 prices). This represented around one-third of the total investment associated with these projects of £316.5m. The average cost-per-job promoted of these projects was just over £20,300. This compares with annual average male earnings in Northern Ireland of £12,800 in 1991. In addition to the costs associated with the direct subsidization of foreign investment projects, the IDB also incurs substantial costs related to promotional and overseas expenditure, in particular the costs of general public relations and the running of its various offices around the world. This totalled £8.5m in 1991–92.

Given the high cost of attempting to attract FDI to Northern Ireland it is important to question whether the opportunity cost in the use of public resources allocated towards the foreign investment effort is too high. In other words could the resources which are being spent on foreign investment policy be more beneficially allocated towards other policy options? Similar questions about the cost effectiveness of foreign investment policy were raised in the Republic in the Telesis Report (NESC, 1982) and more recently in the Culliton Report (1992). The latter report recommended that while the policy of trying to attract foreign investment should not be stopped completely the amount of public funds which it consumes should be significantly reduced.[17] No such firm conclusions have been made about the continuing promotion of FDI in Northern Ireland, where the debate on the issue has been relatively low level and uninformed. However, it would be misleading to suggest that there has been a clear shift away from the attraction of foreign investment in the Republic. The reality appears to be that the limitations of depending heavily on foreign investment as the main route to greater industrial development and the proposal to cut back on the average level of grants appear never to have been fully accepted at the level of government in the Republic (Fitzpatrick and Storey 1991).

CONCLUSIONS

This chapter has highlighted some of the major trends, characteristics and general issues resulting from the increased globalization of production in recent years. For Northern Ireland the extent of FDI in terms of employment has been presented. In particular, the analysis has shown that FDI is a significant but falling component of the regional economy. Overall, the rate of decline in employment in externally-owned plants has been greater than the general fall in manufacturing employment. The basic problem for industrial policy is that after the success of attracting large amounts of FDI in the 1960s it became virtually impossible to sustain the policy with the onset of the 'troubles' in the 1970s. The continuing decline in the contribution of FDI and the associated contraction of the manufacturing sector shows that FDI, even in times of success, did not form the basis of sustainable industrial development. Many of the concerns which have been raised in connection FDI in peripheral economies have, therefore, been realised in Northern Ireland.

In the case of the Republic the costly but substantial increase in

FDI, as in Northern Ireland, helped to expand the industrial sector from its relatively underdeveloped base. However, with indigenous companies continuing to operate largely in domestic markets or in low value-added products, the Republic faces the same problems to those in Northern Ireland in earlier periods – the difficulty of continually replacing foreign plants that contract or close. At least in the Republic FDI is of a higher quality than it has ever been in Northern Ireland in terms of being in modern high-technology industries such as electronics, computers and pharmaceuticals. However, despite efforts, local linkages by TNCs are still relatively weak (though this is as much a function of the weak indigenous base) and profit repatriation continues at an excessive rate.

The experience and the issues which FDI has raised for the industrial development of a peripheral economy such as Northern Ireland raises the question as to what, if any, should be the correct policy towards FDI. Given the increasing globalization of production it appears that small peripheral economies have no option but to accept inward flows of FDI, even if there is no active foreign investment policy. Foreign ownership of a large component of the manufacturing sector in a small open economy such as Northern Ireland appears to be inevitable given current global trends. However, policy makers should be very clear about the potential shortcomings of FDI as a source for industrial development. If a policy is carried out then decisions on whether to attract FDI should not be based on short-term gains in terms of employment creation. This would seem to be a major lesson of the past for Northern Ireland. The consequence of this stance is that policy should be much more selective and focused in its approach in terms of the type of projects that are targeted. While the IDB, to some extent, already follows such an approach, there are aspects which appear not to have been fully considered, such as the degree of technological activity, capital intensity or export propensity.[18]

Tied to this concept of increased selectivity is the need to place policy towards FDI in a wider strategy for the economy which clearly delineates the requirements of the economy and the detailed aims of policy. Despite the increased thinking that has been applied to economic strategy in Northern Ireland, reflected in 'Competing in the 1990s' (DED, 1990) and the operational strategy of the IDB (1990), such a strategic approach has yet to be fully developed. As a result a number of basic questions still require answering: what industries should be developed in the regional economy; what mix of FDI and indigenous industry can best achieve this; how can FDI contribute to a more flexible, creative and dynamic economy which is not only able to sustain development, but can also protect itself from adverse shocks from the outside; and how can FDI contribute to the development of flexible production techniques and industrial districts or clusters which some have argued are central to the successful development of regional economies (Piore and Sabel, 1984). These are just some of the questions which should be addressed in any future formulation of policy towards FDI. However, the conclusion of this chapter is that FDI by itself cannot form the basis for sustainable industrial development. Without direct, positive and coherent support for the indigenous sector of the economy Northern Ireland will not be able to match the rapid and successful industrialization experienced by economies in East Asia (Wade, 1990).

One final issue that has received increased attention, and which has implications for policy towards FDI, is the potential for increased cooperation and coordination between the north and south of Ireland (Quigley, 1992 and Anderson and Shuttleworth, 1992). In terms of FDI policy, such co-operation could involve a single promotional agency for the island of Ireland. This would reduce the current duplication of effort and wasteful competition for mobile foreign investment. The establishment of single promotional agency for Ireland again stresses the need for a detailed strategy for industrial development which prioritizes industries, products, locations and firm types. In addition an all-Ireland approach to foreign investment policy would require not just alterations to economic institutions, but also fundamental changes to the wider political framework within which industrial policy operates. Such changes to the political economy of Ireland could potentially increase industrial development significantly in both the north and south of Ireland (Hamilton, 1993).

A move in the above direction would require a far greater knowledge and understanding of the role, contribution and impact of FDI in Northern Ireland than there is at present. Much more needs to be known about how foreign plants operate in Northern Ireland: does the particular form of FDI – branch plants or cross-border mergers for example – have any differential effect; what are the extent of linkages between foreign and indigenous plants; how detrimental are the effects on local communities of a high dependence on FDI; what is the impact of FDI on the composition of employment in terms of religion and sex and what effects does it have on skills, pay and working conditions; is the degree of profit repatriation as high as in the Republic and how extensive is transfer pricing; what are the effects of different types of incentives on the attraction of FDI; is there a relationship between profitability levels and incentives; and, perhaps most fundamentally is there actually the potential to attract substantial levels of FDI to Northern Ireland given the likely continuation of the 'troubles' and worldwide trends in FDI? These are just some of the crucial issues around which a research agenda on FDI in Northern Ireland could be usefully developed.

NOTES

1. This is in contrast with the situation in the Republic of Ireland, where a much more extensive literature exists on the role and contribution to economic development. See for example NESC (1982), O'Malley (1989), Foley and McAleese (1991) and Culliton (1992).
2. The author was the principal researcher on NIEC (1992).
3. See, for example, Caves (1982), Dunning (1985), Cowling and Sugden (1987), NESC (1981) and Graham and Krugman (1991).
4. For an analysis of this effect on the Repuplic of Ireland see Foley (1991).
5. For the seminal work on dependency theory see Frank (1967). For a discussion of the Irish economies north and south which is placed in the context of dependency theory see Munck (1993).
6. The employment information presented here relating to foreign-owned companies in Northern Ireland was compiled from data provided to the Northern Ireland Economic Council by the Northern Ireland Economic Research Centre from its industrial databases and refers to three main observation points – 1973, 1986 and 1990. While these three years give a far from complete time series of information the data allow a picture of the recent level and changes in FDI to be made, and also show the important longer-term trends which have occured over the seventeen-year period since 1973. It should also be noted that the information presented in this chapter only refers to foreign-owned companies operating in the manufacturing sector. Information pertaining to the Republic was provided by the Industrial Development Authority. There are, of course, many companies in the service sector, such as retailing and financial services, where the country of ownership lies outside Northern Ireland. Unfortunately data availability only allows analysis of manufacturing firms. However, since policy towards foreign investment has been almost exclusively targeted at manufacturing firms over the period analysed here, this sector is of prime interest. It is also important to note that the information on foreign-owned plants presented here *excludes* the aerospace company Short Brothers. The privatization of Shorts and its takeover by a Canadian company, Bombardier, in 1989 greatly distorts the analysis of external ownership because of the size of the company in relation to the rest of the regional economy (in 1990 the company employed 7,500 making it by far the largest manufacturing employer in Northern Ireland). This

distortion is particularly evident when the data on external ownership are disaggregated to the level of the industrial sector, nationality and location. By excluding Shorts from the 1990 figures a clearer picture of the underlying structural changes in the foreign-owned component of the manufacturing sector is able to be presented, especially in the more recent period 1986 to 1990. Finally the term externally-owned refers to all plants in which the ownership lies outside Northern Ireland. Therefore for the purposes of the statistical analysis companies which are from either the Republic or Britain are classified as externally-owned.

7. Note that the information is classified by the number of plants rather than companies. The number of externally-owned companies would be slightly below that given in Table 7.1 because some companies operate more than one plant.
8. Gudgin *et al.* (1989) estimated that 24,000 jobs were lost in Northern Ireland due to the 'troubles' for the period 1971 to 1977.
9. Canning, Moore and Rhodes (1987) estimated job losses of 40,000 due to the 'troubles' for the period 1969 to 1983 while Rowthorn and Wayne (1988) estimated that 46,000 jobs were lost during the period 1970 to 1985.
10. In terms of actual job losses in existing plants, however, a study of branch factory closures in Northern Ireland during the 1980s found that the 'troubles' were not 'a cause of substantial numbers of plant closures in the 1980s' (Fothergill and Guy, 1990b, p. 16).
11. It is important to note that information for the Republic refers to the number of companies while for Northern Ireland it refers to plants.
12. See, for example, Ruane and McGibney (1991) and O"Malley, Kennedy and O'Donnell (1992).
13. NESC (1982) compared the incentives packages available in Northern Ireland and the Republic and concluded that, despite the methodological difficulties involved, the two were comparable. especially for larger investment projects. NIEC (1990) also compared European incentives packages and concluded that the level, range and flexibility of incentives available in Northern Ireland were generous compared with most of the other regions of the EC.
14. See NIEC (1991) for a full account of the evolution of economic policy in Northern Ireland over the period 1945 to 1990.
15. Before the establishment of the IDB in 1982 the responsibility of attracting inward investment lay jointly with the Northern Ireland Development Agency and the Department of Commerce.
16. Such difficulties are the larger size of the Republic's economy (in terms of population it is over twice as large), the problems involved in compiling comparative information on the amount of public resources expended and the lack of information on the proportion of job promotions and approvals which are subsequently created.
17. O'Malley, Kennedy and O'Donnnell (1992) warn that a cautious approach should be adopted to cutting the incentives for foreign investment because of the dangers of missing out on badly needed employment.
18. See NIEC (1992) for a discussion of some of these.

REFERENCES

Anderson, J. and Shuttleworth, I. (1992) 'Currency of Cooperation', *Fortnight*, December.

Canning, D., Moore, B. and Rhodes, J. (1987) 'Economic Growth in Northern Ireland: Problems and Prospects', in Teague, P. (ed.), *Beyond The Rhetoric*, Lawrence and Wishart, London.

Caves, R. (1982) *Multinational Enterprises and Economic Analysis*, Cambridge University Press, Cambridge.

Cowling, K. (1990) 'The Strategic Approach to Economic and Industrial Policy', in Cowling, K. and Sugden, R., (eds), *A New Economic Policy for Britain – Essays on the Development of Industry*, Manchester University Press, Manchester.

Cowling, K. and Sugden, R. (1987) *Transnational Monopoly Capitalism*, Wheatsheaf, Brighton.

Culliton, J. (1992) *A Time for Change: Industrial Policy for the 1990s*, Report of the Industrial Policy Review Group, The Stationery Office, Dublin.

Daniel, P. (1991) 'Foreign Investment Revisited', *IDS Bulletin*, Vol. 22, No. 2, April, Institute of Development Studies, Sussex.

DED (1990) *Competing in the 1990s – The Key to Growth*, Department of Economic Development, Belfast.

Department of Industry and Commerce (1990) *Review of Industrial Performance*, The Stationery Office Dublin.

Dunning, J.H. (ed.) (1985) *Multinational Enterprise, Economic Structure and Competitiveness*, Wiley, London.

Fitzpatrick, J. and Storey, A. (1991) 'Changing Policy towards Overseas Investment', in Foley, A. and McAleese, D., (eds), *Overseas Industry in Ireland*, Gill and Macmillan, Dublin.

Foley, A. (1991) 'The Export and Foreign Exchange Contribution of Overseas Industry', in Foley, A. and McAleese, D., (eds), *Overseas Industry in Ireland*, Gill and Macmillan, Dublin.

Foley, A. and McAleese, D. (eds) (1991) *Overseas Industry in Ireland*, Gill and Macmillan, Dublin.

Fothergill, S. and Guy, N. (1990a) *Retreat from the Regions – Corporate Change and the Closure of Factories*, Jessica Kingsley, Regional Studies Association London.

Fothergill, S. and Guy, N. (1990b) *Branch Factory Closures in Northern Ireland*, Northern Ireland Economic Research Centre, Belfast.

Frank, A.G. (1967) *Capitalism and Underdevelopment in Latin America*, Monthly Review Press, London.

Graham, E.M. and Krugman, P.R. (1991) *Foreign Direct Investment in the United States*, 2nd Edition, Institute for International Economics, Washington.

Gudgin, G. *et al.* (1989) *Job Generation in Manufacturing Industry 1973–1986*, Northern Ireland Economic Research Centre, Belfast.

Hamilton, D. (1990) 'Industrial Development Policy in Northern Ireland – An Evaluation of the IDB', *The Economic and Social Review*, Vol. 22, No. 1, October

Hamilton, D. (1993) 'Current Issues in Irish Industrial Development', in Collins, N. (ed) *Political Issues in Ireland Today*. Manchester, University Press, Manchester.

Harris, R.I.D. (1991) 'Technology and Regional Policy: A Case Study of Northern Ireland', *Applied Economics*, Vol. 23, pp. 685–696.

IDB (1990) *Forward Strategy 1991–93*, Industrial Development Board, Belfast.

Julius, D. (1991) 'Direct Investment among Developed Countries: Lessons for the Developing World', *IDS Bulletin,* Vol. 22, No. 2, April, Institute of Development Studies, Sussex.

Munck, R. (1993) *The Irish Economy: Results and Prospects,* Pluto Press, London.

NESC (1982) *A Review of Industrial Policy,* Report No. 64, National Economic and Social Council, Dublin.

NIEC (1986) *Economic Strategy: Industrial Development Linkages,* Report 56, February, Northern Ireland Economic Council, Belfast.

NIEC (1990) *The Industrial Development Board for Northern Ireland: Selective Financial Assistance and Economic Development Policy,* Report 79, February, Northern Ireland Economic Council, Belfast.

NIEC (1991) *Economic Strategy in Northern Ireland,* Report 88, July, Northern Ireland Economic Council, Belfast.

NIEC (1992) *Inward Investment in Northern Ireland,* Report 99, November, Northern Ireland Economic Council, Belfast.

O'Malley, E. (1989) *Industry and Economic Development – The Challenge of the Latecomer,* Gill and Macmillan, Dublin.

O'Malley, E., Kennedy, K. and O'Donnell, R. (1992) *The Impact of the Industrial Development Agencies,* Report by the Economic and Social Research Institute to the Industrial Policy Review Group, The Stationery Office, Dublin.

OECD (1992) *Economic Outlook,* No. 51, June, Organisation for Economic Cooperation and Development, Paris.

Piore, M.J. and Sabel, C.F. (1984) *The Second Industrial Divide – Possibilities for Prosperity,* Basic Books, New York.

Quigley, G. (1976) *Economic and Industrial Strategy for Northern Ireland,* Report by Review Team, HMSO, Belfast.

Quigley, G. (1992) *Ireland – an Island Economy,* Speech to the Confederation of Irish Industry, Dublin, February.

Rowthorn, B. and Wayne, N. (1988) *Northern Ireland: The Political Economy of Conflict,* Polity Press, Cambridge.

Ruane, F. and McGibney, A. (1991) 'The Performance of Overseas Industry, 1979-89', in Foley, A. and McAleese, D. (eds) *Overseas Industry in Ireland,* Gill and Macmillan, Dublin.

Vickery, G. (1992) 'Global Industries and National Policies', *The OECD Observer,* 179, December, Organisation for Economic Cooperation and Development, Paris.

Wade, R. (1990) *Governing the Market – Economic Theory and the Role of Government in East Asian Industrialisation,* Princeton University Press, New Jersey.

8
THE LABOUR MARKET IMPACT OF NEW AND SMALL FIRMS IN NORTHERN IRELAND

Mark Hart

INTRODUCTION

New firm formation, survival and growth have become increasingly important aspects of economic development in recent years. The poor performance of the national UK economy over this period called into question many of the underlying assumptions related to the traditional mechanisms of industrial policy. In particular, the large-scale labour-shedding activities of externally controlled branch plants and firms were having a devastating effect on local and regional labour markets. It became widely accepted that the successful development of local economies depends on competitive, indigenous firms, most of which start as small companies (Storey and Johnson, 1987). Consequently, UK government policy since the late 1970s, and in particular since 1979, has actively encouraged new and small firms as a means to create jobs. The onset of the current recession in 1989 has further underlined the importance of this shift in emphasis for regional economic development.

The purpose of this chapter is to provide an assessment of the contribution of new and small indigenous manufacturing firms to the Northern Ireland economy in recent years. The focus on the manufacturing sector is predicated on the belief that it is this sector which is of crucial importance to the achievement of long-term sustainable economic growth in the Northern Ireland economy. This chapter is structured as follows. The first section briefly outlines recent trends in the small-firm sector and new firm formation in the UK against the background of the discourse on the 'enterprise culture'. The following section discusses the process of job generation in the manufacturing sector in Northern Ireland over the period 1973–86. The importance of new and small firms in this process will be highlighted. Then the development of small firm policy in Northern Ireland is detailed and the principal findings set out of a recent major evaluation of the Local Enterprise Development Unit (LEDU): the small business agency for Northern Ireland. The chapter concludes with an examination of the future role of small-scale indigenous development for the revitalization of lagging peripheral economies.

THE UK CONTEXT: THE RE-DISCOVERY OF AN ENTERPRISE CULTURE?

It is now widely accepted that the 1980s in the United Kingdom, as in other developed industrial economies, was a highly favourable decade for enterprise and the small firm sector in particular. The renaissance of the small business sector over this period has been widely documented with a great deal of attention being paid to the rapid rise in the numbers of self-employed and in the number of firms registering for VAT (Curran and Blackburn, 1991). In addition, since 1979, the creation of the 'enterprise culture' was one of the dominant principles of the Thatcherism project. Against the background of major economic, social and political change in Britain in the 1980s, the proponents of the enterprise culture have sought to present it as an antidote to these deep-rooted restructuring processes. The justification and validity of this connection has yet to be adequately debated; yet it remains an integral part of government policy for the 1990s (Burrows, 1991a). The spirit of enterprise has thus become closely associated with economic renewal. Such a strategy is seen as being of particular significance for the lagging peripheral regions, which include Northern Ireland.

The Enterprise Initiative, which was set out in the Department of Trade and Industry's White Paper in January 1988, demonstrated the commitment of the Conservative government to new and small firms, as part of their strategy to promote enterprise and reduce unemployment (DTI, 1988). Within Northern Ireland, the Department of Economic Development (DED) had produced a similar document in 1987 known as 'Pathfinder' (DED, 1987). In essence, this document concentrated on the means by which indigenous potential could be harnessed in the regeneration of the regional economy. Arising out of Pathfinder, the Enterprise Taskforce produced a major initiative to foster a more positive attitude to enterprise in Northern Ireland. The Enterprising Northern Ireland Campaign was launched in July 1988, with the task of promoting and developing new small firms. The objective was both to improve existing levels of entrepreneurial activity and to release new sources of enterprise ability: young people, women, people in employment and the unemployed. Continued support for enterprise has been acknowledged in the most recent strategy document from the Department of Economic Development (DED, 1990). The whole question of public support for the small-firm sector will be explored in greater detail in the fouth section.

As the creation of a more positive policy environment towards the small-firm sector was developed in the 1980s in the UK, the growing importance of this sector was reflected in a number of key statistics. For example, between 1981 and 1991 in Great Britain self-employment increased by 1.1 million (52 per cent), to a total of 3.3 million (Campbell *et al.*, 1992). Over the period 1980–90 the annual numbers of firms registering for VAT rose from 150,000 to 235,000[1] with a positive annual balance of registrations over deregistrations throughout the period. However, in 1990 there was a marked change in this trend with a decline in the number of registrations and an increase in the number of deregistrations which would tend to indicate the early effects of the current recession. Nevertheless, the total stock of VAT businesses increased by 420,000 or 32.6 per cent from 1.29 million in 1980 to 1.71 million in 1990 (Daly, 1991). In Northern Ireland the numbers of self-employed increased by 13,000 across all sectors between 1980 and 1990. Over the same period the number of firms registering for VAT rose by 39,300, representing a net increase of 21.8 per cent in the stock of VAT businesses.

Further insights into the relative position of Northern Ireland in terms of new firm formation can be gained from looking at an analysis of regional variations in VAT registrations across the UK between 1980 and 1990. The analysis draws upon the Department of Employment's VAT registration data as an indicator of new firm formation. The indicator used in this analysis is the number of new manufacturing (production) registrations for VAT. All companies with a turnover of over £25,400 per annum (threshold in 1990) are required to register. Although some wholly owned subsidiaries and established businesses which have been trading without previously being liable for VAT (turnover below the threshold) are included in the figures, the vast majority of new VAT registrations are made by new small independent companies. Nevertheless, to allow for this discrepancy the analysis here calculates formation rates by using the number of manufacturing employees in the base year as the denominator. (Thus the assumption is that the vast majority of new business founders in the manufacturing sector have a background of employment in that sector.)

Two measures of new firm formation have been created: *gross* and *net* formation rates. These two variables are taken to broadly represent different stages in the process of new firm formation. *Gross* formation represent an areas ability to generate new firms, while *net* formation is taken as a measure of an area's ability to help new firms survive once they have been established. Thus, as a measure of gross new firm formation we have taken the cumulative number of new registrations between 1980 and 1990 in each county[2] divided by the number of manufacturing employees in 1980. Net new firm formation is calculated as the number of new registrations less deregistrations in each county divided once again by the number of manufacturing employees in 1980.

Table 8.1 Gross and net new firm formation rates 1980–90: UK Regions

Region	Gross formation rate	Rank	Net formation rate	Rank
South East	42.3	1	4.9	6
South West	38.8	2	10.6	2
East Anglia	36.1	3	11.2	1
West Midlands	17.8	9	4.8	7
East Midlands	27.2	4	7.4	5
North West	20.7	8	3.0	11
Wales	25.3	5	8.1	3
Yorks and Humb.	21.3	7	3.9	9
N. Ireland	22.2	6	7.5	4
Scotland	17.1	10	3.7	10
North	15.3	11	4.3	8
UK Average	28.2		5.3	

Source: Department of Employment

Table 8.1 presents data on both gross and net formation rates over the period 1980–90 per thousand manufacturing employees in each of the UK regions. The data for gross formation clearly reveal that the recent growth of new and small manufacturing businesses in the UK has been geographically uneven, with the South East, South West and

East Anglia recording much higher rates than northern regions such as the North, Scotland, and North West. The performance of Northern Ireland (ranked sixth) is a surprising exception to this crude north–south split, as indeed is the relatively high ranking of Wales. Superficially, both Wales and Northern Ireland could be considered to possess broad similarities in industrial structure to that of Scotland and therefore the differences in formation rates would not be expected. Nevertheless, all three peripheral regions recorded a gross formation rate below the UK average.

With respect to net formation rates the regional ranking exhibits some interesting changes within the overall north–south pattern (Table 8.1). First, the South East region now has a formation rate below the UK average and is ranked only sixth compared to its top rank on gross formation rates. Second, both Wales and Northern Ireland recorded above UK average net formation rates and are now ranked third and fourth respectively. The implication here is that while these two regions are below average in generating new firms they do have a better record in maintaining them once formed. The opposite is true for the South East which clearly had a relatively poor record of new firm survival in the 1980s. An important factor in the higher net formation rates in Northern Ireland is the Local Enterprise Development Unit (LEDU) which since 1971 has been active in the support of new and small firms through the provision of selective financial assistance (Hart, 1984; 1989; Gudgin *et al.* 1989). The activities of this agency will be evaluated below.

The extent to which these trends can be associated with the increased political discourse on the 'enterprise culture' stemming from the 'New Right' has been the subject of a great deal of debate (Curran and Blackburn, 1991; Keat and Abercrombie, 1991; Burrows, 1991b). Whilst this is an attractive argument for some, it is perhaps more convincing to see these trends as part of the broader processes of economic change operating since the late 1970s.

Evidence from the manufacturing sector suggests that the enterprise development patterns of the 1980s are a function of more long-term trends. Hughes (1990) provides a comprehensive overview of recent statistics on new and small firms and seeks to place them in their historical context. He argues that the trends observed in the 1980s have their roots prior to 1979 and indeed, can be traced back to the late 1960s and early 1970s. For example, the long downward trend in the employment share of manufacturing establishments employing less than fifty persons in UK manufacturing industry was halted and then reversed between 1973 and 1981: in 1973 the share was 11 per cent rising to 17 per cent in 1981 (Hughes, 1990).

Furthermore, in attempting to understand the determinants of the supply of entrepreneurs or new firm founders consideration must be given to a combination of economic and non-economic factors. These factors may be categorized as follows:

1. Macroeconomic factors (ie. demand-led formation);
2. Microeconomic factors (ie. expected profit to be made);
3. Personal skills (including experience and qualifications) and access to capital;
4. Environmental factors (eg. industrial structure of an area or the degree of rurality).

Each of these categories, either individually or collectively, have been used extensively in the many recent studies which have sought to explain the pattern (temporal or spatial) of new firm formation (see for example Ashcroft *et al.*, 1991; Hart and Gudgin, 1992). A number of key variables do consistently emerge from the multivariate regression analyses, which would suggest that we are moving closer to a better specification of a model which explains the spatial variations in new firm formation. It is clear that the spatial variations in new firm formation are indeed a '... product of a wide variety of social, cultural, structural and economic factors which combine to influence the emergence of new firm founders' (Mason, 1992, p. 154).

The nature of the explanatory variables (for example, firm size, occupation, earnings, growth in demand, degree of rurality, education, house prices, house tenure, population growth and government assistance) would immediately suggest that the notion of an 'enterprise culture' in the 1980s being directly related to increased levels of new business start-up is somewhat misleading. Without doubt government support for the small business sector, either through national schemes such as the Loan Guarantee Scheme, or through the enterprise development activities of specific agencies (for example, LEDU in Northern Ireland), has had an important effect on changing the environment within which new and small businesses operate. Further, as Mason (1992) argues, a direct consequence of increased government activity in this area of economic development may well have been a rise in the social esteem attributed to the small business owner-manager. Confirmation of this effect can be seen in a number of the regression analyses which attribute a positive and statistically significant impact of dummy variables for government assistance in the explanation of spatial variations in new firm formation (Ashcroft *et al.*, 1991; Hart and Gudgin, 1992; Hart *et al.*, 1993).

However, other more deeply-rooted structural effects within local areas have clearly emerged as dominant factors which affect the supply of potential new firm founders. In particular, the industrial and social structures of an area have been consistently identified as key explanatory variables in the uneven spatial pattern of new business start-ups. These factors do not necessarily change quickly, and can reflect earlier patterns of spatial economic development. This conclusion does not ignore the effect of short-term trends in the market place upon regional formation rates (such as the rise in real incomes in the UK in the latter half of the 1980s), but the consistency of the structural effects over time and across different national contexts perhaps testify to a more rigid process of new firm formation than perhaps most government ministers and policy makers would accept. As Ashcroft *et al.* (1991, p. 405) conclude:

> if the government is serious about raising firm formation rates in Scotland and in other peripheral regions of the UK, it would do better to focus on certain aspects of the regions' economic structure than on repeated exhortations to local residents to embrace the 'enterprise culture'.

A major impact upon regional economic structure in the 1980s has been the effect of the twin processes of corporate restructuring and technological change. These processes have had quite drastic effects upon local labour markets, but at the same time they have provided market opportunities for both new and existing small businesses (Keeble, 1990; Mason, 1992). Perhaps it would be more fruitful for government to seek to understand and harness these developments, and their spatial impacts, than simply to tell individuals to take responsibility for their own 'job creation'.

Irrespective of the interpretation placed upon the factors driving these trends it is overwhelmingly clear that the fortunes of the small-firm sector has undergone a major transformation during the 1980s. The task now is to assess the importance of these trends in the process of economic regeneration by examining the economic impact of new and small firms within Northern Ireland.

JOB GENERATION IN NORTHERN IRELAND

Birch (1979) heralded a decade of research and debate in the area of the contribution of small firms to employment. His study, which has been subject to considerable controversy since its publication (see

Storey and Johnson, 1987; Armington and Odle, 1982), discovered that most new jobs were provided by small firms. This overall conclusion has been largely substantiated by a plethora of 'job generation' studies conducted throughout the 1980s (Mason and Harrison, 1990).

Table 8.2 Net job generation by size of firm and broad sector, 1987–89

Size band	Services			Production		
	A	B	C	A	B	C
1–4	250	35.4	13.2	107	25.4	4.0
5–9	103	14.6	14.6	62	14.8	7.1
10–19	44	6.2	15.5	48	11.4	11.7
20–49	46	6.5	8.7	30	7.1	9.3
50–99	46	6.5	7.1	39	9.2	8.5
100–499	75	10.6	12.2	48	11.3	14.5
500–999	26	3.7	3.4	28	6.7	4.2
1,000–4,999	36	5.0	6.7	7	1.6	7.7
5,000–9,999	9	1.3	4.0	4	0.9	2.8
10,000+	72	10.1	14.7	49	11.7	30.0
Total	708			421		

Source: *Employment Gazette*, August 1992

Note: A Net job generation (thousands)
 B Share of total net Generation (per cent)
 C Share of 1987 employment (per cent)

The most recent analysis of the job generation behaviour of firms in the UK (Daly *et al.*, 1992) covered the period 1987–89 and confirmed that smaller firms (i.e. those employing less than ten persons), across all sectors, have accounted for a disproportionately large share of total job creation in relation to their overall share of employment (Table 8.2). This point is reinforced by Table 8.3 which presents a 'net fertility ratio' comparing each size band's share of net job generation with its share of total employment in 1987 (columns B and C in Table 8.2). A value greater than 1 indicates a disproportionately large share of job generation, and a value less than 1 a disproportionately small share. Furthermore, this analysis demonstrated that it was size rather than sector which was most important in determining employment change in a firm.

Table 8.3 Net fertility ratio by broad sector 1987–1989

Size band	Services	Production
1–4	2.7	6.3
5–9	1.0	2.1
10–19	0.4	1.0
20–49	0.8	0.8
50–99	0.9	1.1
100–499	0.9	0.8
500–999	1.1	1.6
1,000–4,999	0.8	0.2
5,000–9,999	0.3	0.3
10,000+	0.7	0.4

Source: *Employment Gazette*, August 1992.

A major job generation study has been undertaken for the manufacturing sector in Northern Ireland over the period 1973–86 (Gudgin *et al.*, 1989). Based on micro-level longitudinal data on individual firms (or establishments)[3] the analysis sought to disaggregate overall manufacturing change in the region into three distinct components of change:

— growth and decline of established firms and branch plants;
— formation of new indigenous firms;
— inward-moving firms and branch plants.

In the following discussion the labour market impact of new and small manufacturing firms in Northern Ireland is highlighted. However, the performance of other groups of companies in Northern Ireland (i.e. larger firms and multinational branch plants) will also be analysed in order to more realistically assess the contribution of the small-firm sector. The wider study incorporated an important comparative dimension in that the performance of each of the above components in Northern Ireland was compared to similar groups of firms in two other areas: Leicestershire (East Midlands) and the Republic of Ireland. Data on these comparator areas will be introduced were appropriate.

The components of change are shown in Table 8.4. The overall conclusion to emerge is that Northern Ireland experienced a severe contraction among its established firms with insufficient gains in the creation of new firms and branches. As a result the level of manufacturing employment fell by just under 40 per cent between 1973 and 1986. The principal cause of Northern Ireland's poor record in job generation is the performance of the externally owned sector. The sector contracted from 92 thousand jobs in 1973 to 42 thousand in 1986. Contraction, amounting to collapse, was particularly acute among those larger firms which had moved into the province between 1945 and 1973 under Northern Ireland's Industrial Development (ID) legislation. These employed 52 thousand people in 1973, within 134 firms, but by 1986 only sixty-five firms remained employing 16 thousand people. During the same period another forty-four firms had moved in, but these were smaller in size and employed only 7 thousand jobs. A fuller account of the pattern and causes of branch-plant closure in Northern Ireland can be found in Fothergill and Guy (1990).

Table 8.4 Components of change in manufacturing employment: Northern Ireland

Component	000s	%[1]
1973 employment	174.3	
Companies established by 1973[2]		
Externally owned	-55.8	(-60.6)
Indigenously owned	-35.0	(-42.8)
Net change	-90.8	(-52.1)
New inward investment	+6.9	(+3.9)
Indigenous new firms	+17.0	(+9.8)
Total change	-66.9	(-38.4)
1986 employment	107.4	

Source: NIERC Industrial Databank

Notes: 1. Percentages are of base year employment in manufacturing except for established firms, where they are of base year employment in each of the 2 categories. 2. Includes closures and expansions/contractions in surviving firms.

Within this severe contraction of employment in Northern Ireland manufacturing we now need to establish what the performance of new and small firms has been. The discussion will focus upon each of these groups of firms in turn.

New Firms

New firms are an important aspect of economic growth as they are often the vehicle for the introduction of new products and new methods of production into the economy as a whole. Whilst these long-term benefits are crucial ingredients to the success of local and regional economies the discussion of the contribution of new firms often centres around their job creation potential.

Table 8.5 Employment in 1986 in new firms formed 1973–86

	No. of firms	Average employment	Total thous.	Employment % of base year manufacturing
Northern Ireland	2,014	8.4	17.0	9.8
Republic of Ireland	3,676	8.1	29.6	13.3
Leicestershire	1,988	10.0	19.9	11.6

Sources: NIERC Industrial Databases, IDA Employment Survey Data

It is estimated that Northern Ireland produced over 2,000 new surviving independent indigenous manufacturing firms in the thirteen years between 1973 and 1986 (Table 8.5). These firms employed 17 thousand people in 1986, which represented 16.5 per cent of manufacturing employment at that date. Thus, new firm formation is clearly an important source of job generation for the Northern Ireland economy and, indeed, has created three times as many jobs as inward investment by externally-owned companies (Table 8.4). Expressed in terms of employment as a percentage of base year manufacturing employment, Table 8.5 also reveals that the performance of Northern Ireland new firms, whilst lagging behind that of the Republic of Ireland, is broadly equivalent to that of new firms in Leicestershire. To put these figures in perspective, if Northern Ireland had generated jobs in new firms at the rate of Leicestershire or the Republic, the regions current employment total would be between 3 and 6 thousand higher. Although this constitutes a significant number of jobs, an addition of this magnitude is not huge in the context of an unemployment level of around 100,000.

Data on formation rates are presented in Table 8.6 for Northern Ireland and the other two areas. A reasonable conclusion to draw would be that Northern Ireland's formation rate, irrespective of the methodology employed to calculate the rate,[4] is somewhat below that of the Republic of Ireland but broadly similar to that in Leicestershire.

Table 8.6 Net formation rates for new firms 1973–86

	Number of new firms surviving to 1986	Formation rate[1]	
		(a)	(b)
Northern Ireland	2,014	9.0	11.6
Republic of Ireland	3,672	11.1	16.3
Leicestershire	1,988	9.9	11.6

Sources: NIERC Industrial Databases, IDA Employment Survey Data

Notes: 1. Formation rate are numbers of new firms per thousand employees: (a) in manufacturing plus 12% of non-manufacturing in 1973 (b) in manufacturing employment in 1973

This is an interesting result in that it has always been assumed that new firm formation has lagged significantly behind that experienced in other regions of the UK (DED, 1987). This is clearly not the case and tends to reinforce the findings from the analysis of gross and net new firm formation based on VAT registrations for the production sector in the UK in 1980–90 (see Table 8.1)[5]. Thus, merely to seek to increase levels of new firm formation to national levels or to those experienced in other economies will not produce significant job gains to the Northern Ireland economy. This then raises the question of the overall contribution of the small-firm sector in terms of its labour market impact. The remainder of this section will concentrate upon this aspect of the job generation debate.

Existing Small Firms

The ability of successive cohorts of small indigenous firms to create jobs is a vital ingredient of economic development. From Table 8.7 it can be seen that employment growth among the established cohort of independent indigenously-owned small firms (i.e, those employing less than fifty people) in Northern Ireland in 1973 has been rather disappointing. This cohort experienced a 42.2 per cent (7 thousand jobs) fall in employment by 1986. Northern Ireland's small firms employed 19 thousand people in 1973 and by 1986 most of these firms had closed. Although the survivors expanded considerably (44.4 per cent), the employment effects were too small to offset large losses through closures. The same conclusions would apply to the performance of the Republic of Ireland's small firm sector over the same period.

However, the performance of the small firm sector in Leicestershire is worthy of comment. In this region the cohort of small firms in 1973 had expanded its total employment by 1986 despite a high rate of closure (Table 8.7). This means, therefore, that the 20 thousand jobs created in new surviving firms between 1973 and 1986 can all be considered net additions to small firm employment (Table 8.5).

Table 8.7 Mode of employment change, 1973–86: small indigenous firms

	Northern Ireland thous.	(%)	Republic of Ireland thous.	(%)	Leicestershire thous.	(%)
All established firms	-7.5	(-42.2)	-21.3	(-40.0)	+1.5	(+7.4)
Survivors	+3.1	(+44.4)	+4.2	(+15.1)	+10.0	(+86.4)
Closures	-10.6	(-59.9)	-25.5	(-47.9)	-8.5	(-42.2)

Sources: NIERC Industrial Databases, IDA Employment Survey Data

A sector by sector comparison of employment change shows that the performance in Northern Ireland was considerably worse than would appear from the aggregate total. In Table 8.8, 'expected' employment changes have been calculated by multiplying base year employment in each sector by the rate of change in each Leicestershire sector. The results show that 'expected' change was very favourable in Northern Ireland, indicating that it had a favourable mix of industries compared with Leicestershire. Allowing for differences between areas in the mix of industries, actual employment change was 68 per cent less than 'expected' on Leicestershire's rates of change.

This difference is dramatic. Had Northern Ireland's small firms been able to expand at the same rate as those in Leicestershire, there would have been an extra 12 thousand manufacturing jobs in the region by 1986. Although these foregone jobs would have been important in themselves, what has also been foregone is a population of established small firms, some capable of further expansion, and most able to hive off additional small businesses via their employees.

Table 8.8 Actual and expected employment change, 1973–86: small indigenous firms

	Actual change		Expected change		Actual less expected change	
	thous.	(%)	thous.	(%)	thous.	(%)
Northern Ireland	-7.5	(-42.2)	+4.6	(+25.9)	-12.1	(-68.4)
Republic of Ireland	-21.3	(-40.0)	+9.2	(+17.2)	-30.5	(-57.2)
Leicestershire	+1.5	(+7.4)	+1.5	(+7.4)	0.0	(0.0)

Sources: NIERC Industrial Databases IDA Employment Survey Data

Note: Expected change is base year employment in each sector multiplied by Leicestershire rate of change in each sector.

The greatest difference between the two study areas came not so much in the rates of closure, but in the growth of surviving firms (Table 8.7). Those firms which survived from 1973 through to 1986 grew twice as rapidly in Leicestershire as in Northern Ireland. Differences of these magnitudes obtained from entire populations of firms, as opposed to small samples, demonstrate a pressing need for an understanding of the processes at work which prevent small firms maximizing their growth potential.

One immediate interpretation of these very large differences in small firm performance is the possibility that local market expansion has constrained growth in Northern Ireland. This may be important in the light of recent studies which have revealed that on average LEDU-assisted small firms sold 63 per cent of their output to customers within Northern Ireland (Scott and O'Reilly, 1992; Hart *et al*, 1993). However, local consumer spending grew considerably more rapidly in Northern Ireland than in Leicestershire (Gudgin *et al.*, 1989). But, despite this apparent advantage in local market growth, Northern Ireland industries serving consumer markets performed as poorly as the other sectors. Slower growth of local industrial and commercial markets in Northern Ireland may have constrained growth particularly in the engineering and chemical industries.

A more plausible argument is that a lack of competitiveness is a greater cause of decline than sluggish market growth. Hitchens and O'Farrell's work (1987; 1988a; 1988b) addressed this issue and has revealed several dimensions to the problem. A wide range of potential influences on growth were examined during lengthy interviews with matched pairs of firms in Northern Ireland, the Mid-West region of the Republic of Ireland, South East England and South Wales.

The most notable and perhaps most important deficiency in Northern Ireland small firms occurred in the quality and price of production. This problem, according to the authors, appears to reflect lower skill and dedication among Northern Ireland workers, but whether the latter is in reality a failure of labour or management is not discussed in the studies. Northern Ireland firms also tended to sell a higher proportion of their output to local markets than did their British counterparts. Hitchens and O'Farrell did not accept that the relatively isolated location of Northern Ireland small firms could explain their findings since they assume that no competitive disadvantages arise from peripherality.

A final possible explanation of the dramatic differences in performance between Northern Ireland and Leicestershire is that new and other small firms rely more heavily on local markets in Northern Ireland. Accordingly, new firm formation and growth becomes, to a significant degree, a 'beggar thy neighbour' process in which start-ups may actually put existing trading companies out of business. Some social gains may accrue since the displacing firms presumably have some competitive advantage over those displaced. However, too large a proportion of all small firms appears to remain vulnerable to displacement by new local competitors, many of whom will have been grant-aided by LEDU. The displacement effects of LEDU assistance will be explored in greater detail in the following section of this chapter. In Leicestershire the apparently lower level of displacement means that new small firms are able to augment the employment growth of existing small firms to create an expanding small firms sector and Act as a seed-bed for the generation of future medium-sized and larger firms.

The most recent research on small firm growth in Northern Ireland tends to indicate that the trends outlined above have *not* continued until the end of the 1980s. Hart *et al.* (1993) have shown that, in contrast to the earlier 1973–86 period, employment growth in Northern Ireland small firms in 1986–90 was faster than in most of the other study areas (Table 8.9). The role of public policy towards small firms in Northern Ireland in the transformation of employment growth in surviving small firms is difficult to unravel, but there are signs that it has not been insignificant. The final section of the chapter investigates this point further by presenting a detailed evaluation of the impact of the activities of LEDU on the performance of the small firm sector.

Table 8.9 Annual employment change 1986–90 in surviving small firms

Area	1973–1986 % pa	1986–1990 % pa
Northern Ireland	2.9	6.8
Leicestershire	4.9	4.5
Republic of Ireland	1.1	3.0
Wearside	n.a.	9.9

Sources: NIERC, IDA and University of Northumbria at Newcastle Industrial Databases

PUBLIC POLICY FOR NEW AND SMALL FIRMS

Economic development strategy in Northern Ireland has not delivered a rate of economic growth sufficient to employ a growing labour force and make inroads into the high rate of unemployment in the region. As a result, a debate has started about how this situation can be reversed. Much of this debate has concentrated within the Department of Economic Development and the main industrial development agencies: the Industrial Development Board (IDB) and LEDU. The concentration upon indigenous potential and enterprise creation seemingly at the expense of any co-ordinated policy on inward investment has attracted some comment (Teague, 1989a; 1989b; Hitchens and Birnie, 1989). In that context, and without wishing to engage in the detail of the debate, it would seem appropriate to investigate the job creation record of the agency charged with the responsibility of promoting indigenous economic growth in Northern Ireland.

Since its inception in 1971 LEDU's primary aim has been the creation of employment in the small firm sector.[6] The jobs objective, revised only slightly differently over the years, has dominated the organization's approach and operations. For the most part, LEDU ties financial assistance to the number of jobs promoted and created in the small firm sector. In the 1980s attention was focused on the fact that not all jobs promoted were created. There was also concern about the quality and duration of the jobs created. Consequently, in the late 1980s the overall objective of LEDU was to *maximize enduring employment*.

Any analysis of the performance of LEDU with respect to its function of providing selective financial assistance during the 1980s must therefore take as its main focus the achievement of the Agency in maximizing enduring employment in the small firm sector. While the policy may have changed[7] in the interim an assessment of the success of past policies is not only of academic interest. Much can be learned from the success, or failure, of past activities while the effectiveness of past policies can also act as a base-line against which to measure the success of the new strategy.

The analysis contained in this section is based upon the recently published NIERC evaluation report on the job creation activities of LEDU in the period 1984/85 – 1988/89 (Hart *et al.*, 1993).[8] In evaluating the overall effect of LEDU's job-related assistance the study concentrated upon four separate issues: Job Uptake; Job Duration; Deadweight; Displacement. The final aim of the study was to arrive at a measure of additionality for LEDU job-related assistance. This would estimate the aggregate number of jobs created with LEDU assistance after allowing for deadweight and displacement. Within the space constraints of this chapter it is only possible to present a summary of the key findings of the analysis.

The study investigated firms receiving assistance during the five financial years from April 1984 to March 1989. In this period 1,345 firms were recorded as receiving job-related assistance from LEDU. Of these, 591 were new firms formed during the period. Another 754 assisted firms were already in existence, employing 6,865 people at the time of assistance. A further 14,000 jobs were 'promoted' in these 1,345 firms, i.e. the firms expected to create these additional jobs in return for financial assistance. By the end of 1990, 993 of the LEDU clients were still in operation employing 16,908 people, and 352 firms had closed. Job creation over the period totalled 10,043. Therefore, for all assisted firms just under three-quarters (72.2 per cent) of job promotions were actually achieved. This low uptake rate was caused by the closure of almost a quarter of assisted firms.

The duration of assisted jobs is considered firstly by measuring the survival and closure of assisted firms, and secondly by examining employment change within surviving firms. A little under three-quarters of the 1,345 companies assisted over the period survived until the end of 1990. The average annual survival rate was 88.6 per cent, indicating that 11.4 per cent of firms closed each year.

The evaluation concluded that over half of the 10,043 jobs created in assisted firms would probably not have been generated in the absence of LEDU's activities. As a result LEDU assistance was instrumental in creating between 4,100 and 5,500 net additional jobs in Northern Ireland over a five-year period.

The level of additionality associated with LEDU job-related assistance is estimated to lie within the range of 41 to 55 per cent. Deadweight is between 8 and 32 per cent. This low level of deadweight is due more to the higher survival rate of LEDU companies rather than to accelerated employment growth in surviving firms. Displacement was determined using data on export sales by LEDU companies and is estimated to be 40 per cent.

Table 8.10 Employment change 1986–90 in surviving small firms

	No. of firms	Empl. in 1986	Empl. change	% change
Current LEDU				
(assisted 85–89)	653	8,212	3,412	41.5
Control groups				
NI non-assisted	1,367	11,717	14,345	22.4
of which:				
Previous LEDU				
(assisted 80–85)	406	4,101	1,989	48.5
Newer LEDU	961	7,616	639	8.4
Leicestershire	1,902	26,115	5,014	19.2
Other areas				
Republic of Ireland	4,076	54,224	6,778	12.5
Wearside	269	3,038	1,388	45.7
Northern Ireland total	2,015	19,929	6,040	30.3

Sources: NIERC, IDA and University of Northumbria at Newcastle Industrial Databases. Northern Ireland Census of Employment.

The major lessons from the analysis of additionality appear to be that larger small firms are most likely to be able to grow without LEDU assistance. In these companies deadweight is an ever-present danger facing LEDU. In the smallest firms private sector finance and assistance is less available and hence deadweight is less of a problem. However, most of these firms produce for local markets and displacement is a greater danger. LEDU, therefore, would need to apply more stringent additionality tests to larger firms, and to focus more on exporters and potential exporters among the smallest and youngest firms.

From Table 8.10 it can be seen that LEDU-assisted firms outperformed average companies in all of the comparator areas. This reflects on LEDU assistance, especially since local demand within Northern Ireland appears to have grown relatively slowly during this period. The favourable growth performance over the period 1986–90 of Northern Ireland's non-LEDU surviving companies can also be said to reflect on LEDU. Much of this favourable performance was achieved in companies which had been former LEDU clients. Some of these firms may also have received grants from LEDU not directly related to employment. In addition these firms were eligible for automatic capital grants for part of the period.

The evidence thus suggests that a regime of intensive grant assistance to small firms does result in higher employment growth even with relatively high deadweight and displacement. LEDU has made a significant and worthwhile contribution to employment creation in Northern Ireland. However, it must be stated that the rate of job creation, at around 1,000 additional jobs a year, during a period when the national economy was experiencing a boom in growth, was not sufficient to make any significant inroads into the region's chronic unemployment problems: in 1990 unemployment in Northern Ireland was just under 100,000 (13.4 per cent).

CONCLUSION

Within the last two decades there has clearly been a resurgence in the fortunes of the small firm sector in the UK and in other developed industrial economies. This analysis of the labour market impact of new and small firms revealed that there is a strong regional dimension to the debate on new enterprise creation and the performance of the small firm sector. Therefore, the greater reliance on general economy-wide policies would not appear to provide the most appropriate framework for the delivery of policy measures to depressed regional economies throughout the UK.

The evidence on the growth performance of small manufacturing firms, taken together with the earlier discussion on the centre-periphery contrasts in the formation rates of new enterprise, strongly suggests that one of the major problems with the depressed peripheral regions lies in their inability to generate sufficient numbers of *successful* small firms. Increasing the levels of enterprise formation does not on its own provide the necessary platform for economic regeneration.

Overall, the role of public policy, as illustrated by the activities of LEDU, has clearly been a significant factor in the job generation process in Northern Ireland. This has especially been the case in the latter half of the 1980s, when there has been a clear reversal of earlier trends in the growth performance of surviving small indigenous firms.

Nevertheless, two points need to be stressed by way of conclusion. First, although there are some encouraging signs in the small firm sector in Northern Ireland with regard to employment growth, the stark fact remains that the absolute number of jobs involved are very small when set aside the severity of the unemployment situation. The estimate of 1,000 net additional jobs created by LEDU each year over the period 1984/85 – 1988/89 illustrates that point very clearly. The question must seriously be asked as to whether it is realistic to expect the small indigenous manufacturing sector to take the lead in revitalizing the local economy.

Second, the evidence from the Northern Ireland job generation study demonstrates that, irrespective of the performance of the small firm sector, the key determinant of employment growth or decline are the activities of larger firms, whether indigenously or externally owned. Accordingly, the argument that the fortunes of the small firm sector are intrinsically linked to those of larger firms has much validity. Any industrial strategy ignores these links at its peril.

NOTES

1. The 1990 figure includes an allowance of 15,000 for the effect of changes introduced in the 1990 budget.
2. The analysis has been conducted for 64 GB counties and Scottish local authority regions as well as Northern Ireland.
3. Full details of the sources and methods used in the construction of the databases referred to in the analysis that follows are contained in Gudgin *et al*, (1989).
4. Calculation of a formation rate is not straightforward, since there is no single unambiguous choice for denominator. The conventional measures the reflect the stock of potential entrepreneurs and use employment in the relevant sectors. Conventionally, this is base year employment in manufacturing. Since, some

founders originate from non–manufacturing backgrounds it is advantageous to include some non–manufacturing employees in the denominator.
5. The formation rates presented here for the period 1973–86 should be regarded as broadly equivalent to the *net* formation rates presented in Table 1.
6. LEDU's budget in 1991/92 was £39.7m, of which £32.5m was programme expenditure mainly in the form of grants to small firms in Northern Ireland, and £7.2m administrative costs. The agency has a staff of 270 persons.
7. Since 1990 the emphasis of policy has changed radically. The DED's document 'The Key to Growth' laid out a new direction for industrial policy to be followed by various agencies including LEDU. In its current Corporate Plan for 1989–94 'Forward Thinking', LEDU describes its policy mission as existing 'to strengthen the Northern Ireland economy by encouraging enterprise and stimulating competitiveness in new and existing businesses. In practice the emphasis on job-creation has been relegated to a background aim. The immediate concern is now to develop stronger businesses in larger numbers.
8. The author gratefully acknowledges the permission of the NIERC to use some of of the analysis in this chapter.

REFERENCES

Armington, C. and Odle, M. (1982) 'Small Business – How many jobs?', *Brookings Review*, Winter pp. 14–17

Ashcroft, B. et al. (1991) 'New Firm Formation in the British Counties with special reference to Scotland', *Regional Studies*, 25.5, pp. 395–409.

Birch, D.L. (1979) *The Job Generation Process*, MIT Program on Neighbourhood and Regional Change, Cambridge, Massachusetts.

Burrows, R. (1991a) 'The Discourse of the Enterprise Culture and the Restructuring of Britain: a polemical contribution'. In Curran and Blackburn (eds) *Paths of Enterprise: the Future of the Small Business*, Routledge, London

Burrows, R. (1991b) *Deciphering the Enterprise Culture,* Routledge, London.

Campbell *et al.* (1992) 'Self Employment: into the 1990s', *Employment Gazette,* June 1992, pp 269–292.

Curran, J. and Blackburn, R. (1991) *Paths of Enterprise: the Future of the Small Business*, Routledge, London.

Daly, M. (1991) 'The growth in enterprise: self employment data from the Labour Force Survey', *Employment Gazette*, March 1991, pp. 109–134.

Daly, M. *et al.* (1992) 'Job Creation 1987–89: preliminary analysis by sector' *Employment Gazette*, August 1992, pp. 387–392.

Department of Economic Development (1987) *Building a Stronger Economy: the Pathfinder Initiative,* HMSO, Belfast.

Department of Economic Development (1990) *Northern Ireland: Competing in the 90s: the key to growth*, HMSO, Belfast.

Department of Trade and Industry (1988) *DTI – the Department for Enterprise,* HMSO.

Fothergill, S. and Gudgin, G. (1979) 'The Job Generation Process in Britain', *Centre for Environmental Studies*, London.

Fothergill, S. and Gudgin, G. (1982) *Unequal Growth: Urban and Regional Employment Change in the UK*, Heinemann, London.

Fothergill, S. and Guy, N. (1990) *Branch Factory Closures in Northern Ireland*, NIERC Belfast

Ganguly, A. (1982) 'Births and Deaths of Firms in the UK in 1980, *British Business*, 9, pp. 204–7.

Gudgin, G. et al (1989) *Job Generation in Manufacturing Industry, 1973–86: a comparison of Northern Ireland with the Republic of Ireland and the English Midlands*, Northern Ireland Economic Research Centre (NIERC), Belfast.

Hart, M. and Gudgin, G. (1992) 'Spatial Variations in New Firm Formations in the Republic of Ireland 1980–1990', paper presented at OECD Workshop, Dec. 1992, Paris: mimeo

Hart, M., Scott, R, Keegan, R. and Gudgin, G.(1993) *Job Creation and Small Firms: An Economic evaluation of Job Creation in Small Firms assisted by the Northern Ireland Local Enterprise Development Unit (LEDU)*, NIERC, Belfast.

Hitchens, D.M.W.N. and O'Farrell, P.N. (1987) 'The Comparative Performance of Small Manufacturing Firms in Northern Ireland and South East England', *Regional Studies*, 21.6, pp. 547–553.

Hitchens, D.M.W.N. and O'Farrell, P.N. (1988a) 'The Comparative Performance of Small Manufacturing Companies in South Wales and Northern Ireland: an analysis of matched pairs', *Omega International Journal of Management Science*, 16.5, pp. 429–438.

Hitchens, D.M.W.N. and O'Farrell, P.N. (1988b) 'The Comparative Performance of Small Manufacturing Companies in the Mid-West and Northern Ireland', *Economic and Social Review*, 19.3, pp. 177–198.

Hitchens, D.M.W.N. and Birnie, J.E. (1989) 'Economic Development in Northern Ireland: Has Pathfinder lost its way? A Reply', *Regional Studies*, 23.5, pp. 477–482.

Hughes, A. (1990) 'Industrial Concentration and the Small Business Sector in the UK: the 1980s in Historical Perspective', Aug. 1990, *Small Business Research Centre*, Working Paper No. 3.

Keat, M. and Abercrombie, J. (1991) *Enterprise Culture*, Routledge, London.

Keeble, D. (1990) 'Small Firms, New Firms and Uneven Regional Development in the UK', *Area*, 22, pp. 234–245.

Mason, C. (1985) 'The Geography of Successful Small Firms in the UK', *Environment and Planning A*, 17, pp. 1499–1513.

Mason, C. (1991) 'Spatial variations in enterprise', in Burrows, R. (ed.) *Deciphering the Enterprise Culture*, Routledge, London.

Mason, C. (1992) 'New Firm Formation and Regional Development in the 1990s', in Townroe, P. and Martin, R. *Regional Development in the 1990s*, Regional Studies Association.

Mason, C.M. and Harrison, R.T. (1985) 'The Geography of Small Firms in the UK: towards a research agenda', *Progress in Human Geography*, 9, pp 1–37.

Mason, C.M. and Harrison, R.T. (1990) 'Small Firms: Phoenix from the Ashes?', in Pinder, D. (ed.) *Western Europe: Challenge and Change*, Belhaven, London.

Scott, R. and O'Reilly, M. (1992) *Exports of Northern Ireland Manufacturing Companies 1990*, NIERC, Belfast.

Storey, D.J. and Johnson, S. (1987a) *Job Generation and Labour Market Change*, Macmillan, London.

Storey, D.J. and Johnson, S. (1987b) 'Job Generation and SMEs', Vols 1–3,

Programme of Research and Actions on Development of the Labour Market, Commission of the European Communities, Luxembourg.

Storey, D.J. (1981) 'New Firm Formation, Employment Change and the Small Firm: The Case of Cleveland County', *Urban Studies*, 18, pp. 335–45.

Teague, P. (1989a) 'Economic Development in Northern Ireland: Has Pathfinder lost its way?', *Regional Studies*, 23.1 pp. 63–68.

Teague, P. (1989b) 'Pathfinder: A reply to Hitchens and Birnie', *Regional Studies*, 23.5 pp. 483–486.

9

THE POTENTIAL AND LIMITS TO NORTH–SOUTH ECONOMIC CO-OPERATION

Rory O'Donnell and Paul Teague

A few years back the consensus was to dismiss the idea of deeper economic links between the North and South of Ireland (O'Malley 1989). Now this accepted view is fragmenting. More and more people are coming to believe that economic co-operation on an all-Ireland basis offers a range of benefits and opportunities. Yet although the idea has gained popularity, a good deal of confusion prevails about what should be the substance of North-South economic co-operation.

Much of this uncertainty is caused by the notion of economic co-operation being open-ended and ill-defined. Experience shows that it can take a number of forms and can be obtained by widely different procedures. In some instances, the launch of co-operation has involved the signing of a treaty or protocol which defined the scope and extent of collaboration and set out the model of economic association which the partners would like to reach. A number of associative models have emerged via this route, ranging from those which are narrowly focused to those which are more expansive, covering various economic and policy functions. Other cases display a type of rolling co-operation in which formal and integrated arrangements arise from a series of discrete collaborative initiatives. The Benelux Economic Union, for example, was the product of a fifteen-year integration process involving individual agreements, protocols, ministerial decisions and so on across the economies (Meade et al., 1962). Economic co-operation can involve a degree of political integration, as characterized by the European Community, but this does not have to be the case. Thus the

Nordic Economic Council has brought about close economic ties between Scandinavian countries without compromising their political independence. Nearer home, a de facto monetary union operated between the United Kingdom and the Republic of Ireland for over fifty years without weakening political sovereignty. Realistically, however, deep and intensive forms of economic integration probably require some formal political co-operation or integration between the participating countries (Schmitter 1992). Conversely, if there is political opposition to economic collaboration then such initiatives are unlikely to reach their maximum feasible potential.

Thus economic co-operation is a fairly malleable notion. This situation holds both benefits and drawbacks for the local debate on the issue. On the positive side, it means that greater economic and commercial links between the North and South of Ireland can take whatever form the policy and business worlds deem appropriate. Initiatives do not have to be shackled by issues which may undermine the active pursuit of policy. On the negative side, however, adopting such an essentially eclectic approach carries the dangers of collaboration becoming a 'muddling through' option. Schemes could be launched here and there with little relation to each other, producing an overall effect which is haphazard and incoherent. Now circumstances may dictate the adoption of such an approach rather than a more ordered and systematic strategy. But it would be preferable for co-ordinated and structured arrangements to emerge for they are more likely to produce worthwhile and positive results.

Thus this chapter examines a number of possible different co-ordinated routes to North-South economic co-operation. The first section discusses the maximalist option, in which the objective of co-operation would be a full-blown recasting of economic institutions and arrangements in Ireland. Then an assessment is made of the opposing minimalist strategy where co-operation would involve relatively low-key and 'negative' initiatives to improve commercial and trading opportunities both sides of the border. The chapter argues that both are inappropriate models to base a concerted drive to improve and intensify North–South economic connections. Whereas a maximalist course would be too disruptive given its excessive harmonization and integration tendencies, a minimalist approach would be too weak to exploit all the potential gains from collaboration. In the light of this conclusion, the final section suggests a co-ordination approach to the question of cross border economic co-operation.

THE MAXIMALIST ROUTE

Conceivably, the purpose of cross-border economic co-operation could be to launch a process aimed at taking Northern Ireland out of an economic union with Great Britain and creating a new economic union in Ireland. If the objective was to introduce such root and branch changes in an orderly and tidy manner, then the programme would in all likelihood be guided by the principles of fiscal federalism. Fiscal federalism is a body of economic theory used to analyse the optimal assignment of economic functions between different tiers of government. For an economic framework to work optimally in the sense of maximizing overall welfare a number of conditions have to be met. First, the relationship between different tiers of government have to be symmetrical and symbiotic. Such a synergy allows economies of scale to be captured in areas such as transportation and communication networks and negative externalities and spillovers to be reduced on matters such as limiting debt accumulation by local government. Second, the framework must have the capacity to adjust to asymmetric shocks so as to maintain stability. For some this capacity involves the economy being free of rigidities so that wages and prices can downwardly adjust when times are bad. Others regard such conditions as unrealistic since they view prices and wages to be relatively fixed in the short-term and thus see stabilization being secured either through a devaluation or by higher taxes or debt. Third, the economy must have redistribution mechanisms to ensure economic and social cohesion. Most economies at some time suffer from some type of income gap involving regions, industrial sectors or specific groups which have to be addressed by fiscal transfers. All in all, an economic framework is seen to be working successfully (or maximizing welfare) when it achieves an efficient allocation of public goods and services, macroeconomic stability and effective re-distributional policies.

In crude terms, these are the key principles of fiscal federalism. To achieve overall co-ordination with regard to allocation, stabilization and re-distribution functions, countries use different constitutional and institutional arrangements. Thus, a priori, no good grounds exist for not considering the establishment of a new economic union in Ireland along fiscal federalist lines. But once the economic realities of modern Ireland are confronted the impracticalities of creating such a new economic union immediately come to light. Economic performance and conditions both sides of the border are fairly gloomy. In these circumstances, it would be short-sighted to pursue a full-blown integration strategy. With regard to Southern Ireland, after about three years of relatively good performance in terms of rapid growth and lower unemployment the economy begin to weaken in the latter part of 1990 and has remained fragile ever since. Nominal indicators such as inflation and exchange rate levels have remained basically sound, but there has been a deterioration in real variables such as employment and output growth. As a result, unemployment started to rise again and now stands at 15.8 per cent of the workforce, one of the worst levels in the EC. Moreover, with growth rates faltering, thus reducing the amount of tax revenue collected, the government found itself in 1991 over-committed on the expenditure front by about IR £200m. In normal times, such a relatively small revenue shortfall could have been met by increasing public borrowing. But against the backdrop of a debt/GNP ratio of 110 per cent such a response was regarded by the government as an option of last resort. Thus to balance the public accounts, it chose to cut back on existing expenditure commitments. In particular, it proposed to hold back promised pay awards to public sector workers. However, this proposal caused a political storm which threatened other crucial areas of economic management, particularly the Programme for Economic and Social Progress.

This episode shows that even on a yearly basis the Irish government is finding it difficult to manage its public finances. A huge overhang of debt caused by cavalier public expenditure policies in the 1970s is the source of the government's fiscal straitjacket. Although not as bad as in the early 1980s when the ratio of debt to GDP was rising exponentially, repaying this debt has had a bruising effect on the economy. Effectively the only way that such repayments can be made is if the country runs a balance of payments surplus, thereby earning extra income from abroad. For most of the 1980s Southern Ireland ran a balance of payments surplus with most of the earned income going to reduce the country's debt burden. But of course this strategy amounts to a net transfer of resources out of the country which places enormous constraints on internal expansion. For instance, in the Republic it has proven extremely difficult to use income earned from the trade surplus to expand employment in the face of a huge job crisis. In other words, servicing the country's debt problem has ruled out the public authorities pursuing 'fiscal activist' strategies to tackle some of its economic problems.

Now this is the very last economic situation Southern Ireland would want to be in before entering an economic union with Northern Ireland. Currently the province is bedeviled by a range of economic shortcomings. Perhaps the chief characteristic of the regional economy is the stark gap between its income and expenditure. Approximately, total public expenditure exceeds locally raised revenue by some 25 per cent, suggesting that the province is living substantially beyond its means. For the most part, this gap is met by a fiscal transfer from the UK exchequer. The UK subvention has resulted in the public sector playing the central role in the economy. Twice as important to the Northern Ireland economy than to any other UK region, the public sector directly employs over 40 per cent of the workforce and many other jobs indirectly depend on government expenditure. Estimates suggest that if the subvention were cut off, local living standards would fall by about a third. Yet despite the large public sector, unemployment has remained persistently high and currently stands at 15 per cent. Moreover, as the manufacturing sector has fallen in absolute and relative terms over the past two decades, the prospect of the province becoming anywhere near self-reliant in the foreseeable future is bleak.

Thus the prevailing economic conditions both North and South could not be worse for a full-blown integration strategy. Strictly speaking, if an all-Ireland economic union were created then the subvention from the UK to Northern Ireland would end. To allow the region to maintain its present income levels, the new union – which in reality means the current government in Dublin – would have to transfer about £2.2 billion annually to the province. In rough terms this amounts to 12 per cent of Southern Ireland's GNP. Given the current state of the public finances such a financial commitment would put the Exchequer Borrowing Requirement and the debt/GNP ratio under intolerable stress. Were it to be attempted, the result would be a massive increase in interest rates which would cause output and employment levels to fall sharply. In all likelihood both parts of the island would experience a deep slump from which it would take years to recover. In the language of fiscal federalism, a stand-alone economic union in Ireland would be unable to realise the stabilization and redistribution functions so necessary to make it a viable economic entity.

Such a conclusion cannot be seriously disputed. To overcome this huge hurdle, advocates of an all-Ireland economic union suggest that such an arrangement could be made viable if an external entity contributed to its public finances. Rowthorn and Wayne (1988), for instance, argue that the British subvention to Northern Ireland should continue to ease the transitional problems of economically integrating both parts of Ireland. But this option is not now being seriously proposed, as it has come to be seen as politically too controversial or unrealistic. Instead, a preference is emerging for the EC, perhaps with the British government, to take on the role of financial guarantor to a new Irish economic union as part of a wider settlement to the political conflict in the province. No legal barriers stand in the way of the EC taking on this role. Article 130b of the new Treaty on Economic Union that emerged from the Maastricht Summit allows for Community action outside the existing Structural Funds to improve economic and social cohesion between and even within member states. However, the practicalities of the Community making such a financial commitment are far less clear cut.

Currently, the Community does not have the budgetary capacity to sustain an annual subvention to an all-Ireland economic union. Such a commitment would use up over half of the Community's resources targeted at regional and social issues. Proposals are now on the table for a sizeable increase in the Community budget, but it remains highly uncertain whether these will be adopted, especially after the post-Maastricht melt-down in European integration. Even if these proposals were adopted, Ireland would be only one of a number of countries or causes claiming a disproportionate share of the extra money. Pitted against the economic problems of eastern Europe and the economic tensions associated with creating European monetary union, it is far from certain that the financial needs of Irish economic integration would win out. Thus in all probability, if the EC were to underwrite the financial costs of creating an Irish economic union, it would have to be the result of a special one-off initiative by the twelve member states. Whether the political will exists amongst EC members to launch such an initiative is at best an open question.

Even if a financial underwriter were secured for an all-Ireland economic union, such an arrangement would still have serious economic shortcomings. Receiving an external subsidiary would certainly reduce the financial problems that would emerge in all Ireland economic union. But there would be a down side to this situation. Experience has shown that where an economy relies on an internal benefactor a series of internal distortions and tensions emerge. One widely recognized problem is that the budget constraint is softened creating asymmetric incentive and signalling structures in the economy. In relation to Northern Ireland, for instance, it is now more or less accepted that while the British subvention acts as an economic lifeline to the province it also triggers negative spillovers such as creating a bloated public sector, entrenching the economy in the non-tradeable sector, dulling entrepreneurial drive in the private (tradeable) sector and more generally generating a climate of dependency.

Similar problems could arise in an all-Ireland economic union dependent on outside economic assistance. With regard to Northern Ireland such an arrangement may simply amount to changing the institutional and political foundations of dependency, which calls into question the economic purpose of the exercise. Potentially, the implications for Southern Ireland are actually damaging. In the past decade or so the main positive feature of the Republic's economy is that it is beginning to create mechanisms and institutions that allow it to face the full vagaries of international economic and commercial life. Thus for instance the recent attempts at wage co-ordination aim at establishing the optimal balance between unemployment, inflation and competitiveness.

By easing the pressures on government, trade unions and employers to reach compromises about economic management, a highly subsidized economic union could undermine the co-ordination mechanisms that have just emerged in the Republic. Hedonistic economic behaviour, as well as unruly economic norms, may come to dominate just as they do in Northern Ireland. Thus whilst an external benefactor may shore up incomes in an all-Ireland economic union, it may also block the establishment of the institutions and arrangements required to create a dynamic and self-reliant economic entity. All in all, it is likely that more economic disadvantages than benefits may arise from the creation of an all-Ireland economic union.

THE MINIMALIST SCENARIO

Over the past few years interest in North–South economic cooperation has grown considerably in the business community on both sides of the border. Perhaps the first clear indication of this interest came in 1990 when the Northern Ireland committee of the Institute of Directors organized a conference on the theme in Belfast. Since then the Confederation of Irish Industry (CII) based in Dublin and the Northern Ireland committee of the Confederation of British Industry (CBI) have established a number of joint working parties and conducted a number of small-scale research projects to improve North–South economic and commercial connections. Recently the two organizations produced a joint report arguing that a huge potential exists for greater North–South trade.

The starting point for this report is the observation that there is relatively little trade between North and South. For example, it points out that manufacturers from the Republic sell only one-third as much per capita in Northern Ireland as they do in the Republic; and manufacturers from Northern Ireland sell only one-sixth as much per capita in the Republic as they do in Northern Ireland. From this it has been inferred that 'total trade between the two parts of the island could at least be trebled from the current level of £1.5 billion to £4.5 billion' (CII, 1992). The employment effect of such an increase has been calculated to be 30,000 additional manufacturing jobs and 75,000 additional jobs in total. This possibility of trebling trade and increasing employment by 75,000 has been cited in many discussions of North–South co-operation (see, for example, Kinsella, 1992; Quigley, 1992).

The central proposition is that by the removal of barriers, and certain positive actions, trade can be increased in a way which has strong mutual benefits. This is a situation which requires the application of the microeconomic approach articulated in the Cecchini report, *The Economics of 1992*, Buigues and Jacquemin's analysis of the strategies of firms in the large internal market and Kay's guide to identifying the 'strategic market'. The Cecchini Report outlined the two channels – 'size' and 'competition' – through which the removal of NTBs influences firms and industries (Emerson, *et al.*, 1988). Buigues and Jacquemin (1989) identify different firm strategies and relate these to a range of structural environments. Kay outlines the concept of the strategic market and shows how its geographic and product dimensions are determined (Kay, 1990). All of these analytical approaches caution against the rhetorical notion of a European market of 320 million consumers. When applied to Ireland they suggest that we should be wary of the idea of an easily available market of 5 million or a 'single Irish market'.

One of the central insights of the literature cited above is that barriers of the sort which are being removed in the 1992 programme are not the only reason for fragmented and segmented markets. The history of the economies of Northern Ireland and the Republic confirm this and provide an important background to the current situation and future possibilities. The two Irish economies have been externally oriented, rather than trading with each other, since at least the nineteenth century. While the North became an important part of the British manufacturing base, serving an imperial market, the South adopted the role of supplier of agricultural produce for the British market. These separate orientations were strengthened in the twentieth century, when the South used tariff protection in an attempt to re-industrialize. In the past thirty years the two economies have become much more similar, but not in a way which fosters intense interaction – since branch plant investment is the basis of both. In this situation some potential for certain synergies probably exists. The key questions are: how much and what are the significant remaining barriers?

A systematic application of the analytical approaches mentioned above suggests that there is limited potential for easy increases in trade between North and South. The method is to consider in turn the three channels through which removal of tariff or non-tariff barriers influences firms and industries: first, traditional inter-industry adjustment, second, exploitation of economies of scale and, third, the effect of increased competition on pricing and innovation.

There must be very little scope for inter-industry adjustment between the two economies, since their economic structures and factor prices are now very similar. Second, though there could be some reduction in costs from the removal of NTBs it is unlikely that this would generate a significant indirect effect via the exploitation of economies of scale. Research by O'Malley (1992) shows that the Republic of Ireland no longer features in most industries in which there are large economies of scale – let alone unexploited economies of scale. This is not so true of Northern Ireland (Enderwick *et al.*, 1988). But the large firms in Northern Ireland have acquired their scale through access over a long period of time to a much wider market, and the 'creation' of a market of 5 million in Ireland is unlikely to allow further exploitation of scale advantages. However, as the NESC have argued, consideration of industries in which there are large economies of scale, and in which scale is the key competitive advantage, is not enough. 'Clearly there are many industries where product differentiation or scientific application, rather than scale, is the key competitive advantage, but where some economies of scale still exist" (NESC, 1989, p. 239). This suggests that in both the Republic and Northern Ireland there are some firms which could exploit scale economies through increased sales across the border. The extent to which this will occur is likely to depend on three factors: (a) whether the most significant barriers are removed, (b) the number of firms whose strategic market falls in the range between the size of the Republic and the size of Northern Ireland, and (c) whether expansion into the Northern or Southern market is seen as the easiest and most profitable route to extra sales. Since these are important general issues, they are discussed below. Overall, consideration of them suggests that we should be cautious in predicting large increases in trade and employment.

The third channel through which removal of NTB works is the effect which increased competition has on innovation. The strength of this effect depends, first, on the degree to which markets are currently segmented and prices are above costs and, then, on the extent to which the response to increased competition takes the form of product differentiation and innovation. In explaining and applying this idea, the NESC said that it 'leads to the expectation that completion of the market, by increasing competition, will have a major dynamic impact on those sectors in which current NTBs are high, technological development is significant and the outlook for market growth is good. Clearly this dynamic process would initially be much stronger in some sectors than others' (NESC, 1989, p. 241). Research has shown that in the Republic, even after EC accession, there remain industries in which the domestic market has some protection and hence firms have scope for pricing above costs (Blackwell and O'Malley, 1984; NESC, 1989). These include large-scale firms in manufacturing industries such as paper and printing, drink and tobacco, non-metallic minerals and some foods, and probably include some firms in financial services. It is probable that similar firms exist in Northern Ireland. The question is the extent to which 1992 or other action will induce cross-border market penetration and consequent innovation. While some cross-border market penetration is likely, several of the relevant industries are slow-growth sectors in which there may be little scope for technical innovation. There may, of course, be scope for product differentiation. The food and drink industries account for a large portion of this 'naturally' protected group. But consideration of their position suggests that there may be limited scope for new trade and net employment increases. First, meat, dairy products and beverages already account for a very significant proportion of existing cross-border trade. Second, further cross-border trade will replace local, rather than foreign production and will be beneficial because it reduces prices and widens choice for consumers, not because it creates employment.

In summary, consideration of the three ways in which removal of NTBs influences firms and industries suggests that the 1992 programme may not increase cross-border trade to the huge extent which is sometimes suggested.

STRATEGIC MARKETS, HOME MARKETS AND SEGMENTED MARKETS

Even if the major barriers were removed, the question remains: how many firms would find their strategic market to coincide with the island of Ireland? The comparison which underlies most of the discussion of possible increases in North–South trade (that manufacturers in the Republic sell only one-third as much per capita in Northern Ireland as they do in the Republic) may be somewhat misleading. The use of these comparisons implicitly assumes that the primary strategic market is the home market – i.e. the national geographic area. It is then further assumed that Northern Ireland can be added to the Republic's home market and vice versa. These assumptions may be incorrect – for several reasons. Many firms do not sell outside a market area with a radius of twenty or so miles – and hence are no more likely to sell to Northern Ireland after 1992 than before it. Other firms have strategic markets which are international and which may or may not include Northern Ireland. The assumption of some of the discussion of trade would seem to be that there is sufficient market segmentation to guarantee a 'home market' on the island of Ireland. What factors could ensure that the Northern Ireland market 'has the potential to purchase three times more production within a few years' (CII, 1992)? Both transport costs and agglomeration economies can create advantages for local suppliers. But are these sufficient to give suppliers from the Republic clear advantages over foreign suppliers? The whole drift of the 1992 programme is to widen the sphere of competition. The extreme openness of both the Republic and Northern Ireland, and research on transport costs, suggest that the island of Ireland is not likely to form an economic entity. Finally, the very thinness of past and current economic and social interaction between North and South indicates that the agglomeration economies which can generate a growth dynamic are unlikely to emerge across the North–South divide in the foreseeable future.

Overall the low current share of cross-border trade reflects economic weakness rather than easy opportunities. The low sales of Irish industry in Ireland, in comparison with sales of Danish industry in Denmark (a fact cited by the CII) reflects the externally oriented and externally controlled nature of both Irish economies – it hardly suggests that 'sales of goods in Ireland manufactured on the island could be increased by at least 50 per cent' (CII, 1992). For producers in the Republic, the Northern Ireland market will be as toughly contested as any other, and vice versa. Indeed, there is no reason to assume that cross-border market penetration, which is bound to increase somewhat, will displace British or foreign producers rather than local suppliers.

TRANSACTIONS COSTS AND INTEGRATION THEORY

Thus although there has been an upsurge in support for North–South economic co-operation, thinking on the issue remains naive and unconvincing. New and more robust ideas are needed on the issue. In the remainder of this chapter the argument will be developed that North–South co-operation should be regarded as essentially about the positive co-ordination of two separate economies to achieve mutual benefits. First of all, the theoretical foundations of this argument are developed.

Recent developments in economic theory emphasizes that most markets are decentralized and endowed with limited information. In limited information markets agents can only explore a very restricted number of potential transactions and are obliged to operate on that basis. (In some discussions, bounded rationality rather than limited information might be the starting point then the key constraint would be the ability to process information rather than its availability, but many of the consequences would be similar). Moreover, because exchange is decentralized, buyers and sellers must themselves establish links with each other and must themselves act as price-makers with all this implies for strategic interactions. Thus in decentralized market structures there are always, actually or potentially, very high transaction costs which are variable and not fixed. Such situations encourages close and repeated 'customer' relations between buyers and sellers. (Transaction costs are here interpreted widely to include all the effects of uncertainty and all the costs of information associated with an exchange rather than the narrower question of opportunism and contract compliance – the expression is thus taken in the sense of New Keynesian theory rather than that of Williamson (1985) and the new institutionalists.)

Limited information markets often fail to clear because potential buyers and sellers do not establish effective communication with each other. On the other hand, their decentralised structure endows them with enormous plasticity and this permits a very close adaption to differentiated conditions whether on the side of supply or demand.

Such markets may therefore be described as self-organizing although they are not self-clearing. Clearly the time dimension conditions all such judgements: if long periods of time elapse without important disturbances then full information may be approached even in a decentralised system which will find a market clearing price on the basis of long experience. When short periods are considered, on the other hand, the decentralized structure in general may be regarded as subject to price inertia rather than volatility. Thus decentralized markets are fragmented and incomplete arrangements and in many cases depend on established social relations that mitigate the uncertainty which would otherwise paralyse economic life. The social links involved are of many kinds – formal and informal associations, ties of common culture in particular – but they are all influenced by history and tradition, usually in a national or local context.

Decentralized markets can be viewed as networks in which each agent only has direct contact with a few others while communication with more remote agents may be considerably impeded by transaction costs. (The notion of distance here is not directly geographical but refers to the complexity and indirectness of existing relations.) In this case the mere removal of barriers to exchange will not necessarily establish new economic relations between separate areas, because only a small subset of potential relationships will even be investigated. This kind of market has a much more palpable geography and history than in the Walrasian case: it is rational, and may be efficient, for a given agent to favour continuing relations with established partners simply because they are established and thus do not necessitate new investment in communication. Similarly cultural, or in some contexts linguistic, homogeneity may be a rational basis for economic relations even in the absence of discrimination because it will tend to lower the cost of negotiation.

Now the classical approach to integration is hardly applicable to situations where there is a range of prices for the same product within each country. As a result, 'negative' integration policies aimed at removing tariff or other governmental barriers to exchange will not be enough to establish a genuinely open market involving separate economies. Transactions costs and lack of information prevent market agents from taking advantage of all exchanges which negative integration has, in principle, made possible.

In these circumstances, positive integration of the market sector itself becomes necessary in the sense that active policies are needed to establish the linkages which sustain market exchange. Integration now takes place via the positive co-ordination of two markets. European Community technology programmes are a good example of this kind of policy. Although, in administrative terms, programmes like ESPRIT or EUREKA help to finance particular research projects by companies from different member states, the essential object of the programme is to establish a network of companies and other organizations which will constitute a European Technological Community and will ultimately be able to generate its own collaborative ventures. The programmes thus aim to reduce transactions costs and to disseminate information so that non-official barriers to free exchange – those within the private sector itself – are removed. Without this kind of positive policy markets would remain too fragmented and unco-ordinated to permit worthwhile integration. As well as positive interventions to make market exchanges more likely, integration may also be encouraged via common or unified public policies. The EC also provides examples of this type of positive integration. One is the Common Agricultural Policy, to the extent that it goes beyond the free movement of farm goods to define a common strategy for intervention in the agricultural sector; another is the imposition of production quotas and minimum prices in the crisis-hit European steel industry during the 1980s.

NORTH–SOUTH ECONOMIC CO-OPERATION AS POSITIVE CO-ORDINATION

Thus from this theoretical standpoint North–South economic co-operation may yield the best results if it involves positive co-ordination measures. Or put another way a co-ordination deficit exists between the two economies which has caused certain economic gains to remain unexploited. To a large extent, this deficit is reflected in the remarkably thin economic relations between the North and the South. The CII note that 'perhaps of greatest importance has been the psychological barrier caused by lack of communications. It is remarkable that the density of telephone traffic is proportionately only one-sixth as great between the Dublin area and Northern Ireland as it is with, say, the province of Munster' (CII, 1992). Moreover, the co-ordination deficit is inseparable from the historical/political, and in the past twenty years, the military situation. It is almost certain that at present the greatest barrier to cross-border economic activity is the IRA war, the political uncertainty which fuels it and the widespread military and security measures which are necessary because of it. The repeated bombing, and eventual closure, of the electricity interconnector between North and South and the continual bombing of the Dublin–Belfast railway line are only the more obvious demonstrations of this.

INDUSTRIAL POLICY

To argue for the need for positive co-ordination should not be taken as a licence to propose co-operative ventures willy nilly. Careful consideration needs to be given to any project before collaboration is mounted. A number of proposals have been made for North–South economic co-operation which would require positive co-ordination schemes but which have not been adequately thought out. One suggestion is for North–South economic co-operation to encourage the merger of existing companies north and south of the border to obtain greater economies of scale effects in Irish industry. Certainly there may be cases where the coming together of certain companies will generate such effects, but it is open to doubt whether this should be an objective of an all-Ireland economic policy. Encouraging Irish industry to pursue economies of scale strategies may be locking it into a production and commercial model which has become outmoded. In particular, the realization of economies of scale crucially depends on producing relatively homogeneous goods in long production runs for relatively stable markets. Yet there is clear evidence in Europe of a real diversity of demand for products, obliging firms to produce more customized goods in small batches.

Consider, for example, the experience of the European clothing industry. This sector has seen a considerable restructuring over the past decade or so in the face of stiff international competition. The mass production of standard goods using long production runs has by and large been relegated to low-wage, less developed countries. European producers have (to different degrees) concentrated more and more on high-quality fashion products, producing an increasingly wide range of goods and turning them over rapidly year by year. Successful firms will be those that cater to the needs of local markets, operating flexible production strategies that respond to diversity in demand. For the most part the quest for economies of scale has given way to the capturing of economies of scope, loosely defined to mean the ability to move from one product market to another with relative ease. To realize economies of scope requires radically different organizational structures, skill levels amongst employees, and commercial strategies from those used to capture economies of scale. Thus it is highly questionable whether North–South economic co-operation should encourage vertical integration strategies amongst Irish companies.

Another popular proposal for North–South economic co-operation is the creation of an economic corridor on the eastern seaboard of the island, roughly running from Belfast to Dublin. This idea is heavily influenced by the emergence elsewhere of dynamic regional economic systems such as Silicon Valley in California, Cite Scientifique around Paris and the M4 corridor in the South-East of England. With regard to an all-Ireland economic corridor, the objective would be to generate agglomeration or external economies through the clustering of interdependent firms. Such agglomeration economies would hopefully allow Irish companies to steal a march on their competitive rivals, particularly inside the European market. Superficially this proposal is attractive but on closer examination it has certain problems. As Saxenian (1989) splendidly shows with regard to the Cambridge phenomena, agglomeration economies cannot be mechanically created by public authorities. Rather they result from peculiar and subtle interconnections between firms and external institutions which take time to foster. Whether Ireland can go from the position of having little cross-border economic collaboration to the situation where it provides agglomeration economies spanning both parts of the island is an open question. The uncommitted would certainly conclude that such a project was too ambitious.

But there may be scope to create strategic alliances between enterprises on both sides of the border. In each part of the island firms face considerable obstacles in penetrating international markets – including the Irish market. It is widely acknowledged that where competitive advantage based on scale cannot be acquired, then a range of strategies involving product differentiation and market segmentation must be considered. It is also acknowledged that innovation, product differentiation and marketing are highly demanding in terms of both finance and management skills. In this situation firms frequently do best by making strategic alliances which give them access to the advantages already acquired by their partner.

Since these problems are particularly acute for firms in both the Republic and Northern Ireland – due to small scale, weak management, few external economies, a poor tradition of R&D and innovation, limited access to equity and venture capital and other problems – it is precisely in this area that the potential for North–South co-operation exists. The proposals for initiatives, by private or public sector bodies, to enhance information, encourage joint promotions, assist co-operative ventures on product development and branding, and to strengthen other strategic alliances, seem sensible. Even then the amount of public resources devoted to these activities should be limited, since these North–South strategic alliances are not essentially any different from alliances with overseas firms. Indeed, there is reason to believe that, on average, alliances with overseas firms will be more advantageous, since the synergy arises precisely from differences rather than similarities.

BORDER REGION INITIATIVES

It is well known that border regions tend to suffer from particular problems due to their isolation within national economies and the effect which borders have in creating different fiscal and labour market regimes and in representing the frontier between linguistic and ethnic communities. This is a phenomenon found in many member states and the Community's INTERREG initiative is an attempt to address some of these problems. There is no doubt that some of these problems arise along the land border between the Republic and the United Kingdom. It is entirely appropriate that the Community and both member states should implement appropriate programmes in the border areas.

However, these initiatives should be seen for what they are – standard border-area regional policies – and should not be subsumed into the rhetoric of an extensive and, as we have seen, questionable programme of general North–South economic and political co-operation. The Community should not allow any such rhetoric to lead it to commit excessive resources to wider cross-border initiatives in the hope that it will thereby assist to ameliorate the conflict in Northern Ireland (see below).

TRANSPORT

Transport is another area in which there is scope for North–South co-operation. The need for co-operation arises for two reasons. First, the intensity and efficiency of economic interaction between the two regions depends, in part, on the density and quality of transport connections. Second, transport between the Republic and Northern Ireland forms an important part of each region's external logistics – especially movement along the route which runs from Rosslare to Belfast (Co-operation North, 1983). What transport problems can be identified and what are their causes? First, the Dublin–Belfast road is not of sufficient quality. This problem arises from insufficient public capital expenditure, reflecting fiscal pressures and policy priorities. Second, the Dublin–Belfast railway line provides a slow and broken service. This problem is, to a very large extent, due to continued IRA bombing of the line. Third, many roads between the Republic and Northern Ireland are closed – greatly reducing the density of transport interconnections. This is a result of the security response to IRA activity. Fourth, there are problems arising from differential regulation of the haulage industry and the management of Dublin Port. The effect of these problems is to give Northern Ireland hauliers an advantage and to route a surprisingly large proportion of freight traffic through the port of Larne. The problem of differences in regulation is a standard problem of economic integration and requires the vigorous measures of both positive and negative integration. The weakness of Dublin Port is a problem of public sector management within the Republic. The final transport problem is the quality of key road and rail links in Britain. This too can be viewed as a standard problem of economic integration – requiring either a co-operative or a supranatural solution.

To what extent does solution of these problems require North–South co-operation? Improvement of the Rosslare–Belfast road requires co-operation between the Irish government, the UK government and the EC. In the context of a general improvement of roads in the Republic, and Structural Fund assistance to both regions, there is a case for investment here. However, the amount of investment should be decided by reference to a realistic assessment of the potential increase in the efficiency and volume of trade.

While improvement of the Dublin–Belfast railway line requires some investment, its efficiency and potential to attract passengers depends essentially on a cessation of violence both to the track and in Northern Ireland. This, and the closure of many roads, depends far more on the removal of political uncertainty by the British government than on any international economic co-operation. Again, the amount of investment should be tailored to the likely density of traffic: Quigley reports calculations which show 'that the propensity for passenger traffic by rail is eight times greater in the case of Dublin–Cork than Dublin–Belfast and four times greater in the case of Dublin Waterford' (Quigley, 1992).

The problems of regulation and transport infrastructure in Britain do not require North–South co-operation, per se. They require co-operation between the Irish and British governments and, in all probability, the involvement of the Community.

ENERGY

The presence of significant economies of scale in the provision of energy infrastructure makes it a natural area for inter-regional and international co-operation. Such co-operation yields the normal benefits of trade – competitive pricing and efficiency – and, in addition, economies of capacity use and scale and decreased vulnerability (McGurnaghan and Scott, 1981). When these principles are applied to the Irish case they are strongly confirmed, but not in a way which reinforces the idea of a single Irish market or the island of Ireland as an economic entity.

In the case of electricity, there is a strong case for interconnection between the grids in Northern Ireland and the Republic. Indeed, an interconnector was built in the late 1960s and operated from 1970. However, after continual damage by bombing, the interconnector went out of operation in 1975. McGurnaghan and Scott calculate that consumers in both the Republic and Northern Ireland pay a high price for the absence of this highly cost-effective device (McGurnaghan and Scott, 1981).

While the gas industries in the Republic and Northern Ireland were traditionally similar, they have evolved in different directions in recent years. This is because of the Republic's exploitation of natural gas and its supply to Dublin via a major pipeline. By contrast, the British government refused a natural gas pipeline from Scotland to Northern Ireland, with its high-cost 'town gas' industry. With the slow rundown of the Republic's natural gas reserves, both the Republic and Northern Ireland face the similar problem of the need for a link to an external source. Indeed, economic logic suggests 'the planning of gas transmission needs to be undertaken in an integrated manner', in that the decision on a link to GB is a matter of common concern for the Republic and Northern Ireland. Once this wider context is appreciated there is, indeed, a possible case for North–South co-operation. Drawing attention to the isolated position of Ireland and its limited resources, McGurnaghan and Scott conclude, appropriately, that 'an integrated approach to the gas industry for these islands seems the logical procedure' (McGurnaghan and Scott, 1981).

CREATING POLICY NETWORKS

To actually realize the economic benefits outlined above, an important first step may be to establish policy networks to promote cross-border economic co-operation. Currently popular in the political science literature, policy networks can be described with regard to economic matters as intermediate arrangements between government and the market and society which involve the institutionalization and formalization of certain economic management functions (Wright, 1989). The type of activity a policy network performs can vary a good deal. It can involve straigthforward consultation and the exchange of information or the co-ordination of otherwise independent action or co-operation in policy formation, implementation and legitimization. Policy networks can be organized by local organizations or can be loose arrangements without any hierarchical centre. But a key feature of networks is that they establish conventions and rules which govern the nature and type of action undertaken by the policy group. In some instances policy networks develop their own 'culture' which allows them to have a more powerful agenda-setting role.

Establishing policy networks across a range of areas would be the first decisive steps towards the positive co-ordination of the two economies. It would ensure that cross border co-operation was not ephemeral but an enduring feature of economic policy-making both sides of the border. Of course, the purpose of the policy networks would differ according to the issue at hand. In certain areas, such as education and social policy, perhaps the objective of a policy network would be to simply increase concertation (a combination of consultation and co-ordination) both sides of the border. Other policy networks may be more ambitious. For instance, technology policy may be a fruitful sphere for cross-border collaboration. Increasingly, the diffusion and application of a growing variety of business and consumer services depends on the type of telecommunication infrastructure in place. New telematic services, for example, are made possible by the interfacing of telecommunications and computing which allows the exchange of information between computer systems through networks. Such networks can unleash the full power of new information technology and have a major impact on areas such as information and communication services, tourism and so on. Now on paper at least, it would seem sensible to develop such telecommunication infrastructures on an all-Ireland basis given the positive externalities that could be captured.

The task here is not to select those areas which are suitable for policy networks and those which are not. Nor is it appropriate to attempt to define the functions of particular networks. The above examples are simply illustrations of the type of activity that networks could pursue. The key point is that a process of institutionalization has to be embarked upon so that formal structures exist for the launching of cross border economic collaboration. The groups and bodies involved in such institutionalization will obviously differ from area to area, but invariably in all cases the relevant government departures on both sides of the border will be involved in the process. Furthermore, the degree of institutionalization will differ from area to area. A body like an all-Ireland Economic Council would probably be required to oversee the establishment of specific policy networks.

THE COMMUNITY DIMENSION AND THE POSITION OF NORTHERN IRELAND

Having considered the main concrete economic issues, it is necessary to look at another dimension of the case for North–South co-operation or integration. This is the view that deepening European integration reveals the anomalous position of Northern Ireland and implies or warrants a change in the relationship North and South. For the most part, this view is based on a number of propositions concerning the representatives of Northern Ireland in EC fora, the apparent success of the Republic in the Community, the advantages of a Europe of the Regions and the effect of European integration in reducing the significance of national identity and national boundaries and thereby, possibly, ameliorating the conflict in Northern Ireland. It is clearly of great importance that the strength and limits of these propositions be evaluated. Indeed, this case may ultimately be of more than British and Irish interest – since it may provide the Community with valuable general information on the effects of economic and political integration on ethnic divisions and conflicts.

The representation of Northern Ireland's interest in Community fora is one of the important themes in Aughey, Hainsworth and Trimble's book *Northern Ireland in the European Community: An Economic and Political Analysis* (1989). Trimble draws attention to what he describes as 'a continuing clash of interests' between Northern Ireland, the UK government and the Commission over the allocation of EC budgetary resources. The question we must ask is whether this conflict can sustain the case for some all-Ireland negotiation and administration of Community regional, agricultural, R&D and competition policies and, more generally, for a change in Northern Ireland's administrative and/or constitutional status. When we do this, we find that these anxieties about Northern Ireland reflect genuine problems. Some of these arise because Northern Ireland does, indeed, have unusual representative and administrative structures; others arise as instances of Community-wide problems concerning the representation of regional and other interests. However, there is little evidence that joint North–South approaches to Community regional and other policies is feasible or, indeed, would do anything but make Northern Ireland's structures even more unusual and probably, unstable.

Trimble's discussion of the 'continuing clash of interests' brings to light a number of special factors which explain it and help to put it in perspective. First, he notes that this exists partly because of 'the British government's perception of Community finances'. This perception is one in which 'the paramount consideration must ultimately be the maximisation of EC receipts' (Trimble, 1990, p. 430). Second, Trimble notes that conflict over the national government's handling of the Structural Funds exists in most British regions, but is most obvious and most acute in Northern Ireland for two special reasons: first, Northern Ireland is unique among British regions in having separate financial accounts (a point which is emphasised by Wilson (1990) also); second, Northern Ireland has consistently had unusual local/provincial government arrangements which, at times, implied a measure of local autonomy. These specific features of the Northern Ireland situation need to be kept in mind when considering the argument that membership of the EC, in and of itself, requires some change in Northern Ireland constitutional or administrative arrangements.

In addition, it is entirely plausible that the representation of Northern Ireland's interests in London and in Brussels is not satisfactory. Northern Ireland is unlike any other region in any other member state in the way its democratic voice feeds into national politics: its politicians are excluded from the main government and opposition parties in the UK and most of its electorate have no option to vote for these parties. One example of the representational and administrative effects of this is the fact that while the Secretary of State for Scotland is, almost invariably, Scottish, the Secretary of State for Northern Ireland is never from Northern Ireland.

The significance of these particular factors in the UK and Northern Ireland must not be underestimated – since the flow of Community resources to Northern Ireland has averaged only two per cent of total public expenditure in Northern Ireland. Indeed, the significance of representation in Westminster is also emphasised by Aughey who says 'it is an illusion to suppose that current or proposed Community funds are a substitute for a sensible and just set of national economic policies' (Aughey, 1989, p. 24).

While problems in the negotiation and administration of Community policies as they apply to Northern Ireland can mainly be traced to the particular situation in the UK, and Northern Ireland's treatment within it, there is a Community dimension also – especially where regional policy is concerned. We know that even where regions are allowed to participate in national politics, and where their representatives are in national government and opposition, problems arise concerning the level at which Community regional policy should be designed and implemented. While this is partly an administrative issue, it also goes to the heart of the political dimension of European integration, since it relates to the principle of subsidiarity and the tension between the intergovernmental, supranational and democratic elements of the Community. To that extent Northern Ireland faces issues with which the whole of the Community is grappling.

If the problems of the negotiation and administration of Community policies as they apply to Northern Ireland can be traced to these Northern Ireland, UK and EC issues, the question is: to what extent is a joint North–South approach feasible and what benefits would it yield? To the extent that the argument for such an approach is based on the unrealistic assessment of the potential increase in trade and economic integration, which has characterized much of the discussion, we must discount it. This suggests that while there would be little benefit from joint approaches to the fundamental task – the execution of regional development policies – there may be some benefit from joint research. In addition, since transport and energy systems are part of regional planning, and since these have a definite international and inter-regional dimension, there is a case for co-operation in these areas. However, the analysis above suggests that the inter-regional dimensions of transport and energy encompass Ireland, Northern Ireland, and GB – rather than just the Republic and Northern Ireland. Consequently, the strongest argument is for a joint approach, in these areas of policy, between the British government, the Irish governments and the Commission.

By contrast, there seems little to gain from a purely all-Ireland approach to Community policy. This is important because there are also formidable political and administrative obstacles to such an approach. The limited concrete gains available suggest that the great difficulties, and even risks, associated with such an approach may not be worthwhile. Indeed, if the whole Community faces problems in defining the political and administrative prerogatives of the Community, the member states and the regions, it hardly seems sensible, or fair, to begin experiments on these relationships in a region which is deeply divided internally and over which sovereignty is disputed by two member states.

THE EFFECT OF INTEGRATION ON NATIONAL IDENTITY AND BOUNDARIES

The view that European integration warrants some change in relations between North and South, and the impulse, at national and Community level, to develop policies which straddle the border, draws support from the idea that the deepening of the Community can ameliorate the conflict in Northern Ireland. This is a most important idea and requires careful examination. While it is impossible to address this issue adequately in this chapter, some of the factors which should be considered can be identified.

At first sight it seems entirely plausible that deepening European integration could ameliorate the conflict in Northern Ireland. We know that a major motivation for the formation of the Community was the desire to heal the historic conflicts which had led European nations into two major wars this century. Furthermore, we can sense that the EC has achieved this to a considerable degree – not only by involving states in continual co-ordination, but also by lessening the enmity between peoples. Nevertheless, the continuation of separate national identities does not seem to have excluded the development of some degree of shared European identity.

In order to assess whether EC integration could have a similar effect on the conflict in Northern Ireland we need to look in some detail at how the Community has influenced national politics, national identities and the significance of national boundaries. This influence may not have occurred solely at the symbolic or ideological level. Significant political implications can arise from practical action at the economic level. In Pelkmans' view, when mixed economies integrate the necessary and sufficient requirement is the believable and permanent constraint of at least some domestic policy instruments, combined with the irrevocable transfer of one or more important elements of national jurisdiction to a common institution. 'The implication is an intense politicization, both of the initial bargaining leading to the basic integration Treaty and of the ensuing process' (Pelkmans, 1984). Indeed, it has been argued that because of the political nature of economic integration some policy domains are likely to be more easily transferred to the union level. In particular, this analysis was used to explain why the early stages of integration tended to consist primarily of the integration of product markets.

This analysis of the political nature of economic integration can throw considerable light on the question in hand. One important implication of the analysis is that the question of integration becomes linked to questions about the 'economic order'. An economic order can be defined as a coherent set of laws, institutions and instances allocating economic decision-making to certain types of participants. As Pelkmans says, 'among integrating mixed economies the resistance to constraints by, or transfer to, the union tier of government is inextricably linked to the prior question, namely about the economic role of the State, whether union or national' (Pelkmans, 1982). While attempts have been made to confine integration to product markets, and hence to preserve the core of 'electoral politics' (macroeconomic and distributive policies) at the national level, Pelkmans was in no doubt that pressure for deeper integration would build up. Subsequently, in reviewing the Commission's internal market white paper, Pelkmans and Robson argued that:

> An undiluted application of the principle of free movement for factors and products – which would involve not merely the negative abolition or restrictions but the elaboration of many 'positive' measures – would inevitably, through its impact on the 'effective jurisdiction' of Member States, drastically undermine the delicately balanced packages of public policy regulation, market intervention, income redistribution measures and macroeconomic policies that are at present determined at the level of national politics. (Pelkmans and Robson, 1987).

What would this lead us to expect in Northern Ireland?

The implication of this analysis is that one of the important political effects of European integration is to remove, or reduce the relevance of, the substance of domestic political competition. In particular, the integration process encroaches further into the substance of the terrain which has been disputed by Christian democratic and socialist parties since the Second World War. Many of the macroeconomic, microeconomic and redistributive issues over which they have competed can no longer be settled at national level. Whether politicians or bureaucrats admit it or not, the sovereignty of member states over these areas of policy has been diminished. But the people, and politicians, of Northern Ireland do not compete over these macroeconomic, microeconomic and redistributive issues. Indeed, they are excluded from political competition on these issues within the UK. European integration has definitely not encroached on the substance of political competition in Northern Ireland. That competition revolves around the more symbolic issues of nationality and identity and the related issue of law and order.

The implication of this argument is that European integration, as it has proceeded to date, may have significant political effects – effects which seem to reduce the significance of national boundaries – everywhere but in Northern Ireland. It also suggests that beneficial political effects of European integration could be expected if the political agenda in Northern Ireland shifted from symbolic to economic and social issues – but that is to say no more than that EC integration will help once the problem is being solved for other reasons. A third, and even more dispiriting, implication is that the erosion of the traditional political agenda in most member states (however necessary) may have something to do with the return to symbolic/ethnic issues, and the aestheticization of politics, which has been evident in many member states in recent years.

CONCLUSIONS

Four main conclusions arise from this chapter. First, those who harbour the notion that somehow increased North–South economic co-operation will create a back door for the creation of a new political and economic union in Ireland are misguided. The economic conditions are simply not in place for such an arrangement and any pursuit of such a strategy would almost certainly result in a dramatic fall in living standards both sides of the border. Second, much of the upbeat discussion within the business community about the unexploited gains that have yet to be captured from North–South co-operation is naive and hugely over-optimistic. While there may be scope for increased trade between the Republic and Northern Ireland, the benefits in terms of new business and employment will be relatively small. Third, the chapter discussed the view that the best way to view increased north–south economic integration is in terms of encouraging positive co-ordination across a range of economic policy functions and ideas. It was supported that a co-ordination deficit exists between the two economies which may be reduced through the creation of policy networks. As a result of these networks, a number of possible spillover and externalities may be captured. However, it is much too early to suggest the exact magnitudes of the economic benefits that may emerge from such a strategy, but they are unlikely to be huge. Fourth, recent talk that the EC may play a key role in fostering North–South economic co-operation was not found to be convincing. The issue of European integration may be a subject for co-operation but is really an aspect of the process.

REFERENCES

Aughey, A., Hainsworth, M. and Trimble, M. (1989) *Northern Ireland in the European Community: an economic and political analysis*, Belfast Policy Institute.

Blackwell, M., and O'Malley, E. (1984) 'Economic Policy in Sweden: Lessons for Ireland', ESRI discussion paper, Dublin.

Buigues, P. and Jacquemin, A. (1989) 'Strategies of Firms and Structural Environments in the Large Internal Market', *Journal of Common Market Studies*, **28**, 1.

Callan, T. and FitzGerald, J.D. (1989) 'Price determination in Ireland: effects of changes in exchange rates and exchange rate regimes', *Economic and Social Review*, **20**, 2.

Chick, V. and Dow, S. C. (1988). 'A Post-Keynesian Perspective on the Relation between Banking and Regional Development', *Thames Papers in Political Economy*, reprinted in P. Arestis (ed.) Post-Keynesian Monetary Economics, Elgar, Aldershot.

CII (1992) 'A Single Market on the Island', *CII Newsletter*, Confederation of Irish Industry, Dublin.

Convery, F. (1992) 'Environmental and Energy', in *Ireland in Europe: a Shared Challenge*, Stationery Office, Dublin.

Co-operation North (1983) *Transport in Northern Ireland and the Republic of Ireland: Common Problems, Common Solutions*, Co-operation North, Dublin.

Cox, P.G. and Kearney, B. (1983) 'The impact of the Common Agricultural Policy', in D. Coombes (ed.) Ireland and the European Communities. Dublin: Gill and Macmillan.

Crowley, J. (1992). 'Transport', in *Ireland in Europe: a Shared Challenge*, Stationery Office, Dublin.

Dow, S.C. (1986) 'The Capital Account and Regional Balance of Payments Problems', *Urban Studies*, **23**.

Durkan, J. and Reynolds-Feighan, A. (1990) 'Irish Manufacturing Transport Costs – Results of Two Surveys' in J. Bradley (ed.) *The Role of the Structural Funds: Analysis of Consequences for Ireland in the Context of 1992*, Policy Research Paper No. 13, ESRI, Dublin.

Economic and Social Committee of the European Communities (1983) *Irish Border Areas: Information Report*, European Communities, Brussels.

Emerson, M., Jacquemin, R., Buiges, P. (1989) *The Economics of 1992*, Oxford University Press, Oxford.

Enderwick, P., Gudgin, G. and Hitchens, D. (1988) 'The Role of the Firm in Manufacturing, in R. Harris, C. Jefferson and J. Spencer (eds), *The Northern Ireland Economy*, Longman, London.

Ergas, H. (1984) 'Corporate strategies in transition' in *European Industry: Public and Corporate Strategy*, A. Jacqumin (ed.), Clarendon Press, Oxford.

Ferris, T. (1991) 'Transport Policy' in P. Keatinge (ed.) *Ireland and EC Membership Evaluated*, Pinter, London.

Fitzgerald, J.D. (1986). 'The Economic Implications of Tax Harmonisation', *The Economic Consequences of European Union*, Policy Research Series, Paper No. 6, Economic and Social Research Institute, Dublin.

Fitzgerald, J.D., Quinn, T.P., Whelan, B.J. and Williams, J.A. (1988) *An Analysis of Cross-Border Shopping*, Economic and General Research Series, Paper No. 137 Economic and Social Research Institute, Dublin.

Fitzpatrick, J. and McEniff, J. (1992) 'Tourism', in *Ireland in Europe: A Shared Challenge*, Stationery Office, Dublin.

Government of Ireland (1992) 'Economic Overview', in *Ireland in Europe, A Shared Challenge*, Stationery Office, Dublin.

Gray, A. (1992) 'Industry and Trade', in Ireland in Europe: a Shared Challenge, Stationery Office, Dublin.

Harris, R.I.D. (1987) 'The role of manufacturing in regional growth', *Regional Studies*, 21, 4.

Harris, R.I.D. (1990) 'Manufacturing Industry' in R. Harris, C. Jefferson and J. Spencer (eds) *The Northern Ireland Economy: A Comparative Study in the Economic Development of a Peripheral Region*, Longman, London.

Harrison, R. (1990a) 'Industrial Development Policy' in R. Harris, C. Jefferson and J. Spencer (eds) *The Northern Ireland Economy: A Comparative Study in the Economic Development of a Peripheral Region*, Longman, London.

Harrison, R. (1990b) 'Northern Ireland and the Republic of Ireland in the Single Market', in A. Foley and M. Mulready (eds) *The Single European Market and the Irish Economy*, Institute of Public Administration, Dublin.

Harrison, B. (1992) 'Industrial Districts: Old Wine in New Bottles?', *Regional Studies*, 26, 5.

Hitchens, D.M.W.N. and O'Farrell, P.N. (1987) 'The Performance of Small Manufacturing Firms in Northern Ireland and S.E. England', *Regional Studies*, 21, 6.

Hitchens, D.M.W.N. (1988) 'The Comparative Performance of Small Manufacturing Companies in South Wales and Northern Ireland', *Omega*, 16.

Honohan, P. (1992) *Intersectoral Financial Flows in Ireland*, Economic and Social Research Institute, Dublin.

Industrial Development Review Group (1992) *A Time for Change: Industrial Policy for the 1990s*, Stationery Office, Dublin.

Kay, J. (1990). 'Identifying the strategic market', *Business Strategy Review*, Spring.

Keatinge, P. (1991) 'Foreign Policy' in P. Keatinge (ed.) *Ireland and EC Membership Evaluated*, Routledge, London.

Keatinge, P. (1991a) *Ireland and EC Membership Evaluated*, Pinter, London.

Keatinge, P., Laffan, B. and O'Donnell, R. (1991) 'Weighing up the gains and losses' in P. Keatinge (ed.) *Ireland and EC Membership Evaluated*, Pinter, London.

Kennedy, K., Giblin, T. and McHugh, D. (1988) *The Economic Development of*

Ireland in the Twentieth Century, Routledge, London.
Kennedy, K. (1992) 'Real Convergence: the European Community and Ireland' paper read to the Statistical and Social Inquiry Society of Ireland, May 1992.
Killen, J. (1993) 'Ireland's Transport Links with Europe' in R. King (ed.) *Ireland, Europe and the Single Market: Geographical Perspectives* GSI Special Publication No. 8, Geographical Society of Ireland, Dublin.
Kinsella, R. (1992) 'Financial Services', in *Ireland in Europe: Shared Challenge*, Stationery Office, Dublin.
Laffan, B. (1991a) 'Sovereignty and National Identity', in P. Keatinge (ed.) *Ireland and EC Membership Evaluated*, Pinter, London.
Laffan, B. (1991b) 'Government and Administration', in P. Keatinge (ed.) *Ireland and EC Membership Evaluated*, Pinter, London.
Laffan, B. (1992) *Integration and Co-operation in Europe*, Routledge, London.
Leavy, A. and Heavy, J.F. (1992) 'Interim Analysis of the Proposed Common Agricultural Policy Reforms', paper read to the Agricultural Economics Society of Ireland.
Lyne, T. (1990) 'Ireland, Northern Ireland and 1992: the Barriers to Technocratic Anti-Partitionism', *Public Administration*, Winter.
Maher, D.J. (1986) *The Tortuous Path: the Course of Ireland Entry into the EEC 1948–73*, Institute of Public Administration, Dublin.
Matthews, A. (1980) *The European Community's External Trade Policy: Implications for Ireland*, Irish Council of the European Movement, Dublin.
Matthews, A. (1988) 'Common Agricultural Policy Reform and National Compensation Strategies', *Journal of the Statistical and Social Inquiry Society of Ireland*.
Matthews, A. (1992) 'Agricultural and Natural Resources' in *Ireland in Europe: a Shared Challenge*, Stationery Office, Dublin.
Matthews, A. and O'Connor, R. (1987) 'The Food Processing Industry' in *ESRI Medium Term Review*, Economic and Social Research Institute, Dublin.
Meade, J. and Wells, J. (1962) *Case Studies in European Economic Union: The Mechanics of Integration*, Unwin Hyman, London.
Moxon-Browne, E. (1992) 'Northern Ireland and the European Community', *Ireland, Europe and 1992*, No. 4, Le Centre d'Etudes Irlandaises de Paris, Presses de la Sorbonne Nouvelle, Paris.
MacIntyre, A. (1981) *After Virtue: a Study in Moral Theory*, Duckworth, London.
McAleese, D. (1975) 'Ireland in the enlarged EEC: economic consequences and prospects' in *Economic Sovereignty and Regional Policy*, J. Vaizey (ed.), Gill and Macmillan, London.
McAleese, D. (1979) 'Intra-industry trade, level of development and market size' in *On the Economics of Intra-Industry Trade*, Symposium 1979, H. Giersch (ed.), Instit für Weltwirstschaft an der Universität, Kiel.
McAleese, D. (1984) 'Ireland and the European Community: the changing pattern of trade' in *Ireland and the European Community*,. P.J. Drudy and D. McAleese (eds) *Irish Studies* 3, CUP, Cambridge.
McAleese, D. and Matthews, A. (1987) 'The Single European Act and Ireland: implications for a small member state', *Journal of Common Market Studies*, 26, 1, September.
McGurnaghan, M. and Scott, S. (1981) *Trade and Co-operation in Electricity and Gas*, Co-operation North, Dublin.
NESC (1984) *The Role of the Financial System in Financing the Traded Sectors*,

National Economic and Social Council, Dublin.
NESC (1989) *Ireland in the European Community: Performance, Prospects and Strategy*, National Economic and Social Council, Dublin.
NESC *(1990) A Strategy for the Nineties: Economic Stability and Structural Change*, National Economic and Social Council, Dublin.
NESC (1992) *The Impact of Reform of the Common Agricultural Policy*, National Economic and Social Council Dublin.
NIEC (1992) *Inward Investment in Northern Ireland*, Northern Ireland Economic Council, Belfast.
O'Donnell, R. (1991a) 'Introduction to Part I: Economic Policy' in P. Keatinge (ed.) *Ireland and EC Membership Evaluated*, Pinter, London.
O'Donnell, R. (1991b) 'External Trade Policy', in P. Keatinge (ed.) *Ireland and EC Membership Evaluated*, Pinter, London.
O'Donnell, R. (1991c) 'The Internal Market', in P. Keatinge (ed.) *Ireland and EC Membership Evaluated*, Pinter, London.
O'Donnell, R. (1991d) 'Monetary Policy' in P. Keatinge (ed.) *Ireland and EC Membership Evaluated*, Pinter, London.
O'Donnell, R. (1991e) 'The Regional Issue' in R. O'Donnell (ed.) *Economic and Monetary Union*, Institute of European Affairs, Dublin.
O'Donnell, R. (1992a) 'The Changing Analytical Foundations of Regional Policy', paper presented to Symposium on European Integration and Regional Policy, University College Galway, May.
O'Donnell, R. (1992b) 'Policy Requirements for Regional Balance in Economic and Monetary Union', in A. Hanneguart (ed.) *Economic and Social Cohesion in Europe: a New Objective for Integration*, Routledge, London.
O'Donnell, R. (1992c) 'Ireland's Competitive Advantage: Conceptual, Definitional and Theoretical Issues', Seminar Paper, 12 November 1992, Economic and Social Research Institute, Dublin.
O'Donnell, R. (1993) 'Ireland and Europe: the Political, Economic and Cultural Dimensions', in R. King (ed.) *Ireland, Europe and the Single Market: Geographical Perspectives*, GSI Special Publication No.8, Dublin: Geographical Society of Ireland (forthcoming).
O'Dowd, L. (1992) 'Borders in the New Europe', paper presented to Sociology Colloquium European Society or European Societies: Sociological Perspectives in a European Context, Trinity College Dublin, 12–13 November 1992.
O'Dowd, L. and Corrigan, J. (1992) 'National Sovereignty and Cross-Border Co-operation: Ireland in a Comparative Context', paper read to the Annual Conference of the Sociological Association of Ireland, Cork.
O'Malley, E. (1989) *Industry and Economic Development: the Challenge for the Latecomer*, Gill and Macmillan, Dublin.
O'Malley, E. (1992) 'Industrial Structure and Economies of Scale in the Context of 1992' in J. Bradley *et al.* (eds) *The Role of the Structural Funds: Analyses of Consequences for Ireland in the Context of 1992*, Policy Research Paper No. 13, Economic and Social Research Institute, Dublin.
Pelkmans, J. (1984) *Market Integration in the European Community*, Nijoff, The Hague.
Pelkmans, J. and Robson, P. (1987) 'The Aspirations of the White Paper', *Journal of Common Market Studies*, Vol. 25, No. 3.
Quigley, G. (1992). 'Ireland – an Island Economy', speech to Confederation of Irish

Industry, Dublin, February 1992.

Reynolds, G. (1992). 'Capital Liberalisation and Strengthening the EMS – an Irish View', *Central Bank of Ireland Quarterly Bulletin.*

Rowthorn, R.E. and Wayne, W. (1988) *The Political Economy of Conflict*, Polity Press, Cambridge.

Rowthorn, R.E. and Wells, J.R. (1987) *De-Industrialisation and Foreign Trade*, Cambridge University Press, Cambridge.

Saxenian, A. (1989) 'The Cheshire Cat's grin: innovation, regional development and the Cambridge case', *Economy and Society*, Vol.18, No. 4.

Schmitter, P. (1992) 'Notes on a Theory of Political Integration', Stanford University mimeo.

Sexton, J., Walsh, B., Hannan, D. and McMahon, D. (1991) *The Economic and Social Implications of Emigration*, National Economic and Social Council, Dublin.

Sexton, J. (1992) 'Human Resources and Health', in *Ireland in Europe: A Shared Challenge*, Stationery Office, Dublin.

Simpson, J. (1988) 'European Community Policies and Northern Ireland', in J. Simpson (ed.) *Northern Ireland and the European Community: An Economic Assessment*, European Commission Office in Northern Ireland, Belfast.

Smith, D. (1991) *National Identity*, Penguin, London.

Spencer, J. E., and Whittaker, J. M. (1990) 'Agriculture' in R. Harris, C. Jefferson and J. Spencer (eds). *The Northern Ireland Economy*, Longman, London.

Stainer, T.F. (1985) *An Analysis of Economic Trends in Northern Ireland Agriculture since 1970*, Department of Agriculture for Northern Ireland, Belfast.

Stohr, W. (1989) *Regional Identity*, Penguin, London.

TEPSA (1991) *Methods for Achieving Greater Economic and Social Cohesion in the European Community*, report to DGXXII of the European Commission of the Trans-European Policy Studies Association.

Trimble, M. (1989a) 'The European Community and Northern Ireland' in A. Aughey, P. Hainsworth and M. Trimble (eds) *Northern Ireland in the European Community*, Policy Research Institute, Belfast.

Trimble, M. (1989b) 'Regional Policy of the European Community' in A. Aughey, P. Hainsworth and M. Trimble (eds) *Northern Ireland in the European Community*, Policy Research Institute, Belfast.

Trimble, M. (1989c) 'The Northern Ireland Agriculture and Sea Fishing Industries' in A. Aughey, P. Hainsworth and M. Trimble (eds) *Northern Ireland in the European Community*, Policy Research Institute, Belfast.

Trimble, M. (1990) 'The Impact of the European Community' in R. Harris, C. Jefferson and J. Spencer (eds) *The Northern Ireland Economy*, Longman, London.

Whyte, J. (1990) *Interpreting Northern Ireland*, Clarendon Press, Oxford.

Williamson, O. (1985) *Economic Institutions of Capitalism*, Collier-McMillan, New York.

Wilson, T. (1990) 'Introduction' in Harris, R., Jefferson, C. and Spencer, J. (eds) *The Northern Ireland Economy*, Longman, London.

Wright, M. (1989) 'Comparative industrial policies: the role of policy communities, *Political Studies*, December, pp. 212–229.

INDEX

Agriculture, Fisheries and Food, Ministry of, 124, 133
aircraft industry, 60
Area Health and Social Service Boards, 124

Barnett formula, 127-9
'branch-plant' manufacturing, 12
'British disease', 25, 33, 39-40
'Broad Focus', 63
Brooke, Basil, 163

Commerce, Ministry of, 61
Community Support Framework (CSF), 134
competitivity, 7, 61, 72
  Neoclassical view, 73-9
  Cumulative Causation Model, 79-83
  Organizational Approach, 83-6
  New Internal Model, 86-93
Confederation of British Industry (CBI), 246
Confederation of Irish Industry (CII), 246
Consolidated Fund, 123
Constitution Act 1973, 123, 126
Culliton Report, 208, 210
Customs and Excise, 123

Defence, Ministry of, 124, 134
Desmond's, 116
Direct Rule, 126
discrimination (religious), 15-18
  employment, 142-166

Economic Development, Department of, (DED), 51-2, 63, 124, 212-9
'Competing in the 90s', 70, 206, 211

Education and Library Boards, 124
Enterprise Initiative, 218
Enterprise Taskforce, 219
'enterprise culture', 218-223
Enterprising Northern Ireland Campaign, 219
European Community of State Aid, 44
European Community, 240, 245, 253, 256, 257, 260-3, 266

Fair Employment Act 1976, 165
Fair Employment Act 1989, 165
Fair Employment Agency, 112, 156
Family Expenditure Survey (FES), 2, 18
Fordism, 114, 151
Foreign Direct Investment (FDI), 191-213

Glass, Milton, 39
Government of Ireland Act 1920, 122
government training schemes, 3
gross domestic product (GDP), 1, 25

Harland and Wolff, 46, 155

Imperial Contribution, 122
Industrial Development Board (IDB), 51-2, 62, 70, 124, 207-9, 211
Industrial Policy Review Group, Report of the, (1992), 50-2
industrial relations, 115-6
Industries Development Act (NI) 1945, 205
inequality (religious), 15-18, 112-3, 141-166
  gender, 179-184
Institute of Directors, 246
IRA, 165, 253

INDEX

Irish Development Agency (IDA), 13

job generation, 223–236

Labour Force Survey (LFS), 15–17
labour market, 3
  and religion, 141–166
  and women 170–185
  and new and small firms, 217–236
Lear Fan, 206
Loan Guarantee Scheme, 222
Local Economic Development Unit (LEDU), 51, 61–2, 70, 124, 218, 221, 230–6
Lord Chancellor's Office, 123, 134

MacBride Principles, 165
manufacturing, 1, 3, 10–12, 20, 60, 66–7, 221
migration, 35

National Institute of Economic and Social Research (NIESR), 40–1
Needs Assessment Study, 129
Northern Ireland Development Agency (NIDA), 62
Northern Ireland Economic Council, 129–130, 171–2
Northern Ireland Exchequer, 122
Northern Ireland Finance Corporation, 61
Northern Ireland Labour Force Survey, 171
Northern Ireland Office, 123, 133
Northern Ireland Railways, 124

O'Reilly, Tony, 39

'Pathfinder', 63–70, 218
'peripherality', 107–110
Policy Studies Institute, 150
Post Office, 124
productivity growth, 8
productivity, 6–9, 25, 28–33, 42, 45

Public Expenditure Survey(PES), 127
public sector, the, 11, 13–15, 65, 102–105, 121–139

Republic of Ireland (ROI)
  comparison with economy of, 24–56
  Exchequer Borrowing Requirement of, 136
  potential economic co-operation with, 240–266
research and development (R&D), 12–13, 41, 109, 110, 194, 206
Revenue Account, 130
Royal Ulster Constabulary (RUC), 151

sectarianism, 112–3
Selective Financial Assistance, 45–6
shipbuilding, 60
Shorts, 46, 116, 155
Single European Market, 192
Sinn Fein (Provisional), 165
Standing Advisory Committee on Human Rights, 179
state intervention, 19
Stormont, 122, 123, 135
strike rate, 48
Structural Funds, 134
subsidies, 43–53, 66, 114

Telesis Report, 42, 51, 204
textiles, 60
trade unions, 115, 158
training and education, 35–44, 64
'troubles', the, 10, 200–201

Ulster Defence Regiment (UDR), 151
Ulsterbus, 124
unemployment, 2–4,
  and religion, 15–18, 47
Unionism, 163
unit labour costs, 6

X-inefficiency, 45, 48, 49